MODERN PUBLIC LAND LAW

IN A NUTSHELL

THIRD EDITION

By

ROBERT L. GLICKSMAN
Wagstaff Professor of Law
University of Kansas

GEORGE CAMERON COGGINS
Tyler Professor of Law
University of Kansas

THOMSON
————*————™
WEST

Mat #40395466

COPYRIGHT © 1995 WEST PUBLISHING
© West, a Thomson business, 2001
© 2006 Thomson/West
        610 Opperman Drive
        P.O. Box 64526
        St. Paul, MN 55164–0526
        1–800–328–9352
Printed in the United States of America

ISBN–13: 978–0–314–16285–4
ISBN–10: 0–314–16285–2

TEXT IS PRINTED ON 10% POST CONSUMER RECYCLED PAPER

To Bertie, the most sophisticated 9-year old ever

To Andrea Margaret Coggins

*

PREFACE

"Modern public land law" embodies the rules and doctrines governing disposition, allocation, and protection of the one third of the nation's surface that is owned in fee by the federal government and of the natural resources those lands contain. This Nutshell cannot offer exhaustive analyses of every issue prominent in this field of study; it instead focuses on the major questions and major authorities in a condensed fashion.

We have keyed Modern Public Land Law in A Nutshell both to the leading casebook in the area (George Cameron Coggins, Charles F. Wilkinson & John D. Leshy, *Federal Public Land and Resources Law* (5th ed. 2002)) and to the only treatise covering the entire area (George Cameron Coggins & Robert L. Glicksman, *Public Natural Resources Law* (1990, supplemented)). With a few exceptions, this Nutshell adopts the basic organization and contents of the casebook, and it cross-references each section to corresponding section(s) of the treatise, cited as PNRL, where more detailed discussions may be found. This edition covers significant legislative, regulatory, and judicial developments through the end of 2005.

Because singling out people to thank for their help risks significant omissions, we offer a blanket thanks to all of those who have contributed to this project.

ROBERT L. GLICKSMAN

GEORGE CAMERON COGGINS

March 2006

OUTLINE

Page

*

TABLE OF ACRONYMS

MSLF:	Mountain States Legal Foundation
MUSYA:	Multiple-Use, Sustained-Yield Act
NEPA:	National Environmental Policy Act
NFMA:	National Forest Management Act
NFSAA:	National Forest Ski Area Act
NHPA:	National Historic Preservation Act
NMFS:	National Marine Fisheries Service
NPS:	National Park Service
NRA:	National Recreation Area
NRDC:	Natural Resources Defense Council
NSO:	No Surface Occupancy
NTSA:	National Trails System Act
NWF:	National Wildlife Federation
NWPS:	National Wilderness Preservation System
NWR:	National Wildlife Refuge
NWRS:	National Wildlife Refuge System
NWRSAA:	National Wildlife Refuge System Administration Act
NWRSIA:	National Wildlife Refuge System Improvement Act
O & C:	Oregon & California
ORV:	Off-Road Vehicle
PNRL:	Public Natural Resources Law
PRIA:	Public Rangeland Improvement Act
RARE:	Roadless Area Review and Evaluation
RNP:	Redwood National Park

TABLE OF ACRONYMS

ROW:	Right of Way
RPA:	Resources Planning Act
RPPA:	Recreation and Public Purposes Act
RRA:	Refuge Recreation Act
SMCRA:	Surface Mining Control and Reclamation Act
SRA:	Surface Resources Act
S-RHA:	Stock-Raising Homestead Act
TGA:	Taylor Grazing Act
TVA:	Tennessee Valley Authority
UIA:	Unlawful Inclosures Act
USCA:	United States Code Annotated
WF-RHBA:	Wild Free-Roaming Horses and Burros Act
WSA:	Wilderness Study Area
WSRA:	Wild and Scenic Rivers Act

TABLE OF CASES

References are to Pages

TABLE OF CASES

TABLE OF CASES

TABLE OF CASES

TABLE OF CASES

TABLE OF CASES

TABLE OF CASES

TABLE OF CASES

TABLE OF STATUTES

UNITED STATES

UNITED STATES CONSTITUTION

UNITED STATES CODE ANNOTATED

5 U.S.C.A.—Government Organization and Employees

XLIX

TABLE OF STATUTES

L

TABLE OF STATUTES

UNITED STATES CODE ANNOTATED
16 U.S.C.A.—Conservation

TABLE OF STATUTES

UNITED STATES CODE ANNOTATED
28 U.S.C.A.—Judiciary and Judicial Procedure

30 U.S.C.A.—Mineral Lands and Mining

TABLE OF STATUTES

TABLE OF STATUTES

UNITED STATES CODE ANNOTATED
42 U.S.C.A.—The Public Health and Welfare

43 U.S.C.A.—Public Lands

TABLE OF STATUTES

UNITED STATES CODE ANNOTATED
43 U.S.C.A.—Public Lands

TABLE OF STATUTES

STATUTES AT LARGE

POPULAR NAME ACTS

———

ADMINISTRATIVE PROCEDURE ACT

CLEAN WATER ACT

ENDANGERED SPECIES ACT

TABLE OF STATUTES

TABLE OF STATUTES

TABLE OF STATUTES

TAYLOR GRAZING ACT

EXECUTIVE ORDERS

CODE OF FEDERAL REGULATIONS

FEDERAL REGISTER

*

MODERN PUBLIC LAND LAW

IN A NUTSHELL

THIRD EDITION

*

CHAPTER ONE

MODERN PUBLIC LAND LAW: AN INTRODUCTION

During most of the 19th century, national policy called for the disposition of lands purchased or conquered by the United States to a variety of beneficiaries. But, through a series of historical occurrences and accidents, the United States still retains fee simple title to more than 660 million acres of the country, roughly 29 percent of America's total surface area. The federal government also owns lesser property interests, such as severed mineral estates and conservation easements; it has record title to over 50 million acres held in trust for Indian tribes; and it asserts jurisdiction (but not ownership) over the outer continental shelf and other offshore lands and resources out to 200 miles. Not counting the lands used for "governmental" purposes, such as forts and post offices, the federal lands have been classified (or zoned) into five "systems" managed by four federal agencies in two executive departments.

The first three land management systems are the National Park, Forest, and Wildlife Refuge Systems. Congressional reservation of Yellowstone National Park in 1872 began the growth and development of the National Park System; that system now encom-

1

passes over 80 million acres of parks, monuments, and other designations and is managed by the National Park Service (NPS), an agency within the Department of the Interior. Congress in 1891 authorized the President to reserve forested lands for timber supply and watershed protection; the resulting National Forest System, under the jurisdiction of the United States Forest Service (FS) in the Agriculture Department, now contains over 190 million acres. Ad hoc presidential and congressional reservations of land for wildlife preservation led to a 1966 law declaring them collectively to be the National Wildlife Refuge System; now aggregating over 90 million acres, the NWRS is run by the Interior Department's Fish and Wildlife Service (FWS).

Homesteading of the "public domain" ended for practical purposes with passage of the Taylor Grazing Act (TGA), 43 U.S.C.A. §§ 315–315r, in 1934. The federally owned lands that had neither been homesteaded nor reserved for federal conservation purposes were withdrawn into grazing districts and later became the fourth system. The Bureau of Land Management (BLM), an Interior Department agency, is in charge of these "public lands," of which about 170 million of the approximately 260 million acre total are in the contiguous western states. Historically, "public lands," or "public domain lands," referred to lands that remained available for homesteading or other forms of disposition; only a tiny fraction of federal holdings now fit that description. Because Congress in the Federal Land

Policy and Management Act (FLPMA) has defined "public lands" to be lands under BLM jurisdiction, 43 U.S.C.A. § 1702(e), this Nutshell uses the phrases "federal public lands" or "federal lands" to mean all of the lands and interests in lands owned by the United States.

See PNRL § 1:2.

The fifth federal land management "system" is composed of specially designated areas within each of the first four systems. Wilderness areas, wild and scenic river segments, and national trails have been superimposed over those preexisting four systems. See § 2D infra. The NPS, FS, FWS, and BLM all manage these areas primarily for preservation or recreational purposes within the boundaries of their preexisting holdings.

A.   THE FIELD OF FEDERAL PUBLIC LAND LAW

Modern federal public land law, like its predecessor fields, is primarily concerned with who is entitled to what in relation to the federal lands and resources. But the nature of modern contests over resource allocation, and the premises by which such contests are resolved, have shifted radically in past decades.

Public land law historically referred to the bodies of rules that defined private entitlement to public lands and resources. It assumed that economic development was the optimal use, and it embodied the processes of privatization whereby private entities could take title to federally owned lands and resources. Within public land law, subspecialties such as water law, mining law, and oil and gas law, developed around what were then the most economically valuable public resources. Typical controversies in traditional public land law were "private"; private entities disputed property rights with the government or between themselves.

The primary concern of traditional public land law was land disposition. As late as 1965, the Supreme Court described the "public land laws" as those "governing the alienation of public land." Udall v. Tallman (S.Ct.1965). Inaccurate even then, that description is now wholly inadequate because very few federal lands remain available for sale or grant. This Nutshell uses the modifier "modern" to distinguish the recent law in this area from what it used to be. Land title transfers are but a small part of the process of determining the right to use or benefit from federal lands. Instead, the emphasis now is on allocation, use, protection, and preservation of the natural resources, broadly defined, found on or in the federal public lands. See PNRL §§ 1:15–1:16.

Modern public land law has also shifted its focus from private to public controversies. While questions of private property entitlement remain important, especially to the disputants involved, the law now centers on the more "public" questions of whether private property rights of any kind should be recognized in public resources, and, if so, under what conditions. In other words, the question whether Bertie or Jaclyn is entitled to graze her cattle on a tract of federal land has been superseded, as an initial matter, by the question whether the tract should be grazed at all, and, if so, to what extent. This, in essence, is a "public interest" inquiry.

Two related developments largely account for the fairly complete transition to modern federal public land law. First, "public interest" or "environmentalist" or "conservationist" or "preservationist" groups have grown, matured, and become highly influential in federal land controversies. Second, general public opinion has become decidedly "environmental," compared to past generations. Which development preceded the other is a debatable but ultimately moot question; the environmental groups have helped to shape public opinion, which in turn has made those groups more influential. The preservation ethic has become deeply entrenched, although it is not immune to criticism as detrimental to the economy and to private property rights. Even the highly commodity-oriented Reagan Administration was unable to swing back the environmental pendulum to any significant degree. The similarly–oriented Bush II Administration apparently has been more successful in turning back the clock.

Because the federal public lands are governmentally owned and operated, all of federal land management necessarily is political. Land users, land managers, and other interested parties have strongly divergent opinions and theories as to the proper or preferable management approaches and philosophies. Even though Congress typically exercises more detailed control over federal land and resource use in modern statutes than it previously did, those laws continue to grant a large degree of discretion to the executive managing agencies. As a result, prevailing political preferences can heavily influence practices in the field. The policies of, say, Secretary of the Interior James G. Watt or Gale Norton simply cannot be reconciled with the policies of, say, Secretary of the Interior Bruce Babbitt. Thus, while federal land law often is gridlocked at the congressional level, it can be quite fluid and changeable in terms of particular management emphases and decisions. See PNRL § 7:2.

Judicial oversight of these decisions is a far more integral part of modern than of traditional public land law. In some instances, the breadth of agency discretion precludes effective challenge by conservation or commodity interests. In other cases, however, noncompliance with statutory procedures or deviation from substantive statutory mandates has prompted courts to enjoin the programs of the land management agencies and to alter their preferred resource allocations.

See PNRL §§ 1:20, 1:26.

B. THE FEDERAL LANDS AND RESOURCES

1. INTERESTS IN LANDS

The United States, from the 1780s to the late 19th century, acquired title to nearly two billion acres of land on the North American continent. By the 1990s, the federal government retained outright ownership of about 662 million acres, and it owned lesser interests (severed mineral and surface estates, easements, reversions, and so forth) in many millions more acres. In addition, the United States claims sovereignty over the continental shelf and submerged lands from three to 200 miles offshore. Only a very small fraction of the remaining federal public lands is used for ordinary governmental purposes such as defense or post offices.

The federal land holdings are heavily concentrated in the eleven western states and Alaska, although every state has some federally owned property. Roughly 30 percent of the Nation's total surface acreage remains in federal ownership for three primary reasons: some was withdrawn from the exploitable public domain and reserved for conservation purposes, beginning with the reservation of Yellowstone National Park in 1872; some went unclaimed by successive waves of homesteaders and other claimants because it could not support any livelihoods under then-prevailing conditions; and the federal government has "reacquired" some lands by purchase or condemnation to serve perceived federal purposes.

2. FEDERAL NATURAL RESOURCES

This Nutshell adopts the classification of the major federal natural resources first propounded in the Coggins, Wilkinson & Leshy casebook. In descending order of traditional (but not necessarily current) direct economic importance, these resources are: water; "hardrock" minerals; "leasable" or "saleable" minerals; timber; grass (or "range"); wildlife (including fish); recreation; and preservation. This classification is more of a spectrum than a series of discrete, exclusive categories.

a. Water

Water is the one resource without which all other resources and uses (and life itself) are valueless. Water shortages are an endemic problem in the West, where most supplies originate on federal lands. Although water allocation law is primarily determined by states, the United States both owns water rights as a proprietor and heavily influences all water uses in the region. Federal water development projects have provided irrigation water, electricity, and recreational opportunities, but at an increasing cost in terms of the destruction of fish resources and the amenities provided by free-flowing rivers.

b. Hardrock Minerals

American mines have yielded immense quantities of gold, silver, copper, tin, iron, and hundreds of other valuable ores, and the federal lands still hold valuable quantities of these minerals. Hardrock minerals, for purposes of the 1872 General Mining Law (GML), 43 U.S.C.A. §§ 22–45, are all of the valuable mineral deposits on public lands other than those that Congress made "leasable" or "saleable." The location system allows private prospectors to stake claims to hardrock minerals on federal lands that have not been withdrawn for other purposes. Discovery of a valuable deposit gives rise to an unpatented claim. The patent process enables the miner to gain fee simple title to not only the minerals, but also the surface estate of the claim. In recent years, however, Congress has placed moratoria on patent issuance. Active hardrock mining operations on federal lands have, for a variety of reasons, declined by roughly two-thirds in the past generation.

c. Leasable Minerals

Coal never was "locatable." In 1920, Congress withdrew oil, gas, oil shale, sulfur, and other fuel and fertilizer minerals from the location system governing hardrock minerals; since then, the withdrawn minerals on federal lands could be obtained only by lease. Mineral Leasing Act, 43 U.S.C.A. §§ 181–287. Congress extended the leasing disposition mechanism to offshore oil and gas in 1953, to geothermal resources in 1970, and to deep seabed mineral resources in 1980. About 41,000 oil and gas leases covered about 33 million acres of federal land in the late 1990s, and onshore production has supplied around five or six percent of total domestic production in recent years. Lately, drilling for coalbed methane has been the hottest area of federal oil and gas leasing. About 390 federal coal leases cover about 800,000 acres of federal land, supplying about one-quarter of total domestic production; the number of leases represents severe declines from historic levels.

d. Timber

The national forests were reserved during 1891–1906 partly to insure a national supply of timber. After the overutilization of private timber lands earlier this century, the national forests now contain nearly half of the total national standing softwood timber inventory. Other federal lands also contain sizable timber reserves. The national forests also provide scenic beauty and recreational opportunities.

The past two decades have seen severe declines in overall timber harvests from public lands, mainly but not exclusively because of the presence of endangered species in the Pacific Northwest. Application of NEPA and the Clean Water Act also impeded planned timber harvests.

e. Grass (or Range)

About 270 million acres in the contiguous states are devoted partly or primarily to domestic livestock grazing. In contradistinction to the productivity of the federal timber lands, however, this immense acreage supports less than two percent of the cattle and sheep in the country. Other animals, including wild horses and burros, antelope, deer, moose, and mountain sheep, also forage on the federal lands. The allocation system for grazing privileges on federal lands has done little to improve range productivity. See § 8B.

f. Wildlife

Because most of the federal lands are undeveloped, they are in general the best remaining wildlife habitat in the country. Many species are entirely dependent upon federal lands for their survival. Hunting and fishing always have been significant commercial and recreational pursuits; in recent years, wildlife viewing alone has become an important source of tourist attraction revenue, and species preservation has become a significant national priority.

g. Recreation

"Recreation" is more than a pastime; it now encompasses many sizable industries and is far more economically important than resource extraction to the West. Outdoor recreation has been a central focus of federal land legislation for four decades. Recreational opportunities are available in each of the five federal land systems, although the prominence of this use differs by system. Use of the conventional resources discussed above long has given rise to conflicts with other potential uses. As recreational use of the federal lands has increased, it has created some of the same kinds of conflicts, both with other recreational uses and with commodity uses.

h. Preservation

Preservation is, essentially, mandated nonuse. As such it is the principal competitor of all commodity land uses. Statutes such as the Endangered Species Act (ESA) are designed to preserve discrete resources, but that law as well as others can also be used to preserve entire ecosystems. Congress created the National Park System for mixed recreational/preservational purposes, but it mandated that all other uses be subordinated to wildlife protection in the national wildlife refuges. The National Wilderness Preservation System (NWPS), now exceeding 100 million acres, is the strongest expression of the preservationist impulse among the federal lands systems, although some commodity uses are permitted to a limited extent.

See PNRL §§ 1:3–1:6.

CHAPTER TWO

HISTORY OF PUBLIC LAND LAW

The history of federal public land law can be divided into three (or more) indistinct, overlapping periods. The Age of Disposition ran from the 1780s to 1934, and a few vestiges of it still remain. The disposition era was characterized by rapid development of the country, fueled by cheap or free land; the United States sold or gave away roughly a billion and a half acres to veterans, states, homesteaders, railroads, miners, and others. The year 1872 ushered in the Age of Conservation, and that Age is still very much alive, even though in some senses it peaked around the turn of the 20th century. "Conservation" in this context means federal reservation and management of the reserved lands for utilitarian purposes. The Age of Preservation has ancient roots, but its official beginning was enactment of the Wilderness Act in 1964. Ensuing years have seen the preservation impulse increasingly translated into legislative, administrative, and judicial policies and decisions. Each of these eras left legacies of influential principles and bothersome problems.

13

A. ACQUISITION OF THE PUBLIC DOMAIN

The traditional "public domain" consisted of those lands that the United States acquired from European and Indian sovereigns and that were available for mineral and non-mineral disposition. Acquisition of the public domain was completed with the purchase of Alaska from Russia in 1867, and the public domain was closed when homesteading ended as a practical matter in 1934 with passage of the Taylor Grazing Act.

Kentucky, Tennessee, Vermont, Maine, and Texas, in addition to the original 13 Colonies, were never considered "public land states" because the federal government never fell heir to any appreciable amount of public domain land within their borders. The United States recognized all grants of land made by prior European and Mexican sovereigns, and those lands, too, never became a part of the public domain.

The United States began nationhood as an owner of roughly half of the land between the Atlantic Ocean and the Mississippi River. The original states ceded to the new nation and in subsequent agreements their claims to lands beyond the Alleghenies as a part of the compromise that became the United States Constitution. President Jefferson in 1803 then negotiated the Louisiana Purchase from France, effectively doubling the size of the country, for about three cents for each of the 523 million acres acquired. Spanish possessions in Florida were acquired in 1819, and the border between Canada and the United States was regularized in the years 1818 to 1846.

Texas achieved independence in 1836 but was refused admission to the Union until 1845. The Republic of Texas had its own highly irregular land disposition system; when it became a state, the federal government purchased lands outside its present borders but refused to assume ownership of the public lands within those borders. The lands acquired from Mexico via cession in 1848 and purchase in 1853 did enter the public domain, as did all of Alaska in 1867.

Cession of sovereignty by European nations did not by itself give the United States full fee title to the lands ceded. Pursuant to then-prevailing principles of international law, the federal government also had to make formal arrangements with the occupiers of the land, the various Native American Indian tribes. In the landmark case of Johnson v. M'Intosh (S.Ct.1823), Chief Justice Marshall held that private individuals could not purchase lands directly from the tribes; only the United States, under the Non–Intercourse Act of 1790, could enter into such transactions, usually by treaty. Questions of Indian title are still being litigated, see Oneida County v. Oneida Indian Nation (S.Ct.1985), but Indian Law generally is beyond the scope of this Nutshell.

B. DISPOSITION OF THE PUBLIC DOMAIN: THE BENEFICIARIES AND THE LEGACIES

From initial nationhood until 1934, the United States generally followed a policy of disposing of the lands it had acquired to diverse groups of beneficiaries. Roughly one-and-a half billion acres were sold or given away to states, veterans, homesteaders, railroads, miners, ranchers, and others. Most of the disposition programs ended long ago, but some title transfer programs are still ongoing on reduced scales.

1. EARLY PUBLIC LAND POLICY AND PROBLEMS

From the beginning, the older eastern states disagreed with the new states in the West over public land policies. States such as Maryland, for example, demanded a share of the benefits of the western territories. Many easterners believed that independent farmers had a "natural right" to uncultivated lands in the public domain, while westerners tended to view land as a commodity to be developed for the benefit of private entrepreneurs. The United States Constitution provided for areas of exclusively federal jurisdiction, art. I, § 8, cl. 17, and gave Congress general authority over federal property, art. IV, § 3, cl. 1. The federal government honored grants from prior sovereigns to individuals totaling some 34 million acres of land, although it took a century to sort out some of the claims.

2. STATEHOOD AND EQUAL FOOTING

Article IV of the Constitution authorizes Congress to admit new states to the Union. As an aspect of the "equal footing" doctrine, by which new states are entitled to all of the political prerogatives and powers of the older states, the Supreme Court ruled in 1845 that new states upon statehood automatically take title to lands underlying navigable waters within their borders. Pollard v. Hagan (S.Ct.1845). Although this holding did not extend to offshore lands, United States v. California (S.Ct. 1947), Congress ceded title to a three-mile offshore belt to the states in the Submerged Lands Act of 1953, 43 U.S.C.A. §§ 1301–1315. The equal footing doctrine does not interfere with the federal government's authority under the Commerce Clause to regulate navigable waters or with its Property Clause powers over the federal lands. Arizona v. California (S.Ct.1963). If it does so clearly, the United States may reserve the beds of navigable waters for federal purposes prior to statehood. Utah Div. of State Lands v. United States (S.Ct.1987). The Court held in United States v. Alaska (S.Ct. 1997) that the state did not receive upon statehood submerged lands within the National Petroleum Reserve and the Arctic National Wildlife Refuge. It later held in Alaska v. United States (S.Ct.2005), that the United States retained title at the time of statehood to submerged lands underneath waters that did not qualify as inland waters and to submerged lands included in a federal reservation before statehood. "Equal treatment" does not prevent

Congress from singling out one state to house nuclear waste. Nuclear Energy Inst. v. EPA (D.C. Cir.2004).

The lands acquired by the states via equal footing come with strings attached. In the landmark case of Illinois Central R.R. Co. v. Illinois (S.Ct.1892), the Supreme Court held that such lands were subject to a public trust doctrine that prohibited states from alienating them in a manner that would deprive the public of their use for fishing, navigation, and commerce. Other aspects of the various public trust doctrines are treated at section 4D.

3.   GRANTS TO STATES

Beginning with the admission of Ohio in 1803, Congress uniformly granted new states certain lands within their borders for specified purposes. All new states received sections 16 and 36 in each township for support of public education; some received far more land under these "in place" grants; and Alaska was allowed to select roughly one quarter of its surface area for state ownership. Those special purpose grants are strictly construed, thereby limiting the uses to which the states may dedicate these lands. States must obtain fair market value for sale or use of "in place" lands and devote the proceeds strictly to the statutory purposes. E.g., ASARCO Inc. v. Kadish (S.Ct.1989). But states may manage trust lands for long-term ecological productivity. Branson School Dist. v. Romer (10th Cir. 1998). Congress also made "quantity" grants to states of "swampland," for internal improvements, and for support of agricultural and mechanical colleges. When, because of prior claim or reservation, or because they were mineral in character, the "in place" lands due to the state were not available to the state, the state was entitled to select "in lieu" lands to replace those foregone.

Early cases treated the state's entitlement as a species of property right immune from federal discretion. When Utah in the 1960s sought to select valuable oil shale lands in lieu of far less valuable non-mineral lands on an acre-for-acre basis, however, the Interior Secretary denied the application because of the gross disparity in value. The Supreme Court, 5–4, upheld the Secretary's decision in Andrus v. Utah (S.Ct.1980). The Court determined that the 1934 Taylor Grazing Act, 43 U.S.C.A. § 315f, granted authority to the Secretary to establish standards for classification of land as suitable for in lieu disposition, and that the Secretary's exercise of that authority to prevent a windfall was consistent with the purpose of indemnity selections.

When the Alaska land selections are final, the transfers of title to the states pursuant to those ancient programs will be virtually complete. States may still obtain lands from the United States under the limited circumstances described at section 4D, however. In addition, the federal government continues to share the revenues accruing from uses of the retained public lands with the states in which those lands are located under statutes such as the Reclamation Act, as amended, 43 U.S.C.A. §§ 371–

616, the Mineral Leasing Act of 1920, 30 U.S.C.A. §§ 181–287, the Federal Power Act of 1920, 16 U.S.C.A. §§ 791a–825r, and the Submerged Lands Act of 1953, 43 U.S.C.A.§§ 1301–1356.

See PNRL §§ 2:7, 5:8.

4. GRANTS TO SETTLERS

The history of federal land grants in America is, to a considerable extent, the story of perjury, fraud, and corruption. The now-glorified homesteaders and ranchers who fought the weather, the Indians, and the banks, probably also stole at least part of their claims from the government.

Congress at first tried to sell the western lands for cash or credit through land auctions conducted under the Land Act of 1796, but speculators dominated the cash sales and farmers did not meet the credit terms. Preemption—semi-legal squatting leading to acquisition of title at modest prices without competitive bidding—became the settlement mechanism of choice in the first half of the 19th century, and Congress retroactively legalized it in 1841. Congress also rewarded war veterans with scrip payable in land, a practice not ended until the 20th century.

In 1862, with the Southerners out of Congress following secession, the landmark Homestead Act was passed. It allowed a settler to obtain 160 acres for free if he established residence on and cultivation of the land for five years. But, due to railroad grants, reservations, and other claims, the supply of arable land was dwindling. Congress reacted by passing a series of more liberal homestead laws, from the Desert Lands Act (DLA) of 1877, 43 U.S.C.A. §§ 321–339 (the only homestead act still on the books), to the Stock–Raising Homestead Act (S–RHA) of 1916, 43 U.S.C.A. §§ 291–301 (repealed 1976). The former authorized settlers to enter on 640–acre tracts by making a minimal payment and to acquire patents upon proof of irrigation. The DLA failed to accomplish its purpose of facilitating irrigation of the arid West because most of the available land was acquired by large corporations for stock raising. The latter statute turned out to be the last homesteading hurrah. Congress reluctantly affirmed the closing of the homesteading frontier in 1934 by authorizing the withdrawal of the remaining vacant, unclaimed lands into regulated grazing districts.

See PNRL § 2:8.

5. GRANTS TO MINERS

Homesteading theoretically was prohibited on "lands chiefly valuable for mining" or "mineral lands." No law governed mineral land disposition until 1866, but that lack did not prevent homestead entrants from laying claim to most of the mineral land east of the Mississippi or hordes of prospectors from occupying and mining the gold fields of California and then mining boom towns all over the West. The Supreme Court later held that Congress granted miners a license to do so by its silent acquiescence in their occupation. Forbes v. Gracey (S.Ct.1876). The miners operated under "the law of the camps," a primitive set of "first in time, first in right" and "use it or lose it" rules. *E.g.*, United States v. Shumway (9th Cir.1999); Morton v. Solambo Copper Min. Co. (Cal.1864).

In 1866, Congress legalized existing trespasses and retroactively validated existing claims, declaring that "mineral lands are free and open to exploration and occupation" under local custom. The Placer Act of 1870 extended these accommodations to placer claims. Two years later, Congress consolidated the 1866 and 1870 acts into the General Mining Law, 30 U.S.C.A. §§ 22–45, to promote mineral development. The GML authorized mineral land disposition by means of a "location" system. In essence, anyone could prospect on any unwithdrawn federal land, and, if he located a valuable mineral deposit, he could both mine it for free and then obtain a patent to the overlying land whether he actually mined it or not. Although Congress has since supplemented or limited the GML, the mineral location system it created remains in effect, and practices conducted under it (and abuses of it) continue to generate conflict with other uses and to interfere with land management objectives and programs.

See PNRL § 2:5, chapter 25.

6.   GRANTS TO RAILROADS

Between 1850 and 1873, Congress directly and indirectly gave railroads perhaps as much as 200 million acres of public lands as incentives to complete regional and transcontinental railroads. For reasons that remain dim, the grants were made in section-by-section checkerboard patterns, some of which still endure as a result of the absence of anticipated homesteading. On access problems stemming from the railroad grants, see section 2E. Federal land reservations within railroad grants gave rise to in lieu selection problems. In a few instances, such as the "O & C" (Oregon and California) railroad grants, title reverted to (or "revested in") the United States upon failure by the grantee to fulfill the grant conditions. In others, abandoned rights of way have been converted to public highways or hiking trails.

See PNRL §§ 2:6, 17:49.

7.   GRANTS FOR RECLAMATION

The Reclamation (or Newlands) Act of 1902, as amended, 43 U.S.C.A. §§ 371–616, embodied the congressional reaction to the failure of homesteading on the arid and semi-arid lands beyond the 100th meridian. The Act authorized construction of what became the massive dam and diversion projects for irrigated agriculture in the West, paid for with proceeds from land sales in the affected 16 states. Congress contemplated that the costs eventually would be repaid by the farmer-beneficiaries of the newly created water supplies, but costs have never been repaid and heavily subsidized sales of water continue. Aside from brief treatment in section 5B, reclamation is beyond the scope of this Nutshell. See generally PNRL chapter 21B; Hamilton Candee, *The Broken Promise of Reclamation Reform*, 40 Hastings L.J. 657 (1989).

8.   LEGACY OF THE DISPOSITION ERA

The section following this one outlines the reasons why, after a century and a half of land sales and grants, the United States retains ownership of as much land as it does; most of the rest of this Nutshell deals with that federal land and the resources it contains. But disposition as well as retention had consequences that still generate legal problems. This subsection expands, preliminarily, on that theme.

The first legacy of the disposition era is imbalance between federal holdings in the East and in the West. Although every state contains some federal land, most such land is concentrated in the eleven western states and Alaska. Second, homesteaders and other grant selectors naturally took the land then perceived as most valuable; consequently, mineral reserves, timber, and, especially, water resources, were appropriated first and foremost, often leaving the United States with dry land lacking access to water. From the standpoint of conventional crop agriculture, the remaining federal lands tend to be the least productive.

Third, the disposition programs left land ownership patterns hardly more coherent than cartographic chaos. State school sections—the "blue rash" on western maps—are scattered among private and federal lands. Many federal lands also have private "inholdings" within their boundaries. Every time a mining claim is located, another potential inholding is created. This geographic state of affairs generates access and management problems despite land exchanges and efforts at cooperation among the various title holders.

Fourth, the disposition era left a psychological legacy in which many Westerners profess to believe that continued federal land ownership is unconstitutional or at least immoral. While attempts to establish the illegality of continued federal land ownership and to "privatize" the federal lands have not succeeded, these attitudes have generated legal and political difficulties, not least of which are the Sagebrush Rebellion of the 1970s and the County Supremacy and Wise Use Movements of the 1990s. Those movements failed, but the reactionary sentiment persists.

See PNRL § 2:9.

C. RESERVATION AND WITHDRAWAL IN THE AGE OF CONSERVATION

A de facto system for classifying the federal lands had existed since the beginning of nationhood.

Withdrawal of lands from the public domain for military purposes or Indian reservations was commonplace during the 19th century. The "Age of Conservation," roughly from 1872 to 1964 (and extending in many ways into the present), was characterized by the creation of new federal zoning mechanisms to serve other federal purposes, notably "conservation." By means of "withdrawals" and "reservations," Congress and the Executive essentially zoned large tracts as off-limits to various land and resource disposition programs. See section 4C.

The Constitution vests the ultimate power over the federal public lands in Congress, which has retained for itself the authority to create national parks, wilderness areas, national trails, and most wild and scenic rivers. The establishment of Yellowstone and Yosemite National Parks first reflected the policy of reserving lands for recreation, conservation, and preservation purposes. Although Congress created several other parks after 1872, it was not until 1916 that it consolidated these holdings into the National Park System. Another form of withdrawal and reservation was (and still is) authorized by the Antiquities Act of 1906, 16 U.S.C.A. §§ 431–433. Congress there empowered the President to reserve as national monuments areas characterized by "historic landmarks, historic and prehistoric structures and other objects of historic or scientific interest." Id. § 431. The NPS usually has assumed responsibility for administering these lands, and Congress has often endorsed executive reservations under the Antiquities Act by transforming national monuments into national parks. No court has ever overturned a monument proclamation. See Tulare County v. Bush (D.C. Cir.2002).

The withdrawal and reservation mechanisms created during the Conservation era also have contributed to the land systems administered by agencies other than the NPS. The 1891 Forest Reserve Amendment to the General Revision Act authorized the President to reserve "any part of the public lands wholly or in part covered with timber or undergrowth, whether of commercial nature or not." 16 U.S.C.A. § 471. Six years later, Congress provided a management mission for these forest reserves in the 1897 Organic Act, id. §§ 473–481 (partially repealed 1976). By 1906, when Congress partially suspended the presidential withdrawal and reservation authority, more than 200 million acres had been set aside as national forests. National forest acreage was augmented by federal reacquisition programs in the 1910s and 1930s. The National Wildlife Refuge System initially stemmed from President Roosevelt's unilateral reservation of Pelican Island as a bird refuge in 1903. Since then, both Congress and the President have withdrawn and reserved lands for refuges.

Congress also "withdrew" certain resources, notably fuel minerals, from older disposition systems and authorized the President to make withdrawals for a wide variety of purposes. Abuses of legislation authorizing the disposition of coal lands prompted President Roosevelt in 1906 to withdraw from all forms of entry 66 million acres of coal-bearing land.

Three years later, President Taft, by presidential proclamation but without supporting statutory authority, withdrew from entry under the General Mining Law lands in California and Wyoming that contained valuable petroleum deposits in an effort to preserve oil reserves for use by the Navy. The Supreme Court rejected a challenge to that withdrawal in 1915, ruling that the long-continued executive practices of making withdrawals for military, Indian, and conservation purposes ripened into a power after Congress with knowledge acquiesced in its exercise. United States v. Midwest Oil Co. (S.Ct. 1915). The legislature's failure to object constituted "an implied grant of power to preserve the public interest" that would continue "until the power was revoked by some subsequent action of Congress."

In the interim, Congress in 1910 had enacted the Pickett Act, 43 U.S.C.A. §§ 141–142 (repealed 1976). It gave the President general authority to withdraw public lands (but not to reserve them) for any "public purposes" from any form of disposition except from "metalliferous" location and entry. Congress went further in 1920, "withdrawing" most fuel and chemical minerals from the location system and decreeing that they would from that point on be available only through federal leases. Mineral Leasing Act, 30 U.S.C.A. §§ 181–287. That form of resource withdrawal continued with the enactment of further leasing and sales statutes in 1947, 1953, 1955, and 1970.

Congress used yet another form of "reservation" in several of the final homesteading statutes, nota-

bly the Stock–Raising Homestead Act of 1916, 43
U.S.C.A. §§ 291–301 (repealed 1976). The liberality
of the surface acreage granted by the S–RHA was
balanced to a degree by the reservation of the
mineral estate in the United States. The Act also
reserved to the federal government the right to
prospect for, mine, and remove the reserved minerals, as well as to occupy the surface to the extent
necessary to facilitate removal.

See PNRL §§ 2:10–2:15, chapter 10D.

D. PERMANENT RETENTION AND MANAGEMENT

1. CONSTITUTIONAL AUTHORITY

The gradual, erratic shift in federal policy from
disposition to retention (by means of withdrawals
and reservations) raised a variety of constitutional
issues around the turn of the 20th century. These
questions implicated both power and procedure.
Courts affirmatively answered the ultimate question: whether the federal government was empowered to retain land for purposes other than normal
governmental functions.

The Fifth Amendment implicitly allows the federal government to acquire land by eminent domain if
it pays just compensation. The implicit limitation
on the implicit power is that the taking be for a
"public purpose." In United States v. Gettysburg
Elec. R. Co. (S.Ct.1896), Congress had authorized
the condemnation of lands comprising the Gettys-

burg Battlefield for inclusion in a national military
park, and the private owner objected. The Supreme
Court upheld the condemnation, ruling that the
congressional determination of public purpose will
be honored "unless the use be palpably without
reasonable foundation." Subsequent constitutional
challenges to the propriety of the purposes of federal condemnations have been futile, although statutes sometimes limit the purposes for which or the
procedures by which the federal government may
acquire lands or interests therein by eminent domain.

See PNRL § 3:19–3:20, chapter 10B.

The notion that the federal government can acquire and retain land for conservation and preservation purposes is now beyond reasonable challenge.
In Light v. United States (S.Ct.1911), the Supreme
Court held that Congress can withdraw large bodies
of land from settlement and reserve them as national forests without the consent of the state in which
they are located. "The United States can prohibit
absolutely or fix the terms on which its property
may be used. As it can withhold or reserve the land
it can do so indefinitely." The Court also decreed
that Congress may administer the trust in which it
holds public lands however it chooses, free of judicial interference. In the companion case of United
States v. Grimaud (S.Ct.1911), the Court upheld the
forest reservation procedure created by the Forest
Reserve Amendment to the General Revision Act of
1891. It ruled that Congress could delegate to the
Forest Service the power to make regulations for

the use of the national forests and that agency regulations requiring a permit for grazing sheep were valid even though Congress had not explicitly prohibited such activity. The Court had already established in Camfield v. United States (S.Ct. 1897), that Congress could regulate conduct off federal lands if the conduct adversely affected the federal lands. See sections 3B, 11B for further discussion of the federal government's constitutional and statutory authority to regulate external threats.

A 1918 decision, Omaechevarria v. Idaho (S.Ct. 1918), illustrates that state laws remain applicable in the absence of federal regulation. In that case, the Court upheld a state law prohibiting grazing of sheep on portions of the public domain previously occupied by cattle. The state statute was not preempted by federal law and did not improperly interfere with any right to graze on the federal lands.

2. THE LEGACY OF THE CONSERVATION ERA

The Taylor Grazing Act of 1934, 43 U.S.C.A. §§ 315–315r, although conceived of as a temporary range management device to shore up the livestock industry and rehabilitate overgrazed public rangeland, in fact closed the public domain, perhaps forever. By authorizing the Interior Secretary to create grazing districts and regulate use of the range, it indirectly resulted in the creation of a new federal land system, now called the "BLM lands" or the "public lands." The TGA also reaffirmed the practical truth that disposition had been displaced as the principal federal lands management objective. The reservations and withdrawals authorized during the conservation era are concrete symbols of Congress' commitment to the view that the public interest is often better served by continuing public land ownership and management than by divestment.

The net result of congressional and legislative withdrawals and reservations, affirmed by judicial decisions, is that the United States owns roughly 660 million acres of the national surface, plus severed estates, easements, and other real property interests. The "nongovernmental" federal lands (i.e., lands not used for forts, courthouses, etc.) are divided into five major "systems" in the charge of four different administrative agencies located in two cabinet departments. Permissible land uses vary by system, ranging from lands governed by the nebulous multiple use and sustained yield mandate (the national forests and the BLM lands) to those dedicated primarily to one or two principal uses (such as the national parks and the national wilderness areas).

See PNRL §§ 2:16–2:23.

a. The National Forest System

The National Forest System contains more than 190 million acres. Most of its acreage is in the West and Alaska, but the System also includes eastern forests acquired under the Weeks Act of 1911, 16

U.S.C.A. §§ 515–521, and national grasslands on the High Plains acquired under the Depression–Era Submarginal Land Retirement Program. The main statutes directing Forest Service management are the Organic Act of 1897, id. §§ 473–551, the Multiple–Use, Sustained–Yield Act (MUSYA) of 1960, id. §§ 528–531, and the National Forest Management Act (NFMA) of 1976, id. §§ 1600–1616. See Chapter 7.

b. The BLM Public Lands

The "public lands" are defined by statute as lands and interests in land under the jurisdiction of the Bureau of Land Management in the Department of the Interior. 43 U.S.C.A. § 1702(e). (This Nutshell refers to them as "BLM public lands" to avoid confusion with normal semantic constructions.) The BLM public lands are those that were not reserved, homesteaded, or otherwise claimed before they were withdrawn into grazing districts pursuant to the 1934 Taylor Grazing Act, id. §§ 315–315r. They tend to be the federal lands that are in the worst ecological condition and the most difficult to manage because of scattered ownership patterns and inholdings and lack of resources. BLM jurisdiction has steadily shrunk since the 1930s as its lands were transferred to other agencies and entities. Still, about 180 million acres in the western states and about 90 million acres in Alaska remain under BLM control. The BLM also oversees mineral leasing and location on the other federal lands systems. Besides the Taylor Act, the BLM's

primary governing statute is the Federal Land Policy and Management Act (FLPMA) of 1976, id.
§§ 1701–1784, which succeeded the expired Classification and Multiple Use Act of 1964, id. §§ 1411–
1418.

c. The National Wildlife Refuge System (NWRS)

The National Wildlife Refuge System Administration Act (NWRSAA) of 1966, 16 U.S.C.A. §§ 668dd–
668ee, consolidated the patchwork of refuges,
ranges, waterfowl areas, etc. into the NWRS. The
System is managed by the Fish and Wildlife Service
(in the Interior Department), which also imple-
ments nationally general wildlife programs such as
the designation of endangered and threatened species. The Refuge System has over 500 units, aggregating over 90 million acres, in nearly every state,
although a majority of its acreage is in Alaska.
Special segregated tax revenues and appropriations
from the Land and Water Conservation Fund have
financed additions to the System. The NWRS is
managed principally for wildlife conservation, although other uses are permitted to the extent compatible with that purpose. The National Wildlife
Refuge System Improvement Act of 1997, 16
U.S.C.A. §§ 668dd–668ee, instituted a hierarchy of
uses and mandated a planning process. See section
9C.

d. The National Park System

Interior's National Park Service manages the 80–
odd million acre National Park System, which is

devoted primarily to recreation and preservation. Half of that acreage was added to the system by the Alaska National Interest Lands Conservation Act (ANILCA) of 1980. The National Park System contains not only national parks but also land categories such as monuments, seashores, recreation areas, lakeshores, urban parks, cultural areas, and military sites. See section 10C. The primary governing laws include the National Park Service Organic Act of 1916, 16 U.S.C.A. §§ 1–18, which requires management "for the enjoyment of future generations"; the Antiquities Act of 1906, id. §§ 431–433, which governs management of the national monuments; and the individual statutes that create each park system unit.

e.   The Preservation Lands

The Wilderness Act of 1964, id. §§ 1131–1136, superimposes the National Wilderness Preservation System on the preexisting land management systems. From nine million acres of "instant wilderness," the system has grown through congressional designations to over 100 million acres. Each wilderness area is managed for preservational purposes by the original managing agency. See section 11D. Similar but more limited in scope are the National Wild and Scenic Rivers Act of 1968, id. §§ 1271–1287, and the National Trails Act, id. §§ 1241–1251. See section 11C. In addition to adding about 50 million acres to both the National Park and Wildlife Refuge Systems, the 1980 ANILCA served preservation objectives by creating more than 50 million acres of additional wilderness and designating thirteen river segments as wild or scenic. One Senator called the Act "perhaps the greatest conservation achievement of the century."

See PNRL § 2:17, chapters 14B, 15.

E. A MODERN LEGACY OF PUBLIC LAND HISTORY: ACCESS TO FEDERAL LANDS

The haphazard nature of settlement, grant, sale, location, withdrawal, and reservation over two centuries resulted in a crazy-quilt patchwork map of land ownership in much of the West. Federal, state, local, and private parcels are interspersed, more or less randomly. The ownership patterns cause various problems, not the least of which is legal rights of access. The primary questions are: who may cross nonfederal land to reach federal land?; and, who may cross federal land to reach federal or nonfederal land? Wilderness designation processes and new attitudes have brought long-dormant access questions to the fore, but no easy answers to these questions have emerged.

The Supreme Court in 1979 unanimously held that the United States did not retain any implied easements for access to its own lands when it made checkerboard grants to the transcontinental railroads in the 19th century. Leo Sheep Co. v. United States (S.Ct.1979). Even though the common law would have provided a private, landlocked owner with an easement by necessity under similar circumstances, the government's power of eminent domain eliminated the necessity for the easement. Because most disposition statutes were silent about retaining access rights, the *Leo Sheep* reasoning means that the United States must condemn access routes over private property for its agents or licensees to have access to retained federal lands. When the United States grants only the surface, however, its dominant mineral estate carries with it a right of access and entry for mineral purposes. E.g., Occidental Geothermal, Inc. v. Simmons (N.D.Cal.1982).

Even though the United States lacks implied easements, it can still force private owners to refrain from fencing their lands in such a fashion as to deny access to federal lands. This regulatory power is exerted in the Unlawful Inclosures Act (UIA) of 1885, 43 U.S.C.A. §§ 1061–1063, which makes obstruction of access by force, threats, intimidation, or fencing a criminal offense. Camfield v. United States (S.Ct.1897), rejected an attack on the constitutionality of the Act as it applied to the use of private checkerboarded sections. Although private owners could fence their own tracts, they could not, under the guise of doing so, enclose adjacent federal tracts.

The UIA is not limited to human access. In United States ex rel. Bergen v. Lawrence (10th Cir.1988) the court extended it to insure access to federal lands for migrating wildlife. The government alleged that construction of a fence to exclude antelope from their winter range (likely so that their presence would not interfere with projected mining activities) violated the UIA. Relying on that statute's prohibition of the prevention or obstruction of "free passage or transit over or through the public lands," the Tenth Circuit upheld the district court's order requiring removal of the fence. The absence of any reference in the UIA's legislative history to wildlife made no difference because the statutory prohibition applied to access for "any and all lawful purposes over public lands," and FLPMA authorized winter forage by antelope.

Problems of access to and across federal lands are further discussed in section 4E.

CHAPTER THREE

CONSTITUTIONAL AUTHORITY ON THE FEDERAL PUBLIC LANDS: CONGRESS AND THE STATES

Congressional power over the use or allocation of public lands and resources derives from several constitutional provisions. The Commerce, Treaty, and Spending Clauses all justify certain kinds of legislation. Most jurisdictional conflicts between federal and state powers are governed by the Enclave, Property, and Supremacy Clauses of the Constitution. This chapter describes the major cases that define the scope of federal power and correspondingly limit the powers of states. The constitutional prohibition against "taking" private property, discussed in the final section, applies to both federal and state sovereigns and represents the preeminent "individual rights" issue raised by management of the federal lands.

A. JURISDICTION WITHIN FEDERAL ENCLAVES

The "Jurisdiction" or "Enclave" Clause of the United States Constitution, art. I, § 8, cl. 17, gives Congress exclusive jurisdiction over the District of

Columbia and "all places purchased by the Consent of the [State] Legislature ... for the Erection of Forts, Magazines, Arsenals, dock-Yards, and other needful Buildings." Lands so acquired are called federal enclaves. Enclaves amount to only about six percent of total federal land holdings.

From an early time, the United States Supreme Court refused to read the Enclave Clause literally or strictly. Had it done so, state authority would have stopped at enclave borders and the states could not have taxed private property or served process within enclaves. Instead, the Court held that the states and the federal government could make whatever jurisdictional allocations they desired and that "needful buildings" encompasses all valid federal purposes. This interpretation resulted in the extension of the Enclave Clause to situations in which the government owned land that it acquired before the states existed or the states attached conditions to cessions of jurisdiction. The leading case is Fort Leavenworth R. Co. v. Lowe (S.Ct.1885). Kansas ceded jurisdiction over Fort Leavenworth to the United States, but reserved jurisdiction to serve process and to tax private property within the federal reservation. The railroad argued that "exclusive" means "absolutely exclusive," and thus that the state could not tax its property, but the Court upheld the reserved state taxing power. In the course of its opinion, the Supreme Court also created an immunity from state law for areas owned and used by the federal government for military purposes. Because the United States owned Fort Leavenworth before Kansas was admitted to statehood, its "cession could be accompanied with such conditions as the state might see fit to annex not inconsistent with the free and effective use of the fort as a military post."

Later cases further liberalized the apparently strict limitations of the Enclave Clause. In Collins v. Yosemite Park & Curry Co. (S.Ct.1938), the Supreme Court determined that the sovereign parties could make jurisdictional arrangements for national parks under the Enclave Clause. "As the National Government may, 'by virtue of its sovereignty' acquire lands within the borders of states by eminent domain and without their consent, the respective sovereignties should be in a position to adjust their jurisdictions [without constitutional objection]."

Within federal enclaves, governing law is assumed to be federal law, unless the federal government has somehow assimilated or acceded to state law in the circumstances. Under the Assimilative Crimes Act (ACA) of 1825, 18 U.S.C.A. § 13, state criminal law is assimilated in enclaves, including state law enacted after the most recent reenactment of the ACA. United States v. Sharpnack (S.Ct.1958). Prosecution nevertheless proceeds in federal court. United States v. Parker (10th Cir.2004). The Supreme Court has established a two-part test for determining whether a particular state criminal law is incorporated into federal law under the ACA. If the defendant's act or omission is not made punishable under any federal statute, assimilation of state law is proper. If, however, it is made punishable by federal law, the issue is whether the applicable federal law precludes the application of the state law in question because, for example, state law would interfere with the achievement of federal policy. Lewis v. United States (S.Ct.1998); United States v. Souza (9th Cir.2004).

Congress also assimilated state wrongful death and personal injury law, 16 U.S.C.A. § 457, but it has not generally assimilated state civil law. In cases where no federal law covers the subject in controversy, the law applicable is the law of the transferor state that was effective on the date of cession. Arlington Hotel v. Fant (S.Ct.1929). The extent to which the states must provide enclave inhabitants with the same rights as citizens of the state is comprehensive but not entirely settled.

Enclave law is mostly obsolete today, because the broad interpretation of the Property Clause in Article IV of the Constitution overshadows any limits on federal powers inferable from the Enclave Clause.

See PNRL §§ 3:5–3:9.

B. THE PROPERTY CLAUSE (ON FEDERAL LANDS)

The Property Clause, art. IV, § 3, cl. 2, recites:

The Congress shall have Power to dispose of and make all needful Rules and Regulations respecting the Territory or other Property belonging to the United States.

Some commentators long have argued that the Property Clause does not mean what it seems to say. The most radical version of this "classical" interpretation is that permanent federal ownership of nongovernmental lands outside the purview of the Enclave Clause is unconstitutional because the United States is subject to a trust duty to dispose of all such lands. They point to dicta in Pollard v. Hagan (S.Ct.1845), and *Fort Leavenworth R. Co. v. Lowe*, supra, as support. This argument was the legal basis for the short-lived Sagebrush Rebellion in the late 1970s. The courts have consistently rejected the radical contention for a century and a half, most recently and emphatically in Kleppe v. New Mexico (S.Ct.1976), and United States v. Gardner (9th Cir.1997).

The more moderate version of the argument that Congress has less than full powers under the Property Clause asserts that the United States, as a (nonenclave) property owner, is only a proprietor and thus is fully subject to all state law like any other private landowner. The upshot of this contention, if ever accepted, would be that federal law can have no preemptive effect—and, indeed, would be itself overridden by contrary state law. Again, obscure references to ancient dicta and assumptions about the intent of the Framers are the only legal support for this position.

The courts have consistently rejected that "moderate" theory as well since 1845. The Supreme Court in *Camfield v. United States*, supra, recognized that the federal government possesses a power over its property "analogous to the police power of the several States"; any other rule would place the public domain "at the mercy of state legislation." In *Light v. United States*, supra, the Court made it clear that Congress not only could withhold public lands from settlement indefinitely, it could carry out its trust however it chose. These rights stemmed from the government's role as a proprietor as well as a sovereign. The opinion in Utah Power & Light Co. v. United States (S.Ct.1917), specifically limited the reach of state law on federal lands to matters not inconsistent with federal power and federal law. The Court in Hunt v. United States (S.Ct.1928), upheld a federal deer control program undertaken in contravention of state law.

Kleppe v. New Mexico (S.Ct.1976), should have been dispositive, but some still argue for implied limitations on congressional Property Clause powers. *Kleppe* involved a challenge to the validity of the Wild Free–Roaming Horses and Burros Act (WF–RHBA), 16 U.S.C.A. §§ 1331–1340, which prohibits the killing, harassment, or sale of such critters on BLM or Forest Service lands. The state argued that it owned the regulated feral beasts, that Congress could act only to protect federal lands, not wildlife, and that the United States is only a proprietor, without legislative power, when it acts as a landowner. The unanimous Court soundly rejected all those contentions. It differentiated between enclave and other lands, noting that cases concerning the former, such as *Fort Leavenworth R. Co.*, supra, were irrelevant to the latter. The requirement that legislation be directed at protection of the public lands applies only to situations in which the federal government is acting "extraterritorially." (See the following section). The United States remains a sovereign when it owns land, and congressional Property Clause power is "without limitations." Federal legislation is preemptive as well as plenary: where "state laws conflict with ... legislation passed pursuant to the Property Clause, the law is clear: the state laws must recede." In Nuclear Energy Inst. v. EPA (D.C. Cir.2004), the court rejected the contention that a congressional resolution selecting a site on federal lands in Nevada for construction of a nuclear waste disposal facility exceeded Congress' power under the Property Clause.

See PNRL §§ 3:10–3:12.

C. THE PROPERTY CLAUSE (OFF FEDERAL LANDS)

The Unlawful Inclosures Act (UIA) of 1885, 43 U.S.C.A. § 1061–1063, prohibits all "inclosures of any public lands." Camfield built a fence on his own lands that had the effect of denying access to checkerboarded federal lands within the fenced area. At the behest of the United States, the Supreme Court required abatement of the fence, even though it was located on private property. *Camfield v. United States*, supra. The Court treated the fence as a species of nuisance because of this exclusionary effect, and opined that:

it is within the constitutional power of Congress
to order its abatement, notwithstanding such action may involve an entry on lands of a private
individual. The general Government doubtless
has a power over its own property analogous to
the police power of the several states, and the
extent to which it may go in the exercise of such
power is measured by the exigencies of the particular case ... so long as such power is directed
solely to [the public lands'] protection.

The Court reaffirmed *Camfield* in United States v.
Alford (S.Ct.1927), upholding the government's authority to prohibit unextinguished fires in or near
the national forests. According to Justice Holmes,
"Congress may prohibit the doing of any acts upon
privately owned lands that imperil the publicly
owned forests."

The *Kleppe v. New Mexico* Court found it unnecessary to decide "the extent, if any, to which the
Property Clause empowers Congress to protect animals on private lands or the extent to which such
regulation is attempted by the [WF–RHBA]." Lower
courts in every other recent case raising the question have held that the Property Clause did apply
"extraterritorially" in the circumstances presented.
The leading instance is Minnesota v. Block (8th
Cir.1981). Congress had outlawed forms of mecha-
nized transportation on all lands, federal, state, and
private, within the boundaries of a federal wilderness reservation. Rejecting various attacks against
such restrictions, the Eighth Circuit characterized
the power to forbid uses of adjacent land that are

potentially injurious to public land use as a "necessary incident" of the power to dedicate federal lands
to particular purposes. It held that the caveat in
Camfield dictates this two-pronged test: "if Congress enacted the ... restrictions to protect the
fundamental purpose for which [the federal area]
had been reserved, and if the restrictions ... reasonably relate to that end, we must conclude that
Congress acted within its constitutional prerogative." In this case, the restrictions were a reasonable means to achieve a proper end. Subsequent
cases have also endorsed regulation of activities off
the federal lands. In Columbia River Gorge United–
Protecting People and Property v. Yeutter (9th Cir.
1992), for example, the court essentially recognized
federal authority in the nature of the power to zone
private land adjacent to a national scenic area by
upholding controls on land development imposed by
an interstate regulatory commission.

The full extent of the Property Clause's reach has
not been determined because the government has
been reluctant to assert it. Nevertheless, it is proba-
ble that other constitutional powers, notably the
Commerce Clause, will suffice to uphold any con-
ceivable regulation respecting the federal lands. The
Supreme Court has revived limits on Congress' regulatory authority under the Commerce Clause in
recent years, see United States v. Morrison (S.Ct.
2000); United States v. Lopez (S.Ct.1995), but it has
indicated that those limits are narrowly circum-
scribed, see, e.g., Gonzales v. Raich (S.Ct.2005),
and, in any event, those limits have not yet directly

affected the powers of the federal land management agencies. But cf. Solid Waste Agency of N. Cook County v. U.S. Army Corps of Eng'rs (S.Ct.2001) (holding that the CWA does not authorize regulation simply on the basis of the presence of migratory birds, in part because of questions as to whether the Commerce Clause would support such regulation). Attacks on regulation of external threats are more likely to succeed if grounded on alleged statutory violations than on the absence of sufficient authority under the Property Clause. The Treaty Clause also may provide authority for some intrusive federal actions. See Missouri v. Holland (S.Ct. 1920).

See PNRL §§ 3:13–3:17.

D. FEDERAL PREEMPTION

On nonenclave federal lands, state law governs unless it has been preempted or otherwise overridden by federal law. The United States Congress has full preemptive powers (*Kleppe*, supra), but the question whether or to what extent Congress intended to exercise those powers often is complicated and difficult. The "federalism" inquiry (which sovereign's law governs what situations?), implicates not only preemption doctrines but also various assumptions, common law principles, and other doctrines such as intergovernmental immunities. In all such inquiries, congressional intent is the decisive factor.

Federal preemption of state law occurs when:

1. Congress says it does (express preemption);

2. Congress occupies the entire regulatory field, to the exclusion of state law;

3. State law directly conflicts with federal law; or

4. State law stands as an obstacle to the accomplishment of a federal purpose.

The first situation, express preemption, seldom occurs in public land law, which is characterized by "cooperative federalism," but it has happened. E.g., 16 U.S.C.A. § 1535(f) (state endangered species laws cannot be less restrictive than federal laws and rules). Similarly, and for the same reason, Congress almost never assumes such total and complete responsibility over a public land regulatory subject as to occupy the field. The usual disputes revolve around the "conflict" and "obstacle" branches of preemption. Those tests, while theoretically distinct, often are condensed into one. See, e.g., National Audubon Soc'y v. Davis (9th Cir.2002) (holding that state law restricting the use of leghold traps was preempted by the ESA and the NWRSIA because of a conflict between federal and state policies).

The leading preemption case in modern public land law now is California Coastal Comm'n v. Granite Rock Co. (S.Ct.1987). To understand its significance, however, mention of its predecessor, Ventura County v. Gulf Oil Corp. (9th Cir.1979), is necessary. The County in *Ventura* required a zoning permit for oil and gas operations, but the holder of a federal lease refused to apply, claiming the local requirement was preempted. The Ninth Circuit agreed, despite a Mineral Leasing Act provision retaining for the states the power "to exercise any rights which they might have," but the court's rationale was murky. It could not find a direct regulatory conflict between the federal and local regulatory schemes, because the County did not have an opportunity to determine which, if any, conditions it would have attached to the permit. Nothing in any of the applicable federal laws pointed toward congressional intent to preempt; to the contrary, the MLA specifically accommodates state regulations in many respects (also negating any intention to occupy the field). The court essentially decided that the existence of the local permit scheme by itself was both a conflict with the federal licensing system and an obstacle to accomplishment of an undefined federal purpose. The Supreme Court affirmed without opinion.

State preemption decisions before and after *Ventura* disagreed with its rationale in the contexts both of mineral leasing and hardrock mineral location. A narrow Supreme Court majority in *Granite Rock* adopted that contrary position in part, but the decision raises far more questions than it answers. In a nutshell, Granite Rock had a location claim to limestone located in a Big Sur national forest and had received all necessary federal clearances (fewer and less strict than in the leasing scenario) to begin mining. The state Coastal Commission, like the County in *Ventura*, contended that Granite Rock could not commence mining without a state permit, and the company, like Gulf Oil, refused to go through the state permit procedure. The five-member Supreme Court majority ruled that the CCC permit requirement was not preempted on its face by regulations implementing the 1897 Forest Service Organic Act or by other federal laws, although subsequent actual conditions imposed might be preempted. The Court could find no specific congressional intent to preempt such state requirements. The CCC argued that it sought not to prohibit mining on federal lands, but merely to impose reasonable conditions to protect the environment. The Court accepted the distinction between land use planning and environmental regulation, which it discerned in FLPMA's planning provisions, 43 U.S.C.A. § 1712, although it conceded the absence of a bright line separating the two. Section 1712(c)(9) instructs the Interior Secretary to abide by state land use planning "to the maximum extent he finds consistent with Federal law." A companion provision, section 1712(c)(8), requires full compliance with state regulation of air, water, and land pollution without qualification. The majority (for unexplained reasons) assumed arguendo that the first provision was preemptive, despite Congress' apparent desire to accommodate state law, but went on to hold that because the permit conditions could be "environmental" (that is, in the nature of general pollution control), no facial preemption occurred. The dissenters would have ruled that the existence of an additional "duplicative" permit system is inherently in conflict with the federal regulatory scheme (Powell and Stevens), or that California's regulation necessarily would be land use regulation which is automatically preempted (Scalia and White). Only Justice Scalia even cited *Ventura,* and that was in passing.

Granite Rock decides very little. Its major impact will be to force federal lessees and permittees to undergo the gauntlet of state regulatory avenues before bringing preemption suits. In such suits, the questions likely will be:

— how can the line between "land use" and "environmental" regulation be drawn?

— what is the real difference between "reasonable regulation" and de facto "prohibition" of the activity?

No complete or even good answers to either question suggest themselves. For an example of a preempted de facto prohibition, see South Dakota Mining Ass'n v. Lawrence County (8th Cir.1998). In addition, preemption analyses will necessarily continue to vary by system and resource. Neither the NPS nor the FWS, for example, is subject to the NFMA or FLPMA provisions that governed the result in *Granite Rock*.

Preemption is not the only label under which interjurisdictional federalism conflicts are resolved. Congress often expressly defers to state law in areas such as water allocation or hunting regulation. Courts will protect federal property interests from hostile, discriminatory, or aberrant state law, however, under the guise of a federal common law of real property, United States v. Little Lake Misere Land Co. (S.Ct.1973), and they will create federal "implied" property rights if necessary for the protection of federal interests. E.g., Cappaert v. United States (S.Ct.1976) (implied reserved water rights).

Further, intergovernmental immunities doctrines are a facet of federalism. Those doctrines essentially provide that states cannot tax federal property (although they can tax private property on federal lands, United States v. County of Fresno (S.Ct. 1977)), and that states cannot regulate or otherwise interfere with federal programs and functions unless Congress has specifically assented. Hancock v. Train (S.Ct.1976). In some cases, the Supreme Court's reluctance to find the necessary evidence of congressional intent to waive sovereign immunity to state regulation is striking. E.g., United States Dep't of Energy v. Ohio (S.Ct.1992). In others, the Court has upheld intrusive state regulation. California v. United States (S.Ct.1978) (regulation of a federal dam).

Another side of the federalism coin is federal financial assistance to states and localities. Most federal commodity resource disposition programs (such as oil, gas, grass, and timber) require that a portion of the federal receipts (up to 90 percent in Alaska) be rebated to the states or local governments of origin. For this reason, states are often more supportive of federal resource development than they otherwise might be. States also are the beneficiaries of various federal resource grant programs, such as the Robertson–Pittman program and the Land and Water Conservation Fund, 16 U.S.C.A. §§ 460*l*–5 to 460*l*–22. Additionally, states and localities receive direct payments wherever federal lands are located pursuant to the Payments in Lieu of Taxes Act, 31 U.S.C.A. §§ 6901–6907. States can and do tax resource exploitation on the federal lands. E.g., Commonwealth Edison Co. v. Montana (S.Ct.1981). All in all, federal land ownership benefits states and localities financially, even if contrary state law must yield to federal dictate.

See PNRL §§ 5:18–5:38.

E. "TAKINGS" LIMITS ON THE EXERCISE OF CONGRESSIONAL POWER

The Fifth and Fourteenth Amendments constrain the regulatory reach of both federal and state governments by prohibiting the taking of private property for a public use without just compensation. After years of quiescence, the takings clauses was revitalized as a basis for avoiding regulatory impositions by Supreme Court decisions in the 1980s and 1990s. The pertinent issue is whether those cases and their lower court progeny will pose obstacles to the accomplishment of the regulatory objectives of the federal land management agencies, which, historically, have been immune to takings challenges.

1.   TAKINGS LAW IN GENERAL

Justice Holmes ruled in 1922 that governmental regulation of property could not go "too far" without requiring the payment of compensation to sustain it. Pennsylvania Coal Co. v. Mahon (S.Ct.1922). *Pennsylvania Coal* established that regulation of private property can "take" that property, but did not delineate the invisible dividing line between noncompensable regulation and inverse condemnation. Subsequent cases and theoretical commentaries have suggested a host of tests, none of which is dispositive in all circumstances. For decades following *Pennsylvania Coal*, the Supreme Court rejected the relatively few takings challenges brought before it. The Court ruled that none of the following federal, state, or local regulatory schemes amounted to a taking:

— a prohibition on sale or barter of legally acquired wildlife artifacts to protect the affected species; Andrus v. Allard (S.Ct.1979);

— institution of severe environmental controls over strip mining, Hodel v. Virginia Surface Mining and Reclamation Ass'n (S.Ct.1981);

— controls on coal mining intended to prevent surface subsidence, Keystone Bituminous Coal Ass'n v. DeBenedictis (S.Ct.1987) (a nearly identical replay of *Pennsylvania Coal*);

— a prohibition on the alteration of a city-designated historic landmark, Penn Central Transp. Co. v. City of New York (S.Ct.1978); and

— automatic lapse of severed mineral interests for nonuse, Texaco, Inc. v. Short (S.Ct.1982).

In cases that did not involve federal land management, the Court concluded that a taking occurred, or may have occurred, in instances when a state or local regulator either denied a permit for development or imposed conditions in the nature of access easements for the benefit of the public, despite the absence of any evidence of adverse economic impact on the owner. In Nollan v. California Coastal Comm'n (S.Ct.1987), the Court found a taking, because the permit requirement was not sufficiently related to the state's alleged regulatory interests and essentially amounted to the imposition of a public access easement. In Dolan v. City of Tigard (S.Ct.1994), the public access and dedication conditions imposed on a building permit applicant amounted to a taking because the city could not demonstrate a "rough proportionality" between the exactions demanded and the anticipated impact of development. The Court later limited *Dolan* to dedications demanded as conditions of development and made it clear that the rough proportionality requirement does not apply to denials of development rights. City of Monterey v. Del Monte Dunes (S.Ct. 1999). It also clarified that a regulation that fails to advance legitimate state interests may amount to a violation of substantive due process, but not a taking. Lingle v. Chevron U.S.A. Inc. (S.Ct.2005) (overruling Agins v. City of Tiburon (S.Ct.1980)).

The Court also has found a taking based on adverse economic impact. In Lucas v. South Carolina Coastal Council (S.Ct.1992), the Court reversed the state court's decision that a beachfront preservation statute that deprived a property owner of all reasonable economic use was not a taking. It enunciated a per se takings rule for regulations that eliminate all economically viable use, excepting only regulations that affect uses that would have been proscribed anyway under "background principles" of preexisting state common law. In another case, the Court rejected the contention that a property owner who acquired the regulated property after the effective date of the regulation is necessarily barred from pursuing a takings claim, although the fact that the takings claimant purchased with knowledge of the restrictions may be relevant to the issue of whether the regulation impermissibly interfered with the owner's reasonable investment-backed expectations. Palazzolo v. Rhode Island (S.Ct.2001). See also Norman v. United States (Fed. Cir. 2005) (stating that it is "particularly difficult to establish a reasonable investment-backed expectation" when title was acquired after the effective date of the challenged restriction).

Many questions remain concerning the circumstances in which a regulation will amount to a taking based on adverse economic impact. *Lucas*, supra, held that a regulation that denies a property owner of all economically viable use is a per se taking. But as Justice Scalia admitted in *Lucas*, the Court has not yet defined the property interest against which loss should be measured in a case alleging a taking based on economic impact. In Tahoe–Sierra Pres. Council, Inc. v. Tahoe Reg'l Planning Agency (S.Ct.2002), the Court held that a temporary moratorium on development did not amount to the kind of categorical taking it had found in *Lucas*, despite the property owner's claim that it had been deprived of all economically viable use during the period in which the moratorium was in effect. In doing so, it retreated considerably from *Lucas*, describing it as a narrow exception to be applied only in "extraordinary circumstances." Another area of uncertainty relates to the status and scope of the principle, endorsed as recently as the *Keystone* case, supra, that regulation of a nuisance-like use is not a taking.

In the wake of the Supreme Court's takings cases during the 1980s and 1990s, litigants raised takings claims with increased frequency and renewed vigor, sometimes successfully. The Court of Appeals for the Federal Circuit ruled in several cases, for example, that the application of the CWA's dredge and fill permit program, 33 U.S.C.A. § 1344, amounted to a compensable taking. See Loveladies Harbor, Inc. v. United States (Fed. Cir.1994); Palm Beach Isles Assoc. v. United States (Fed. Cir.2000). Cf. Florida Rock Indus., Inc. v. United States (Fed. Cir.1994) (reasoning that because partial physical invasions are takings, regulations that reduce but do not eliminate economically viable use also might be takings to the extent of the reduction in value). But see Good v. United States (Fed. Cir.1999) (denying taking claim based on absence of reasonable investment-backed expectations).

See PNRL §§ 4:5–4:15.

2. TAKINGS IN MODERN PUBLIC LAND LAW

Thus far, there is little evidence that the Supreme Court's increased interest in takings issues will significantly impair the scope of the federal land management agencies' regulatory authority. A property interest must exist before it can be taken. In most taking scenarios, the plaintiff concededly has fee title, usually to land. Private property interests in public lands or resources seldom rise to the level of a fee simple absolute. In Freese v. United States (Ct.Cl.1981), for example, congressional denial of the opportunity to obtain patents on mineral locations in a specified area was not a taking because denial of the opportunity to patent did not amount to divestment of a property interest. Even the filing of a patent application does not create compensable property rights; only final approval of a patent has that effect. Swanson v. Babbitt (9th Cir.1993). Similarly, a decision reducing the number of cattle permitted to graze in a national forest was not a taking because a grazing permit is revocable at the will of the government. McKinley v. United States (D.N.M.1993). See also Colvin Cattle Co. v. United States (Fed.Cl.2005) (stating that "a grazing permit does not rise to the level of a protectable property interest" so as to sustain a takings claim). See section 8A.

Even where property rights have vested, it has been difficult to demonstrate a taking because the tradition of extensive government regulation of private rights in public resources reduces the reasonable, investment-backed expectations of the property owner. That factor, along with the economic impact of the regulation and the character of the government action, are the determinative factors in the ad hoc approach to resolving takings questions enunciated in *Penn Central*, supra. In United States v. Locke (S.Ct.1985), the leading public natural resources law takings case, plaintiffs owned valuable unpatented mining claims to sand and gravel deposits on public land. FLPMA, enacted after perfection of the claims, required an annual filing by claimants *before* December 31 of each year; plaintiffs filed on December 31. The penalty for failure to file was forfeiture of the claim; these claims could not be relocated because sand and gravel were no longer locatable.

Plaintiffs argued, inter alia, that if the statute was construed so as to deprive them of their property, then it constituted a taking for which compensation was due. The Supreme Court summarily rejected that contention. It instead held:

> This power to qualify existing property rights is particularly broad with respect to the "character" of the property rights at issue here. Although owners of unpatented mining claims hold fully recognized possessory interests in their claims, we have recognized that these interests are a "unique form of property".... The United States, as owner of the underlying fee title to the public domain, maintains broad powers over the terms and conditions upon which the public lands can be used, leased, and acquired ... Claimants

thus take their mineral interests with the knowledge that the Government retains substantial
regulatory power over those interests.

In this case, the burden of compliance was minimal,
and the statute and its purposes were reasonable.

Regulation of property rights does not "take"
private property when an individual's reasonable,
investment-backed expectations can continue to
be realized as long as he complies with reasonable
regulatory restrictions the legislature has imposed.

Other takings claims arising from the decisions of
the federal land management agencies also have
foundered. In Bass Enter. Prod. Co. v. United
States (Fed. Cir.2004), for example, the court held
that the BLM's delay in ruling on a drilling permit
did not amount to a temporary taking, but rather a
"normal," noncompensable delay in permit processing. The potential adverse impact of drilling near a
nuclear waste disposal site also supported the conclusion that the BLM's action did not result in a
taking. In Appolo Fuels, Inc. v. United States (Fed.
Cir.2004), the court held that restrictions imposed
by the Office of Surface Mining (OSM) on surface
coal mining under the Surface Mining Control and
Reclamation Act did not amount to either a categorical taking based on *Lucas* or a partial regulatory
taking based on *Penn Central*. Cf. Rith Energy, Inc.
v. United States (Fed. Cir.2001) (OSM's denial of
mining permit in light of risk of acid mine drainage
was not a taking).

Theorists have long conceived of fee simple ownership as a bundle of rights consisting of the right to possess, use, and dispose of the land or other property owned. In *Minnesota v. Block*, supra, inholders in a federal reservation unsuccessfully relied on this theory in alleging that a statute that gave the United States a right of first refusal at the sale of any inholding in the area was a taking. The plaintiffs argued that the provision created a cloud on title, diminished land value by deterring potential buyers, and divested the owner of an option in the property. The Eighth Circuit disagreed on all counts, concluding that "the mere conditioning of the sale of the property cannot rise to the level of a taking." Whatever diminution in value the statute caused was minimal, and the statute did not interfere with the owner's ability to use, possess, or give away the property. See also Clajon Prod. Corp. v. Patera (10th Cir.1995) (holding that state limitation on hunting on private land was not a taking because it did not destroy all beneficial use of regulated land and right to hunt was not a segregable property interest). In Preseault v. United States (Fed. Cir.1996), however, the court held that approval of a rails-to-trails conversion constituted a taking because it amounted to a government-authorized physical invasion of the property of the holders of the reversion of the railroad's easement.

Efforts to characterize as takings the government's failure to stop wildlife from damaging private property have not fared well. In Mountain States Legal Found. v. Hodel (10th Cir.1986), the court rejected the contention that protections afforded wild horses by the WF–RHBA amounted to a permanent government occupation of private ranches, even though consumption of forage by horses reduced the value of ranch property. Similarly, the Ninth Circuit held that a prohibition on killing threatened grizzly bears that preyed on the plaintiff's sheep was not a taking. Christy v. Hodel (9th Cir.1988).

Not all takings claims leveled against the federal land management agencies have failed, however. The Court of Federal Claims refused to grant summary judgment to the government on a claim that the Forest Service had taken a grazing permit holder's water rights recognized under state law. Hage v. United States (Fed.Cl.1996). See also Walker v. United States (Fed.Cl.2005) (refusing to dismiss takings challenge based on the Forest Service's cancellation of a grazing permit, even though a federal district court had previously ruled that the permit holders lacked any title in the surface estate of the allotment). The same court ruled subsequently that the plaintiff rancher had no compensable rights in the land covered by their Taylor Act grazing permits or in the permits themselves. Hage v. United States (Fed.Cl.1998). The court in Colvin Cattle Co. v. United States (Fed.Cl.2005), read the first *Hage* decision narrowly, stating that it is the only case to find a right to graze in connection with the Mining Act of 1866, that it explicitly concluded that the Mining Act does not address property rights in the public lands, that it did not hold that the plaintiff's water rights included a right to graze on land adjacent to the water, and that it dealt only with a situation in which the government had allegedly limited the rancher's access to water.

An area likely to generate future takings claims is the application of land use restrictions arising from the ESA § 9 takings prohibition. In Tulare Lake Basin Water Storage Dist. v. United States (Fed.Cl. 2001), the Bureau of Reclamation restricted water withdrawals from a reclamation project upon the recommendation of the FWS, which had concluded that operation of the project was likely to jeopardize listed fish species. The court ruled that the withdrawal restrictions constituted a physical taking because they completely eviscerated the water rights of the plaintiff water districts. The court rejected the government's argument that the application of the public trust doctrine and the common law of nuisance rendered the water loss noncompensable. In a later case, a different judge on the Court of Federal Claims criticized *Tulare Lake*, on the grounds, among others, that the court in that case failed to consider whether the water districts' contract rights were limited in times of water shortage and to consider whether the plaintiffs' claimed use of water violated accepted state doctrines, including those designed to protect fish and wildlife. Accordingly, *Tulare Lake* awarded compensation "for the taking of interests that may well not exist under state law." Klamath Irrigation Dist. v. United States (Fed.Cl.2005). In another case, the Federal Circuit rejected the contention that the FWS's denial of an incidental take permit under the ESA, which it later rescinded, was a temporary taking. Seiber v. United States (Fed. Cir.2004).

Public natural resources law traditions and the nature of the competing public and private interests may serve to distinguish cases such as *Nollan*, *Lucas*, and *Dolan*, in which the Supreme Court found compensable regulatory takings. To date, few cases contradict the notion that the federal government has broad discretion to condition use or availability of its resources however it chooses without fear of liability for just compensation. Although recent cases almost unanimously reject takings claims in various circumstances, the holders of private property rights in public natural resources are certain to continue to file these claims with some frequency, and decisions such as *Tulare Lake* indicate that litigants should not assume that the claims will fail.

See PNRL §§ 4:16–4:27.

CHAPTER FOUR

AUTHORITY ON THE PUBLIC LANDS: THE EXECUTIVE AND THE COURTS

Congress has the constitutional power to manage federal lands and resources, but the executive branch must carry out the legislative commands, and courts must decide whether it has done so in a manner consistent with statutory delegations. This tripartite division of responsibility among the three branches of government raises a variety of constitutional and practical questions in the federal public land law context.

The first question is allocation of decisional power. Section A discusses the ability of Congress and the agencies to delegate or subdelegate their legal authorities. Possibly the most important general question implicates the respective roles and powers of the executive and the judiciary. Section B of this chapter addresses this question, which is subsumed into the heading of judicial review of administrative agency decisions. Conflict between the Executive and the Congress, the focus of sections C and D, is highlighted in the areas of withdrawals, reservations, and land title transfers. Section E deals with access problems. Whether or to what extent any branch of the federal government is subject to a "public trust" duty is the subject of section F of this chapter. Section G describes the ubiquitous National Environmental Policy Act (NEPA), 42 U.S.C.A. §§ 4321–4370d, a pervasive influence on modern public land law.

A. DELEGATION

Any power over federal property exercised by the President or an administrative agency must be delegated to them by Congress. The Supreme Court has upheld very broad delegations. United States v. Grimaud (S.Ct.1911). The Court apparently buried the nondelegation doctrine as a meaningful constraint on statutory delegations in Whitman v. American Trucking Ass'ns, Inc. (S.Ct.2001), holding that a provision of the Clean Air Act authorizing EPA to issue national ambient air quality standards "requisite to protect the public health" contained the requisite "intelligible principle." Powers delegated to the Interior Secretary may be subdelegated to inferior agencies or officials, but the subdelegation must be express. United States v. Gemmil (9th Cir.1976).

The recent movement for "devolution" of agency decision-making power and "collaborative" decision-making raises another delegation issue: can agencies delegate their powers to groups of private citizens? Two judicial opinions answer that question in the negative. NRDC v. Hodel (E.D. Cal.1985) (*Ramirez*) arose when the Interior Department proposed, as part of its "cooperative management program," to allow selected grazing permittee-ranchers to manage their federal allotments by themselves, virtually without federal supervision. The court found this variety of delegation unlawful under all of the pertinent statutes:

> it is for Congress and not [the BLM] to amend the grazing statutes. In the meantime, it is the public policy of the United States that the Secretary and the BLM, not the ranchers, shall retain final control and decision making authority over livestock grazing practices on the public lands.

The 1999 decision in National Park and Conservation Ass'n v. Stanton (D.D.C.1999), involved a different sort of delegation/abdication. The National Park Service decided to hand over all management responsibilities for the Niobrara National Scenic River to an independent local council. That council took no action for an extended period. The court ruled that the delegation was invalid because the agency did not retain final reviewing authority.

Most federal land laws require consultation and cooperation; but decisional authority must remain where Congress has placed it.

B. JUDICIAL REVIEW

Judicial review of administrative actions is a central component of administrative law, a topic mostly beyond the scope of this Nutshell. But because legal controversies in modern public land law almost invariably involve federal land management agencies, the operations of which are governed to a significant extent by administrative law doctrines, the subject cannot be avoided entirely. This section summarizes several such doctrines with particular relevance to the federal lands.

Judicial review of administrative actions has been transformed since the decision in Citizens to Preserve Overton Park, Inc. v. Volpe (S.Ct.1971), initiated the so-called "hard look" doctrine. The movement toward meaningful judicial review of agency decisions took longer to reach federal public land law than other types of administrative endeavors because courts long accorded almost super deference to the federal land management agencies. That degree of deference is relatively rare now, but the transformation is not complete. Various administrative law doctrines still allow courts to avoid the merits of some public land lawsuits. Even when a decision is subject to review, the courts remain inclined to defer to certain kinds of determinations, such as those based upon the exercise of scientific expertise.

1. STANDING TO SUE

Standing is a judge-made doctrine, said to stem from the "case or controversy" jurisdictional reference in art. III, § 2 of the Constitution. The standing doctrine defines who is entitled to seek judicial review of administrative (or legislative) action. Because federal courts cannot issue advisory opinions, the plaintiff must have suffered some concrete injury to his, her, or its interest that is attributable to the agency decision being challenged and redressable by the relief sought. The statute that provides the plaintiff with a cause of action may impose additional standing requirements, beyond those stemming from article III. Because most federal land laws do not have "citizen suit" provisions (although the ESA does), most cases involving federal lands are filed pursuant to the APA. Finally, the courts themselves may conclude that a plaintiff lacks standing for "prudential" reasons.

Persons whose property or financial interests are directly and adversely affected by the action at issue have always had standing to challenge the action. In federal land and resources law, standing also presented no significant problem for environmentally oriented plaintiffs from 1972 to 1990. The Supreme Court issued its landmark ruling in Sierra Club v. Morton (S.Ct.1972) in 1972. The Court there ruled that an institutional interest in the conservation and sound management of national parks and forests alone was insufficient to confer standing, but that an organization whose members "used" the affected area, even for solely aesthetic or recreational purposes, had standing to sue on their behalf. The injury in fact requirement was further liberalized in United States v. SCRAP (S.Ct.1973), which held that extremely attenuated and speculative injury was sufficient to satisfy minimum standing criteria. In some subsequent cases, the Court almost totally ignored standing requisites when confronted with cases it felt necessary to decide. E.g., Bryant v. Yellen (S.Ct.1980).

The Court also distinguished during this period between constitutional standing requirements and statutory or prudential standing criteria. The statutory requirements included the requirement, derived from § 702 of the APA, that the plaintiff's alleged injury fall within the zone of interests that Congress intended to protect. The court-created, prudential limitations on judicial review included the requirements that the plaintiff assert its own rights, rather than those of third parties, and assert something other than a generalized grievance. None of these tests posed burdensome obstacles to public interest litigants seeking review of the decisions of the federal land management agencies.

A reaction of uncertain extent set in with the decision in Lujan v. NWF (S.Ct.1990). Plaintiff organization (the nation's largest conservation group) sued to enjoin implementation of the Interior Department's efforts to reclassify lands and to revoke withdrawals on some 180 million acres; the implementation was reflected in 1250 or so land orders issued without observance of NEPA or FLPMA procedural requirements. Plaintiff originally introduced affidavits from several of its members stating that their use of lands "in the vicinity" of the rezoned lands would be adversely affected. The district court granted summary judgment for the government, denying the plaintiffs the opportunity to submit further affidavits, and it dismissed the case for lack of standing. The D.C. Circuit reversed, but the Supreme Court, 5–4, reinstated the dismissal on standing grounds.

Justice Scalia, writing for the majority, ruled that exclusion of the additional affidavits was permissible, that a higher standard governs summary judgment than an initial motion to dismiss, and that plaintiff's original affidavits did not adequately set out "specific facts" demonstrating an injury. In most respects, however, the majority did not purport to tamper with *Sierra Club* standing requirements and definitions. The decision is odd (and of uncertain materiality) for several reasons. The degree of procedural inflexibility endorsed by the majority is contrary to most trends in civil procedure. The NWF, as all concerned realized, in fact had members who likely had "used" every single acre at issue. Additionally, Justice Scalia in dicta went far beyond the questions presented to opine that "the so-called 'land withdrawal review program' " was not final agency action or even agency action within the meaning of § 704 of the APA because it was merely a collection of a multitude of decisions concerning discrete parcels. Further, the majority opined that the case would not be ripe for decision even if it were final agency action. Finally, the NWF lacked standing in its own right because it failed to show that any particular administrative decision harmed its organizational purposes. The decision appears to reflect concern over the appropriateness of judicial intervention into policy matters for which the other two branches of government are responsible under the Constitution.

In a somewhat similar 1992 case, also decided 5–4, the Court reached a similar conclusion. Plaintiffs in Lujan v. Defenders of Wildlife (S.Ct.1992), challenged an Interior Department regulatory modification that limited the obligations of federal agencies to consult with it pursuant to the Endangered Species Act when undertaking actions in foreign countries. Again, Justice Scalia deemed the affidavits of the organizational plaintiff's members to be deficient because they did not specify a date certain when they would return to the foreign countries to study the species that might be adversely affected by the lack of consultation. This time, however, the failure to demonstrate injury in fact flouted constitutional rather than prudential statutory requirements. Only three members of the Court agreed with Justice Scalia that the plaintiff also failed to prove that its alleged injury was redressable by the relief it sought. Although the Court did not purport to reject the prevailing liberal standing tests, it elaborated on them in a manner likely to make it more difficult for future plaintiffs to plead if not prove injury in fact. It insisted that injury in fact be "concrete and particularized" as well as "actual or imminent," it limited the ability of plaintiffs to rely on procedural injury resulting from agency violations of statutes such as NEPA and the ESA, and it cast doubt on the continuing vitality of *SCRAP*.

Some commentators speculated that the Scalia-led faction of the Supreme Court was attempting to shut the courthouse door in the face of environmentalist litigants, and the 1990 and 1992 decisions

certainly invited more rigorous judicial scrutiny
than the courts had previously engaged in concerning the question of whether the plaintiff has a
sufficient stake in the controversy to give it standing to sue. Long after the two *Lujan* decisions,
however, the result feared by environmental groups
had not occurred. Litigation over the standing to
sue question naturally has risen in volume and
heat, but lower courts have concluded that environmental challengers had standing in all but a hand-
ful of tenuous cases, and the Supreme Court has
backtracked. The 7–2 decision in a non-federal
lands case, Friends of the Earth, Inc. v. Laidlaw
Envtl. Serv. (TOC), Inc. (S.Ct.2000), construed
broadly the injury in fact requirement on behalf of
environmental plaintiffs, concluding that injury to
the plaintiffs, not to the environment, is the essential requirement to establish injury in fact. It also
recognized that ongoing injury may be redressed by
the payment of civil penalties to the government
because such payment could avert future injury to
citizen suit plaintiffs due to its deterrent impact.

The Supreme Court's shifting receptivity to the
standing allegations of public interest groups has
not made it more difficult for economic interests to
establish standing. In Bennett v. Spear (S.Ct.1997),
the Court ruled that ranchers and irrigation districts that might lose water because of an ESA
biological opinion were within the ESA's zone of
interests, and therefore had standing to challenge
that opinion, even though the diversions they

sought would have made less water available to listed fish species.

See PNRL §§ 8:5–8:13.

2. TIMING AND PRECLUSION

Several administrative law doctrines flexibly define the appropriate time to bring a suit challenging agency action. If no time is specified in the governing statute, the general statute of limitations for suits against the government is six years. 28 U.S.C.A. § 2401(a). Even if it sues within the limitations period, a plaintiff may be precluded by the equitable doctrine of laches (sitting on one's rights for too long to the detriment of others), but laches is a disfavored defense in environmental and natural resources litigation. Coalition for Canyon Preservation v. Bowers (9th Cir.1980). In Apache Survival Coalition v. United States (9th Cir.1994), however, the court barred an attack on the legality of an astronomical observatory on the basis of alleged noncompliance with the National Historic Preservation Act due to plaintiff's "inexcusable tardiness."

Exhaustion of administrative remedies, the final order rule, and primary jurisdiction all are flexible doctrines requiring the plaintiff to first make his complete case before the agency to the extent possible before bringing suit. See, e.g., Southern Utah Wilderness Alliance v. BLM (10th Cir.2005) (holding that determination of the validity of R.S. 2477 rights-of-way is not within the primary jurisdiction of the BLM). The allied ripeness doctrine requires a plaintiff to refrain from suing until the issues have become sufficiently concrete for judicial resolution. In the 1990 *Lujan* case, supra, which was decided on standing grounds, the Supreme Court majority commented in dictum that the legality of a regulation ordinarily is not ripe for review until it has been applied concretely. See also Sierra Club v. Peterson (5th Cir.2000). In Ash Creek Mining Co. v. Lujan (10th Cir.1991), the failure of the owner of the surface estate in coal lands to accept an exchange proffered by the Interior Department precluded it on ripeness grounds from challenging the agency's refusal to consider competitive leasing.

The ripeness doctrine became a significant procedural obstacle to judicial review in 1998. Plaintiff had challenged a Forest Service land use plan on the ground, inter alia, that its clearcutting prescriptions violated NFMA limitations. A unanimous Supreme Court threw out the lawsuit as unripe. Ohio Forestry Ass'n v. Sierra Club (S.Ct.1998). To determine the "fitness of the issues," the Court considered

(1) whether delayed review would cause hardship to the plaintiffs; (2) whether judicial intervention would inappropriately interfere with further administrative action; and (3) whether the courts would benefit from further factual development of the issues presented.

The land use plan was not ripe for review because further decisions had to be made before any clearcutting actually took place. See also Park Lake Resources Ltd. Liability Co. v. United States Dep't of Agric. (10th Cir.1999) (holding mining associations' challenge to Forest Service designation of Research Natural Area not ripe). The *Ohio Forestry* Court indicated, however, that parts of plans that were immediately effective may be ripe for review. Piecemeal review thus becomes more likely. See Neighbors of Cuddy Mountain v. Alexander (9th Cir.2002) (allowing challenge to forest-wide management practices when they affect the lawfulness of a particular final agency action, such as a timber sale).

The Supreme Court addressed another ripeness challenge to a federal land management agency decision in National Park Hospitality Ass'n v. Department of the Interior (S.Ct.2003). A nonprofit trade association representing concessionaires doing business in the national parks initiated a facial challenge to an NPS regulation stating that the Contract Disputes Act of 1978, 41 U.S.C.A. §§ 601–613, does not apply to concession contracts. The Court held that the case was not ripe because the regulation amounted to a general statement of policy that did not create "adverse effects of a strictly legal kind" or affect the primary conduct of concessionaires. It stated that mere uncertainty as to the validity of an agency regulation does not constitute hardship for ripeness purposes. In addition, the issue was not fit for judicial resolution because further factual development would significantly advance the courts' ability to resolve the legal issues.

The flip side of ripeness is mootness; the personal interest that must exist at the outset of the suit must continue throughout its existence. Southern Utah Wilderness Alliance v. Smith (10th Cir.1997); Fund for Animals v. Babbitt (2d Cir. 1996). Issues that are "capable of repetition yet evading review" are justiciable. See, e.g., Alaska Ctr. for the Env't v. United States Forest Serv. (9th Cir.1999) (NEPA challenge to extension of expired special use permit authorizing skiing and hiking tours in a national forest).

Sovereign immunity no longer bars suits against the United States for nonmonetary relief. 5 U.S.C.A. § 702. Monetary relief against the government is available only for breach of contract, 28 U.S.C.A. §§ 1346, 1491, negligence torts, id. §§ 2671–2680 and section 10F, inverse condemnation, see section 3E, or attorneys fees where statutes grant them or the Equal Access to Justice Act, 28 U.S.C.A. § 2412, applies.

See PNRL §§ 8:4, 8:14–8:22, chapter 10A.

3. REVIEWABILITY AND SCOPE OF REVIEW

Judicial review of agency action is available "except to the extent that (1) statutes preclude judicial review; or (2) agency action is committed to agency discretion by law." 5 U.S.C.A. § 701(a). Only very rarely do federal public land statutes preclude judicial review, but many are phrased in highly discretionary terms. E.g., Multiple–Use, Sustained–Yield Act of 1960, 16 U.S.C.A. §§ 528–531. For decades, courts were very reluctant to pass on the arbitrariness of land management agency actions, deeming the subject one of expertise beyond the understanding of courts. E.g., Hi–Ridge Lumber Co. v. United States (9th Cir.1971). That insulation from judicial review began to break down with the decision in *Citizens to Preserve Overton Park, Inc. v. Volpe*, supra, holding that agency actions are presumptively reviewable. Actions in the nature of prosecutorial discretion, however, are presumed unreviewable. Heckler v. Chaney (S.Ct.1985). In either instance, clear congressional intent can rebut the presumption. Since *Overton Park*, courts seldom find a matter so committed to agency discretion that all review is precluded. E.g., Sierra Club v. Glickman (5th Cir.1998); Christianson v. Hauptman (2d Cir. 1993); Perkins v. Bergland (9th Cir.1979).

Litigants pursuing challenges to an agency's failure to act may face significant reviewability obstacles. The APA authorizes reviewing courts to compel agency action that has been "unlawfully withheld or unreasonably delayed." 5 U.S.C.A. § 706(1). In Norton v. Southern Utah Wilderness Alliance (S.Ct.2004), the Supreme Court held that a § 706(1) claim may proceed only if the plaintiff asserts that "an agency failed to take a *discrete* agency action that it is *required to take*." Applying that test, the Court held that none of the plaintiff environmental group's claims was reviewable. The plaintiff had asserted that the BLM had violated its obligation under FLPMA to manage wilderness study areas in a manner so as not to impair their suitability for preservation as wilderness by failing to take action to prevent degradation of the areas by ORV use. According to the Court, the relief sought—compliance with the nonimpairment mandate—was not discrete. The second claim, which asserted that the BLM failed to conduct monitoring of ORV use pursuant to the applicable resource management plan, also was not justiciable because, according to the Court, land use plans usually do not create binding commitments of the type that can be compelled under § 706(1). The third claim was that the BLM failed to supplement its EIS to account for increases in ORV use since promulgation of the initial land use plan. That claim was not justiciable because the BLM was no longer under any NEPA obligations. Once the BLM approved the land use plan, no "major federal action" remained to be taken, and NEPA no longer applied.

The scope of judicial review is a far more central question to federal public land law than the availability of review. The APA, 5 U.S.C.A. § 706, sets out six standards under which courts "shall" set aside agency actions. These standards break down into the following questions in most disputes concerning review of federal land management agency decisions:

— did the agency comply with statutory and regulatory procedures? (§ 706(2)(D));

— did it act within the bounds of its statutory authority? (§ 706(2)(C));

— did it properly implement its statutory authority, or did it abuse its discretion by acting
arbitrarily or capriciously? (§ 706(2)(A)).

The canons concerning the scope and depth of
judicial review resemble self-fulfilling prophecies. A
reviewing court is more or less free to choose which-
ever principles it wishes to buttress its foreordained
conclusion as to the legality, arbitrariness, or wisdom of the administrative action. Generalizations
are nevertheless possible. Because Congress has
conferred on the land management agencies the
authority to implement statutory delegations,
courts tend to be highly deferential to administrative findings and conclusions. Challengers ordinarily bear a heavy burden of demonstrating a violation
or an abuse of discretion, although the courts generally seem more inclined to engage in rigorous scrutiny of procedural than substantive compliance.
That burden is lessened as the statute at issue is
worded more specifically.

Deference has limits, however. It is important
initially to distinguish between challenges to agency
statutory interpretations and to agency decisions
that implement a statute whose meaning is agreed
upon. In Wilderness Soc'y v. Morton (D.C. Cir.1973)
(en banc), the District of Columbia Circuit ruled
that when a statute is clear on its face, that law
must be applied as written without inquiry into its
wisdom or workability, and regardless of contrary
administrative construction. The court reasoned
that judicial deference is distinguishable from "judicial inertia," and that the latter "make[s] a mock-

ery of the judicial function." Accord: TVA v. Hill (S.Ct.1978). The Supreme Court later adopted that ruling in Chevron USA, Inc. v. NRDC (S.Ct.1984). Under the first step of *Chevron*'s two-part inquiry, "[i]f the intent of Congress is clear, that is the end of the matter; for the court, as well as the agency, must give effect to the unambiguously expressed intent of Congress." If, however, the statute is not clear on the precise question at issue, the court must defer to any reasonable agency interpretation under the second prong of the *Chevron* test. The courts have struggled to determine the circumstances in which the *Chevron* test for review of statutory interpretations applies. See, e.g., High Sierra Hikers Ass'n v. Blackwell (9th Cir.2004) (interpretation rendered in course of issuing special use permit not entitled to *Chevron* deference); Wilderness Soc'y v. FWS (9th Cir.2003) (Solicitor's opinion not entitled to *Chevron* deference).

The courts tend to be even more deferential to agency interpretations of their own regulations than to agency statutory interpretations. A leading case is Udall v. Tallman (S.Ct.1965). At issue was the construction of several executive orders governing the withdrawal of federal lands from mineral leasing. The Supreme Court deferred to the administrative interpretation, even though it was semantically questionable. According to the Court:

When faced with a problem of statutory construction, this Court shows great deference to the interpretation given the statute by the officers or agency charged with its administration. . . . When the construction of an administrative regulation rather than a statute is in issue, deference is even more clearly in order.

Judicial review of agency statutory implementation is governed by a different line of precedents. The landmark case is *Overton Park*, supra, which requires the reviewing court to inquire whether

the decision was based on a consideration of the relevant factors and whether there has been a clear error of judgment.... Although this inquiry into the facts is to be searching and careful, the ultimate standard of review is a narrow one. The court is not empowered to substitute its judgment for that of the agency.

Courts in the public land circuits still tend to review circumspectly the implementation of statutes that afford considerable discretion to the land management agencies. In Perkins v. Bergland (9th Cir. 1979), the court refused to overturn the agency's decision to reduce grazing allotments under multiple use, sustained yield legislation absent proof that there was "virtually no evidence in the record to support the agency's methodology in gathering and evaluating data." Decisions in conflict with agency precedent or based on nonstatutory political factors tend to trigger more demanding judicial review. E.g., International Snowmobile Mfrs. Ass'n v. Norton (D.Wyo.2004) (vacating NPS decision to bar snowmobile use in national park because it was a "radical departure" from previous policy and a "predetermined," politically based decision).

Many land management agency decisions are governed by manuals originally compiled before the enactment of the APA, often without public notice or participation. Some manual provisions have subsequently been published for comment in the Federal Register or otherwise reissued as formal regulations, but others have not. Judicial treatment of the degree to which an agency is bound by manual provisions has been inconsistent. In Foundation for N. Am. Wild Sheep v. United States Dep't of Agric. (9th Cir.1982), the court suggested that manual provisions are binding. Hi–Ridge Lumber Co. v. United States (9th Cir.1971), is apparently to the contrary. Most cases hold that manuals do not have the force and effect of law; they are instead evidence of agency custom and practice. Western Radio Serv. Co. v. Espy (9th Cir.1996); Stone Forest Indus. v. United States (Fed.Cir.1992).

When a reviewing court determines that an agency has abused its discretion, the remedy often but not always is an injunction against the proposed agency action. If the statute or issue dictates a result, the courts must impose it. TVA v. Hill (S.Ct. 1978). Otherwise, equitable principles apply. Kleppe v. Sierra Club (S.Ct.1976). Mandamus relief also is available in some circumstances. In re American Rivers and Idaho Rivers United (D.C. Cir.2004). Cf. Kootenai Tribe v. Veneman (9th Cir.2002) (challenge to Forest Service's roadless area conservation rule).

See PNRL §§ 8:23–8:24.

C. EXECUTIVE WITHDRAWALS, RESERVATIONS, AND CLASSIFICATIONS

1. HISTORICAL DEFINITIONS AND PRACTICES

Early on in this Nation's history, most leaders realized that some limits on the disposition policies of the day were necessary to protect certain federal purposes. Because the "public domain" was generally available to homesteaders, miners, and their ilk, and because the federal government found it necessary to take some land out of the "available" category for forts and Indian reservations, the complementary processes of "withdrawal" and "reservation" evolved. Use of those processes to deny access to federal lands and resources has generated conflicts between the Congress and the Executive for over a century. Along with land use planning, withdrawals, reservations, and classifications are the primary zoning mechanisms of modern public land law.

A "withdrawal" is a statute or order that temporarily or permanently changes the status of a defined parcel from "available" to "unavailable" for certain types of disposition or use. A withdrawal is a negative action in that it prohibits some uses without prescribing other uses. A "reservation," on the other hand, means a legislative or executive designation of a withdrawn tract as primarily or exclusively suitable for specified federal purposes, such as wildlife conservation. Virtually all of the federal lands now have been withdrawn from the operation of the homesteading and similar disposition laws, and most (including all of the National Park, Wildlife Refuge, and Forest Systems) have been reserved or dedicated more or less permanently for various purposes. The lands now managed by the BLM were withdrawn from homesteading availability pursuant to the 1934 TGA, 43 U.S.C.A. §§ 315–315r, but, according to one court, they never have been officially "reserved" as well. Sierra Club v. Watt (D.C.Cir.1981).

Classification involves parcel-by-parcel categorization of lands according to their beneficial use. It is a discretionary agency decision to label a tract as suitable for a specified use. Many 19th century laws distinguished between "mineral" and "non-mineral" land, and other statutes made other distinctions that similarly required classification. Congress in 1934 authorized the Interior Secretary to classify public lands for various purposes, including disposition. 43 U.S.C.A. § 315f. The 1964 Classification and Multiple Use Act (CMUA), 43 U.S.C.A. §§ 1411–1418 (expired 1970), extended that authority, which now is subsumed into BLM planning processes under FLPMA. Id. § 1712(e). The Interior Department's categorization of lands for in lieu selection by states also involves classification.

The ways in which withdrawals, reservations, and classifications are accomplished vary. Congress itself withdrew Yellowstone National Park in 1872 and has continued to arrogate unto itself the exclusive authority to designate national parks and wil-

derness areas. Congress in 1891 delegated to the
President the power to withdraw forested lands as
forest preserves, 16 U.S.C.A. § 471, but it essentially revoked that power in 1907. In 1906, Congress
also gave the Executive powers to create national
monuments out of lands containing historical or
scientific resources. Antiquities Act, id. §§ 431–33.
The Antiquities Act was used originally to preserve
Indian ruins and artifacts, but the courts have
interpreted the scope of the withdrawal authority it
delegated to the President broadly to uphold designation of the Grand Canyon and Jackson Hole,
Wyoming as national monuments. Cameron v. United States (S.Ct.1920); Wyoming v. Franke (D.Wyo.
1945). Congress has reaffirmed many such designations by converting them into national parks. President Carter relied on the Antiquities Act as the
ostensible legal justification for reservation of 56
million acres in Alaskan national monuments. The
ANILCA rescinded these withdrawals, but included
almost all of the affected lands in various preservation systems.

President Clinton used the Antiquities Act authority extensively in 1996–2000. He created the 1.7
million-acre Grand Staircase–Escalante National
Monument in 1996, a decision later affirmed by
Congress, and in 1999–2000, the President designated or proposed nine more new national monuments. The D.C. Circuit upheld a series of these
designations, rejecting the contentions that the
President's authority to declare national monuments is limited to rare and discrete man-made

objects, such as prehistoric ruins and ancient artifacts, that the Antiquities Act does not embrace environmental values, and that the Wilderness Act provides the exclusive means of protecting wildlife, wildlife habitat, and wilderness values. See Mountain States Legal Found. v. Bush (D.C. Cir.2002). See also Tulare County v. Bush (D.C. Cir.2002) (rejecting claim that the President unlawfully withdrew land from the National Forest System in creating a national monument); Utah Ass'n of Counties v. Bush (D. Utah 2004) (the Antiquities Act delegated decisionmaking authority to the "sound discretion of the President").

From an early time, Presidents unilaterally had designated forts and similar military reservations, Indian reservations, and (beginning in 1903) bird sanctuaries. President Taft in 1909 went one step further; he withdrew three million acres from the operation of the General Mining Law insofar as it covered oil and gas exploration without any statutory authority to do so. A challenge to this withdrawal by an oil company which had ignored it resulted in the landmark *Midwest Oil* decision. United States v. Midwest Oil Co. (S.Ct.1915). Although the Supreme Court refused to rule on the existence of inherent presidential withdrawal authority, it upheld Taft's withdrawal on the ground that Congress, by its knowing acquiescence in the earlier executive withdrawals, had created an implied power in the Executive to continue withdrawing lands until Congress expressly revoked the power.

In 1910, Congress passed the Pickett Act, 43 U.S.C.A. §§ 141–142 (repealed 1976), which allowed Presidents to withdraw lands "temporarily" for any public purpose, except that such lands would not be withdrawn from entry for "metalliferous" minerals. Millions of acres subsequently were withdrawn from the public domain under the Pickett Act. For decades, the question whether the Act precluded all nonstatutory Executive withdrawals was unresolved. In Portland Gen. Elec. Co. v. Kleppe (D.Wyo. 1977), the court ruled that Executive withdrawal of lands from all mineral entry, including metalliferous metal entry, rekindled the President's implied power by congressional acquiescence. The court found it significant that Congress had enacted legislation placing express limits on the Executive's power to withdraw lands for military purposes, but had imposed no similar constraints on non-military withdrawals. Congress repealed the Pickett Act, and purported to repeal the implied power created by congressional acquiescence (referring to *Midwest Oil* by name), when it enacted FLPMA in 1976. The courts have not yet had occasion to decide whether congressional silence in the face of post-FLPMA extra-statutory withdrawals would regenerate an implied presidential withdrawal power.

Another form of withdrawal occurs when Congress removes particular resources from types of availability, unaccompanied by a reservation. The Mineral Leasing Act of 1920, 30 U.S.C.A. §§ 181–287, for example, decreed that fuel and fertilizer minerals would no longer be subject to location claims on any of the federal lands; they could only be leased thereafter. Congress also "reserved" mineral estates for the United States in several disposition laws.

By 1976, the park, forest, and wildlife refuge systems had pretty much assumed their present shapes, except in Alaska. All of the lands within them were both withdrawn and reserved—and some tracts doubly or triply so. The BLM public lands all had been withdrawn but, accordingly to one court (in dicta), they had not been reserved generally. Sierra Club v. Watt (D.C.Cir.1981). That ruling is questionable because the 1976 FLPMA arguably amounts to a de facto reservation. Many individual BLM tracts had been specially withdrawn for various purposes over the years, however, and evidently no one knew which or why. In addition, most BLM lands had been "classified" as suitable for multiple use management pursuant to the CMUA before it expired in 1970. One major purpose behind enactment of FLPMA was to clear up this confusion in federal tract designation and zoning.

See PNRL §§ 3:22–3:23, chapter 10D.

2. FLPMA WITHDRAWALS

FLPMA consolidates executive withdrawal authority, delegating it directly to the Interior Secretary, who must seek the consent of other departments before withdrawing lands under their jurisdiction. Although it retains the substantive executive discretion earlier prominent, FLPMA hedges that discretion by mandating detailed procedures that the Executive must follow. One of those procedures, the legislative veto, likely is unconstitutional.

FLPMA defines withdrawal as:

withholding an area of Federal land from settlement, sale, location, or entry, under some or all of the general land laws, for the purpose of limiting activities under those laws in order to maintain other public values in the area or reserving the area for a particular purpose or program; or transferring jurisdiction over an area of Federal land ... from one department, bureau or agency to another department, bureau or agency.

43 U.S.C.A. § 1702(j). This definition obviously blurs the distinction between reservations and withdrawals by including the former within the latter. Generally, FLPMA's reforms of withdrawal policy apply only prospectively, but the statute mandated review by 1991 of pre–1976 withdrawals of lands in eleven western states from the mining and mineral leasing laws. FLPMA directed the President to transmit to Congress the Interior Secretary's recommendations as to the fate of those withdrawals, based on the continuing validity of the original withdrawal purposes. Id. § 1714(*l*). Executive proposals for termination of these withdrawals would take effect unless vetoed within 90 days by concurrent resolution.

Instead of pursuing the statutory review process, the Interior Secretary in 1981–1985 implemented a

Land Withdrawal Review Program, pursuant to which he unilaterally "revoked" (rather than terminated) withdrawals covering tens of millions of acres on the basis that original withdrawal purposes were no longer being served. The Court of Appeals for the District of Columbia Circuit ruled that the revocations were invalid because the Department failed to provide public participation, as required by FLPMA section 1739(e) for programs for the management of the public lands. The court did not reach the even stronger claims that the revocations flew in the face of section 1714(*l*) procedures. NWF v. Burford (D.C.Cir.1987). The Supreme Court later dismissed the litigation, concluding that the plaintiffs lacked standing to sue. See supra section 4.B.1. Because of the Court's failure to reach the merits, the status of those pre–1976 withdrawals remains uncertain.

For post–1976 withdrawals, FLPMA offers the Executive three routes. First, the Secretary may make small withdrawals (less than 5000 acres) for any purpose at any time for periods up to 20 years. 43 U.S.C.A. § 1714(d). Second, the statute requires prior submission of withdrawals of parcels over 5000 acres, also limited to 20 years, to Congress, either House of which can "veto" such a large-tract withdrawal within 90 days. Id. § 1714(c). The Interior Department cannot make de facto permanent withdrawals (for storage of nuclear waste) under this authority. New Mexico v. Watkins (D.C.Cir. 1992). Third, the Secretary may make "emergency" withdrawals of any size for up to three years "to

preserve values that would otherwise be lost";
these, too, must be reported to Congress. 43
U.S.C.A. § 1714(e). President Carter used this authority to withdraw tens of millions of acres in
Alaska pending legislative action. FLPMA requires
the Secretary to make an emergency withdrawal at
the request of designated congressional committees.
Id.

The congressional/executive interactions contemplated in several FLPMA sections, including the
opportunities for congressional veto of large and
emergency withdrawals, probably are unconstitutional. The Court in INS v. Chadha (S.Ct.1983),
struck down a somewhat similar legislative veto
because it required neither passage by both houses
(bicameralism) nor presentment to the President
for signature or veto. The provision of section
1714(e) requiring the Secretary to make an emergency withdrawal upon the recommendation of congressional committees conceivably could pass constitutional muster under the notion that the public
land laws are more like directions to an agent than
normal legislation and therefore are exempt from
constitutional bicameralism and presentment procedures. The sparse authority makes even that limited validation unlikely, however. NWF v. Watt
(D.D.C.1983). If the courts ever declare the FLPMA
legislative vetoes unconstitutional, they will have to
address difficult questions of severability.

Courts have twice ruled that the failure of the
agencies to act on lease applications constituted a
withdrawal requiring compliance with FLPMA pro-

cedures. MSLF v. Andrus (D.Wyo.1980) (BLM's inaction on applications for oil and gas leases in national forest roadless areas amounted to "de facto withdrawals" subject to FLPMA procedures); MSLF v. Hodel (D.Wyo.1987). The Ninth Circuit later specifically rejected the reasoning of these cases in deciding whether NEPA required the Forest Service to consider the "no action" alternative of not issuing any oil and gas leases. Bob Marshall Alliance v. Hodel (9th Cir.1988). Section 1712(e)(2) of FLPMA addresses such a situation by requiring that the Interior Secretary report to Congress on an agency management decision to implement land use plans, including a decision to exclude any "principal or major use" for more than two years on a tract of 200,000 or more acres. FLPMA makes such a decision subject to a congressional veto by concurrent resolution. This, too, probably is unconstitutional.

See PNRL §§ 10D:13–10D:18.

D. LAND EXCHANGES, SALES, AND OTHER TRANSFERS

Although homesteading ended for all practical purposes in 1934, and Congress in 1976 declared that the United States would retain its public lands unless public policy dictated disposition of particular tracts, 43 U.S.C.A. § 1701(a)(1), the map of federal land ownership is not static. The United States regularly sells, grants, swaps, buys, and condemns interests in real estate. Most BLM and Forest Service disposition and exchange authority is now centralized in FLPMA section 1716, but Congress has delegated acquisition powers to agencies in a wide variety of programmatic statutes.

1. LAND EXCHANGES

The exchange mechanism is congressionally favored as an equitable way to rationalize the western land ownership map; Congress thus has authorized large-scale swaps between federal agencies and between federal and state governments. Each federal land management agency has statutory authority to exchange public for private or state lands under some circumstances as a means of consolidating fragmented holdings. Virtually all such laws require at a minimum that the exchanging agency receive lands of at least roughly equal value and that it find that the proposed exchange is in the "public interest."

Before the more stringent standards of recent legislation, courts were reluctant to review the merits of federal land exchanges. E.g., Red Canyon Sheep Co. v. Ickes (D.C.Cir.1938). While still reticent to interfere with managerial discretion, some courts have looked more closely at proposed exchanges. A possible harbinger of future developments in this sphere is National Audubon Soc'y v. Hodel (D. Alaska 1984). Interior Secretary Watt made a formal finding that an exchange of St. Matthew Island for Alaskan Native easements in wildlife refuges (so that the exchanging Natives could lease the Island to energy developers) was in the public interest and thus permissible under AN-ILCA section 1302(h), 43 U.S.C.A. § 3192(h). The reviewing court agreed that the Secretary used the correct procedures and that he properly interpreted the public interest criterion to include potential benefits to national economic vitality and oil production capabilities, as well as to wilderness values. It disagreed, however, with his findings on the merits. The administrative decision arbitrarily inflated the benefits of easements to be acquired and unduly downplayed the detriments attributable to the loss of the Island as a wildlife refuge.

Congress streamlined exchange requirements in the 1988 Federal Land Exchange Facilitation Act, an amendment to FLPMA. The new Act provides more uniform rules for land appraisals and establishes procedures for resolving appraisal disputes.

In 1982, Utah's governor proposed a massive exchange proposal, dubbed Project Bold, to exchange scattered, landlocked state school sections for federal lands. Although it did not enact it in the form originally proposed, Congress passed a more modest version in the Utah Schools and Land Improvement Act of 1993. That statute could presage similar efforts in other western states. After President Clinton designated 1.7 million acres in southern Utah as the Grand Staircase–Escalante National Monument, the federal and Utah governments reached a massive land exchange agreement whereby the United States acquired state-owned inholdings in the Monument and in other federal preservation areas in return for lands and other benefits.

Land exchanges became more prominent in the 1990s because, unlike outright land sales, the management agencies could keep the transfer "proceeds." Judicial reaction was mixed. Compare Lodge Tower Condo. Ass'n v. Lodge Properties, Inc. (10th Cir.1996), with Muckleshoot Indian Tribe v. U.S. Forest Serv. (9th Cir.1999). Recurring reports indicating that the United States often did not receive fair market value in land exchanges could prompt more stringent judicial review. One court has rejected a contention by the owners of mineral interests that the appraisal of lands to be exchanged should be based on the "potential value" of the mineral interests. Mt. St. Helens Mining & Recovery Ltd. P'ship v. United States (9th Cir.2004). In another case, the court enjoined a land exchange that had already been consummated on the ground that the BLM's appraisal failed to take into account the general market for land development as part of the process of determining the highest and best use of property that the exchange recipient intended to use as a landfill. The agency also failed to consider changes in zoning laws that increased the likelihood that the property would be devoted to a landfill. Desert Citizens Against Pollution v. Bisson (9th Cir.2000).

See PNRL §§ 10C:24–10C:41.

2. LAND SALES AND ACQUISITIONS

FLPMA section 1713 authorizes federal land sales to private parties only after land use planning has determined that the tract for sale is not needed for federal purposes. Other limitations include fair market value, a legislative veto (of dubious constitutionality) for large sales, and retention of mineral estates. FLPMA section 1721 authorizes the transfer of unsurveyed islands and omitted lands managed by the BLM to state and local governments.

Federal law with respect to land title transfers is more generous to states, localities, and nonprofit entities. They can proceed via FLPMA sections 1713 and 1720. In addition, the Federal Property and Administrative Services Act of 1949, 40 U.S.C.A. §§ 471–493, allows these entities to claim surplus federal real estate from the General Services Administration in some instances. Further, the Recreation and Public Purposes Act (RPPA) of 1926, 43 U.S.C.A. §§ 869 to 869–4, allows localities to obtain land that is of no national significance for any "recreational or ... other public purpose," subject to several limitations and conditions on the Interior Secretary's discretion. The courts tend to interpret the Secretary's discretion broadly. Humboldt County v. United States (9th Cir.1982). If the locality ceases use of the tract for its intended purpose, the tract reverts to the United States. Classification of land as suitable for RPPA disposition effectively withdraws it from availability for other uses, including mining location. Under a 1988 RPPA amendment intended to reduce the federal government's exposure under the pollution control laws, the reversion does not occur if the site was used for hazardous waste disposal; in those circumstances, the municipality retains ownership and liability.

Congress has not laid out an overall land acquisition program. Still, acquisition continues, usually for one of three purposes. Congress sometimes authorizes the management agency to acquire lands within a special management area. In some cases, agencies have general authority to acquire land to meet some legislative goal, such as waterfowl propagation. Third, Congress has encouraged consolidation of federal holdings for management or access purposes. The Land and Water Conservation Fund Act of 1965 is the major funding source for such purchases.

Federal ownership of large bodies of land often has been a controversial issue in the West. The Sagebrush Rebellion was premised on the notion that such ownership was, if not unconstitutional, at least immoral. See section 3B. Secretary Watt attempted to dispose of millions of federal acres through the mechanism of a Property Review Board, but that experiment failed and soon was abandoned. Legislation was introduced in Congress in 2005 to privatize federal lands, including some of the national parks, but it did not even reach a vote. Large-scale land disposition seems unlikely in the immediate future, in part because erstwhile supporters stand to lose federal revenues, subsidies, and other benefits that accompany federal retention. Sales, exchanges, and acquisitions nevertheless will likely continue as the western maps slowly are redrawn to consolidate public and private holdings and to rectify other management problems.

See PNRL §§ 10C:1–10C:50.

E. ACCESS ACROSS FEDERAL LANDS

Determining rights (or licenses) of access across federal land is a complicated inquiry. Before 1976, various users could acquire access rights by various means. After 1976, most users are required by FLPMA, 43 U.S.C.A. §§ 1761–1771, to obtain and pay for "rights-of-way." Special provisions and principles govern some specific situations.

In general, the United States as a proprietor can exclude others from its lands just like any other landowner. Congress has seldom done this on any large scale. Instead, Congress in 1866 granted rights-of-way for construction of public roads on unreserved land to anyone without administrative permission, R.S. 2477 (repealed 1976), and similar legislation granted others access rights for other particular purposes. The 1877 Desert Lands Act, 43 U.S.C.A. § 321, for example, authorized easements for water diversion works. The courts also determined that congressional acquiescence in the use and occupation of federal lands for mining, grazing, water diversions, and recreation resulted in implied licenses or easements for those purposes; all but the "recreation license" were later canceled by affirmative regulatory legislation.

The relationship between access interests acquired before 1976 and modern management priori-

ties promises to be a vexing problem for some time
to come. A leading case is Sierra Club v. Hodel
(10th Cir.1988). The BLM agreed with Garfield
County that the County could upgrade an old dirt
trail into an improved two-lane road for better
access to a marina. Plaintiff challenged the project
because of its potential effect on wilderness study
areas along the route. The court held that FLPMA
preserved pre–1976 access rights, but that state law
governed the question of the scope of an R.S. 2477
road. In this case, Utah law allowed expansion of
the right-of-way when "reasonable and necessary"
to accommodate increased demand. Road improvement could not, however, unduly degrade the wilderness study areas.

The Tenth Circuit returned to the subject of R.S.
2477 access rights in Southern Utah Wilderness
Alliance v. BLM (10th Cir. 2005). In a lengthy and
ultimately inconclusive opinion, the court ruled that
the BLM lacks the authority to make binding determinations on the validity of R.S. 2477 claims in the
first instance, based on the doctrine of primary
jurisdiction; that, although federal law governs the
question of the validity of a R.S. 2477 right-of-way,
federal law borrows from state law to the extent
that the latter provides convenient and appropriate
principles for effectuating congressional intent; and
that the burden of proof lies on the parties seeking
to enforce R.S. 2477 rights-of-way against the government. The court also rejected the assertion by
the BLM and the environmental group plaintiff that
mere public use cannot suffice to establish an R.S.

2477 right-of-way, and that some form of mechanical construction must have taken place to construct or improve the highway. It nevertheless held that a court may consider actual construction (appropriate to the historical period in question), or lack thereof, as evidence of the required extent of public use even though it is not a necessary or sufficient element. Finally, the BLM had invalidated the R.S. 2477 claims in that case on the ground that the claims had not been established before a 1910 coal withdrawal. The court held, however, that the withdrawal did not amount to a reservation for public use because it narrowly and temporarily removed potential coal lands from certain kinds of private appropriation rather than dedicating the land to a specific public purpose.

Although the land management agencies cannot prohibit use of R.S. 2477 roads, they can regulate that use. Wilkenson v. Department of the Interior (D.Colo.1986). The uncertainty attributable to the scope of access rights under R.S. 2477 has created clouds on title as a result of possible unrecorded access rights and may disrupt agency land use planning efforts. See, e.g., Adams v. United States (9th Cir.2001); United States v. Jenks (10th Cir.1997).

The Bush/Norton Administration has attempted to liberalize R.S. 2477 standards so that private and municipal entities may more easily acquire access rights. As of 2005, that effort has been inconclusive. See SUWA v. BLM (10th Cir.2005), an extensive discussion of R.S. 2477 law without a conclusive resolution.

Inholders in national forests also have by statute a regulatable right of access across the federal lands. The court in Montana Wilderness Ass'n v. United States Forest Serv. (9th Cir.1981), held that a provision of ANILCA, 16 U.S.C.A. § 1323(a), gave such a right to inholders nationwide, while subjecting them to applicable rules and regulations. Whether a similar section applicable to BLM public lands also applies nationwide seems dubious, but the question has not been answered conclusively. Whether landowners have prescriptive easements is also not clear. Compare Bunyard v. United States (D. Ariz.2004), with Barnes v. Babbitt (D. Ariz. 2004). In Mountain States Legal Found. v. Espy (D. Idaho 1993), the court upheld Forest Service restrictions on inholder access that jeopardized a threatened fish species. The ANILCA access provision does not excuse the agency from environmental evaluation responsibilities under the National Environmental Policy Act in determining what constitutes reasonable access. Alpine Lakes Protection Soc'y v. United States Forest Serv. (W.D.Wash. 1993).

The United States (and, presumably, its licensees) does not have an implied right to cross private section corners to reach its own checkerboard lands. Leo Sheep v. United States (S.Ct.1979). But private landowners cannot fence their lands in a fashion that denies people or wildlife access to federal lands. United States ex rel Bergen v. Lawrence (10th Cir.1988).

Since 1976, federal land users without preexisting rights of access, other than casual recreationists, must obtain and pay for official rights-of-way (ROWs) from the managing agency. The ROW mechanism is the all-purpose means of allowing federal land use for such disparate purposes as microwave towers, livestock trails, canals and pipes, power lines, roads, and so forth. In a questionable decision, the Ninth Circuit in California v. FERC (9th Cir.1992), held that applicants for hydroelectric licenses from the Federal Energy Regulatory Commission are exempt from FLPMA ROW requirements.

The issuing agency must limit ROWs under FLPMA to the size necessary for the project, avoiding unnecessary environmental damage. Applications to construct facilities in wilderness study areas are unlikely to be approved. The recipient of a federal ROW is required to pay fair market value for it, as determined by the agency, and also to reimburse the agency for its costs in processing the application, including environmental assessment costs. The substantive standards for ROW grant or denial are relatively strict. 43 U.S.C.A. §§ 1761–1771. See County of Okanogan v. NMFS (9th Cir. 2003) (upholding Forest Service's authority to restrict use of ditch right-of-way by requiring maintenance of minimum instream flow to protect endangered fish).

See PNRL chapter 10E.

F. THE PUBLIC TRUST DOCTRINES IN PUBLIC NATURAL RESOURCES LAW

The "public trust" is an idea that is manifested in various ways. Ultimately, however, it has had relatively little practical impact on federal public land law. The states upon statehood succeeded to the prerogatives of the English sovereign, one of which was to hold ownership of certain properties and resources in trust for the people. In Pollard v. Hagan (S.Ct.1845), the Supreme Court ruled that the trust resulted in automatic state ownership of lands underlying navigable waters. In Illinois Central R.R. Co. v. Illinois (S.Ct.1892), the Court held that those trust lands were burdened with trust duties; specifically, the states cannot alienate trust properties if the title transfer will unduly interfere with public fishing, navigation, and commerce rights. That rule still is good law. Similarly, federal land grants to states create trust duties whereby the states must devote all benefits from the lands to the intended beneficiaries (usually public schools), and states must obtain fair market value for their use.

Public trust doctrines and their impacts have mushroomed at the state level since 1970. The leading case is National Audubon Soc'y v. Superior Court (Cal.1983). The California Supreme Court there held that appropriative water rights are (and always were) subject to a public trust that requires curtailment of the water right if necessary to protect trust resources (in this case, the ecological integrity of Mono Lake and its associated wildlife). Although each state has a different version or variant of the public trust doctrine, the general notion is that, where agencies fail to impose restrictions on private development that threatens to destroy public access to important public resources, the courts should imply and enforce those restrictions. See also In re Water Use Permit Applications (Haw.2000) (public trust covers groundwater resources and excludes private commercial use as a protected trust purpose).

The main question for present purposes is whether any sort of public trust doctrine or duty applies in relation to ownership and management of federal lands. From an early time, the Supreme Court and lower courts have referred to the Interior Secretary as a trustee of the public lands. Those references, however, were meant to buttress the Secretary's power to take the action at issue, not as a limitation on his discretion. In *Light v. United States*, supra, the Supreme Court said that Congress was the entity to determine how the trust would be administered.

Commentators have argued for a generation that the public trust doctrine should act as a limitation on the discretion of land management agencies, making them obtain express congressional sanction for any action that arguably harms trust resources and values. See, e.g., Joseph Sax, *The Public Trust Doctrine In Natural Resources Law: Effective Judicial Intervention*, 68 Mich. L. Rev. 471 (1970); Charles F. Wilkinson, *The Public Trust Doctrine in*

Public Land Law, 14 U.C.D. L. Rev. 269 (1980). Only one case directly supports that theory. In Sierra Club v. Department of the Interior (N.D.Cal. 1974), Sierra Club v. Department of the Interior (N.D.Cal.1975), and Sierra Club v. Department of the Interior (N.D.Cal.1976), Judge Sweigert determined that a public trust duty transformed a discretionary power into a mandatory duty. Timber operations on private lands adjacent to the irregularly shaped Redwood National Park (RNP) had deleterious aesthetic and physical effects within the park. The NPS Organic Act commanded the Secretary to preserve the resources within the parks, 16 U.S.C.A. § 1, and the specific RNP Act gave him discretion to deal with external threats. Id. § 79a. The Secretary refused to take any effective action to safeguard the Park. In the first decision in a suit brought to force secretarial action, the court held that the complaint stated a claim for relief:

> We are of the opinion that the terms of the statute ... impose a legal duty on the Secretary to utilize the specific powers given to him whenever reasonably necessary for the protection of the park and that any discretion vested in the Secretary concerning time, place and specifics of the exercise of such powers is subordinate to the paramount legal duty imposed, not only under his trust obligation but by the statute itself, to protect the park.

The second opinion reaffirmed the existence of the trust duty, found that the Interior Department violated it, and entered an affirmative injunction requiring compliance. Compliance required the cooperation of other entities, all of whom refused to cooperate, so the court in the third opinion "purged" the Department of noncompliance and dismissed the action. See section 11B.

Since the *RNP* case, all courts faced with similar public trust questions have either distinguished the *RNP* holding or ruled that an agency's statutory duty is exclusive (i.e., that the public trust duty does not exist in this context). E.g., Sierra Club v. Andrus (D.D.C.1980). In the latter case, the district court concluded that a 1978 amendment to the NPS Organic Act reflected Congress' intention to eliminate extra-statutory trust duties and that FLPMA is the exclusive embodiment of the BLM's management responsibilities. The allied argument that the public trust should be a central guiding tenet of judicial review of decisions concerning management of the federal lands and resources has not yet received a sympathetic hearing from any court.

See PNRL § 8:27.

G. AN INTRODUCTION TO PUBLIC LAND USE PLANNING: THE NATIONAL ENVIRONMENTAL POLICY ACT

The BLM and the Forest Service are subject to formal land and resource allocation planning procedures under the Federal Land Policy and Management Act and the National Forest Management Act respectively. See Norton v. Southern Utah Wilderness Alliance (S.Ct.2004) (refusing to review alleged noncompliance with BLM land use plan requirements). The NPS and the FWS also have statutory land use planning responsibilities. All of the federal land management agencies also are subject to the environmental assessment and planning requirements of the National Environmental Policy Act (NEPA), 42 U.S.C.A. §§ 4321–4370d. Compliance with NEPA has been at issue in a significant percentage of modern public land law litigation since the statute's adoption in 1969. NEPA applies well beyond the formal planning context, although the land management agencies must comply with it in the implementation of formal planning processes. Despite its generality, the cool reception afforded it by the Supreme Court, and the established principle that the statute has no substantive bite, NEPA has had a significant impact in forcing federal agencies to incorporate environmental considerations into decisionmaking processes and in delaying projects in which environmental assessment has been superficial.

1. THE PURPOSES OF NEPA AND THE LIMITS OF JUDICIAL REVIEW

Section 101 of NEPA sets forth several vague but ambitious objectives, including the use of all practicable means to create and maintain conditions under which man and nature can coexist in productive harmony. Id. § 4331. That section, which has been all but ignored by the courts, also establishes a continuing responsibility of the federal government to improve and coordinate federal plans and programs so that the nation may, among other things, fulfill the responsibilities of each generation as trustee of the environment for succeeding generations, attain the widest range of beneficial uses of the environment without degradation, and preserve important historic, cultural, and natural aspects of our national heritage.

The core of the statute is section 102(2)(C), id. § 4332(2)(C), which imposes on all federal agencies the responsibility to include in "every recommendation or report on proposals for legislation and other major Federal actions significantly affecting the quality of the human environment" a detailed environmental impact statement (EIS). Each EIS must assess the environmental impact of the proposed action, any adverse environmental effects which cannot be avoided if the proposal is implemented, alternatives to the proposed action, the relationship between local short-term uses of the environment and the maintenance and enhancement of long-term productivity, and any irreversible and irretrievable resource commitments involved in implementation of the proposal. Id.

Although the legislative history of NEPA does little to amplify Congress' goals, the courts have discerned two principal statutory objectives. First, NEPA was designed to require agencies that otherwise might not be inclined to do so to consider the potential environmental consequences of contemplated actions. The EIS preparation requirement of section 102(2)(C) is the principal "action-forcing" mechanism for ensuring that agencies take a "hard look" at potential environmental consequences. Second, Congress envisioned NEPA as an "environmental full disclosure law." The statute, the Council on Environmental Quality (CEQ) regulations with which all federal agencies must comply in implementing NEPA, and in some instances the NEPA regulations issued by individual federal agencies require those agencies to circulate draft EISs for comment among other federal and state agencies and to provide opportunities for public review. In theory, these processes make possible congressional and public scrutiny of administrative decisions that are poorly reasoned or that threaten significant adverse environmental consequences with inadequate justification. If political opposition among legislators, other executive branch officials, and voters is sufficiently high, these forces may be able to forestall the proposed project or convince the agency to alter it in a manner that mitigates the objectionable environmental effects.

NEPA also facilitates litigation for stopping proposals the environmental effects of which were ignored by a federal land management agency. The statute itself creates no private cause of action, but litigants adversely affected by an agency project nevertheless typically have access to the federal courts under the Administrative Procedure Act and other jurisdictional bases. Although judicial review of NEPA compliance is therefore widely available, the scope of that review is limited. The Supreme

Court held in Strycker's Bay Neighborhood Council, Inc. v. Karlen (S.Ct.1980), that the judicial function is confined to determining whether an agency complied with its procedural obligations under NEPA. Subsequently, in Robertson v. Methow Valley Citizens Council (S.Ct.1989), the Court confirmed that

> NEPA itself does not mandate particular results, but simply prescribes the necessary process. If the adverse environmental effects of the proposed action are adequately identified and evaluated, the agency is not constrained by NEPA from deciding that other values outweigh the environmental costs.... Other statutes may impose substantive environmental obligations on federal agencies, but NEPA merely prohibits uninformed—rather than unwise—agency action.

Likewise, according to the *Methow Valley* Court, NEPA dictates neither that agencies mitigate the adverse effects of their actions nor that they include in every EIS a detailed explanation of specific mitigation measures. Finally, the Court upheld the validity of an amendment to the CEQ regulations intended to eliminate the responsibility of agencies to include in an EIS a "worst case analysis" when they are uncertain about the extent of reasonably foreseeable environmental consequences as a result of the unavailability or cost of obtaining more complete information.

The unavailability of substantive review has not prevented opponents from using NEPA to induce courts to halt objectionable projects. It is not difficult for litigants to state a colorable claim either that the agency failed to prepare an EIS when it should have done so or that the EIS it prepared was inadequate. Such suits often result in project delays and sometimes lead to outright cancellation. The fear that the courts will demand strict compliance with NEPA procedures undoubtedly has contributed to more conscientious environmental assessment by the federal land management agencies.

See PNRL chapter 10G.

2. JUDICIAL REVIEW OF THE THRESHOLD PREPARATION QUESTION

NEPA vests in the CEQ the task of assessing the extent to which the programs of other federal agencies comply with their environmental assessment responsibilities under section 102. The CEQ regulations establish a process, called an environmental assessment (EA) or a "mini-EIS," for resolving the threshold question of whether an EIS is necessary. If, after performing an EA, the agency determines that it need not prepare an EIS, it must issue a Finding of No Significant Impact (FONSI). Initially, the courts disagreed on whether judicial review of an agency's decision not to prepare an EIS was governed by the arbitrary and capricious standard of review or the less deferential reasonableness test. After the Supreme Court in Marsh v. Oregon Natural Resources Council (S.Ct.1989), rejected the reasonableness standard in the context of review of the decision not to prepare a supplemental EIS, the courts generally have agreed upon the arbitrary and capricious standard. See, e.g., Sierra Club v. Lujan (10th Cir.1991). But one court still thinks that the reasonableness standard is appropriate when the agency decides not to prepare an EIS without even conducting an EA. High Sierra Hikers Ass'n v. Blackwell (9th Cir.2004).

a. Proposals for Legislation

Relatively few cases deal with the obligation to prepare an EIS in connection with legislative proposals. In Andrus v. Sierra Club (S.Ct.1979), the Supreme Court held that an appropriations request need not be accompanied by an EIS because appropriations bills are not legislation. The Ninth Circuit in Trustees for Alaska v. Hodel (9th Cir.1986), subsequently enjoined the Interior Secretary from submitting to Congress a legislative EIS to accompany a report on mineral potential in an Alaskan wildlife refuge because the EIS had not been circulated to interested agencies and the public for comment.

b. Proposals for Agency Action

When a plaintiff claims that an agency improperly failed to prepare an EIS on a proposal for action, the courts typically must make one or more of a series of threshold determinations: does the proposal involve an "action"; is it major and federal; and will it significantly affect the quality of the human environment? A negative answer to any of these questions excuses the proposing agency from the requirement in § 102(2)(C) to prepare an EIS.

Absent an agency proposal, compliance with the environmental assessment responsibilities of NEPA section 102(2)(C) is unnecessary. Kleppe v. Sierra Club (S.Ct.1976). Issuance of regulations, preparation of land use plans, granting of permits, and like activities all qualify as proposals for action. A more difficult question is whether an agency's failure to act can amount to agency "action," and, if so, when it does. The CEQ regulations state that a failure to act qualifies as an agency "action" for NEPA purposes if the failure to act is judicially reviewable. The D.C. Circuit concluded otherwise in Defenders of Wildlife v. Andrus (D.C.Cir.1980), because there was no "overt act." Failure to exercise discretion usually is not an "action." Fund for Animals v. Mainella (D.D.C.2003) (failure to exercise discretion to restrict hunting of black bears in national recreation area).

In *Kleppe*, supra, the Interior Department conducted studies to help determine whether to resume coal leasing in the Northern Great Plains following a moratorium on leasing. Although the agency was preparing an EIS on the effects of the national coal leasing program, and promised to prepare site-specific EISs at the leasing stage, the plaintiff claimed that NEPA also required preparation of a regional EIS. The Supreme Court disagreed, holding such an EIS unnecessary because the Department never proposed an action of regional scope. In the absence of a regional plan of development, the subject of a regional EIS evaluation simply did not exist. The court in High Sierra Hikers Ass'n v. Blackwell (9th Cir.2004), distinguished *Kleppe* in a case involving a challenge to the Forest Service's issuance of multi-year multiple use permits to commercial packstock operators. NEPA applied because the Forest Service contemplated a specific proposal for action through the issuance of the permits and a related wilderness plan.

c.   Federal Actions

Several courts have devised tests for determining the degree of federal participation necessary to trigger section 102(2)(C) obligations. According to one court, the key inquiry involves the extent of the federal agency's authority to influence significant nonfederal activity. Sierra Club v. Hodel (10th Cir. 1988). NEPA typically applies to major state and private actions that require federal permission or financing. In Sierra Club v. Penfold (9th Cir.1988), the court held that BLM review of "notice" placer mining operations did not require an EIS because mine operators did not receive federal funding and BLM approval was not a prerequisite to the commencement of operations. The agency's obligation to monitor operations and enforce regulatory responsibilities did not constitute major federal action.

An agency need not prepare an EIS if it lacks the statutory discretion to consider the environmental consequences of its action. See Department of Transp. v. Public Citizen (S.Ct.2004). Similarly, compliance with NEPA is not required where it would result in an irreconcilable conflict with an agency's obligations under another statute. Flint Ridge Dev. Co. v. Scenic Rivers Ass'n (S.Ct.1976). The courts have split on the question of whether the FWS must comply with NEPA when it designates critical habitat under the ESA. Compare Douglas County v. Babbitt (9th Cir.1995) (Congress intended ESA procedures to replace NEPA procedures) with Catron County Bd. of Comm'rs v. United States FWS (10th Cir.1996) (the ESA's critical habitat designation process does not duplicate NEPA analysis). One court held that the NMFS's issuance of an incidental take statement under the ESA is a major federal action for purposes of NEPA. Ramsey v. Kantor (9th Cir.1996).

d. Major, Significant Actions

NEPA environmental assessment responsibilities are confined to major actions with significant effects on the human environment. The CEQ has ruled that whether an action is "major" is part and parcel of the significance question. Significance involves both the context and intensity of a proposal. The Supreme Court held in Metropolitan Edison Co. v. PANE (S.Ct.1983), that an agency proposing an action that will not have a reasonably close causal connection to a change in the physical environment need not prepare an EIS. A controversial proposal is more likely to result in a finding of significance than a non-controversial one, although the existence of public opposition of itself does not necessarily require an EIS. E.g., Cold Mountain v. Garber (9th Cir.2004).

An agency's promise to mitigate the potential adverse consequences of its proposal may avoid NEPA procedures. Spiller v. White (5th Cir.2003) (endorsing the concept of a "mitigated FONSI"); Cabinet Mountains Wilderness v. Peterson (D.C.Cir. 1982). In National Parks & Conservation Ass'n v. Babbitt (9th Cir.2001), however, the court took issue with the NPS's failure to substantiate its assertion that proposed mitigation measures would provide an adequate buffer against the adverse effects of increasing the number of cruise ships allowed to enter Glacier Bay National Park. In particular, the agency neither studied the anticipated effects of the mitigation measures nor provided criteria for an ongoing examination of them or for taking needed corrective actions.

The most troublesome issues concerning significance tend to occur in connection with federal programs that proceed in steps. The "chronological tiering" question involves determining when in the multi-step process the agency must perform its environmental assessment. In cases such as Sierra Club v. Peterson (D.C.Cir.1983), and Conner v. Burford (9th Cir.1988), the courts refused to permit the Forest Service to defer EIS preparation until the submission of site-specific exploration and development plans for onshore oil and gas leasing, unless the agency retained the authority at the time of leasing to preclude all surface-disturbing activities pending sufficient environmental evaluation. See section 6B(3). Likewise, some courts have looked unfavorably upon deferral of EIS preparation to later stages when implementation of the project's early stages may create a momentum toward project completion that the agency will be unable to reverse regardless of the significance of the environmental consequences later revealed. Others, assuming that agencies will maintain objectivity, have permitted early stages to proceed in the absence of an EIS. The courts tend to take a dim view of agencies that commit to proposals before undertaking the environmental evaluation required by NEPA. E.g., Metcalf v. Daley (9th Cir.2000), or based on "tiering" to an unreleased EA. Montana Wilderness Ass'n v. Fry (D.Mont.2004) (EIS tiered to earlier EA on oil and gas leasing program insufficient).

"Geographical tiering" relates to the relationship between a programmatic EIS and subsequent site-specific evaluation. The leading case is *Kleppe*, supra, where the Supreme Court indicated that a programmatic EIS may be necessary for concurrently pending projects with cumulative or synergistic impacts. The Court also concluded, however, that the agency is responsible for assessing whether such impacts will occur, thereby affording considerable discretion to the agency to decide whether more than one EIS is necessary. Another court required an EIS to assess the cumulative impact of a series of individual projects in the context of BLM approval of placer mining. Sierra Club v. Penfold (9th Cir.1988). Similarly, in Save the Yaak Comm. v. Block (9th Cir.1988), the Forest Service was required to consider in a single EIS the impacts of improving a logging road and of the logging activities enabled by it. In Muckelshoot Indian Tribe v. U.S. Forest Serv. (9th Cir.1999), the court halted a Forest Service exchange of land with old growth, commercial grade timber for heavily logged inholdings on the ground that the EIS afforded inadequate consideration to the cumulative effects of logging on lands involved in previous and reasonably foreseeable planned future exchanges. Vague assurances of future evaluation will not suffice. Although an agency need not prepare a single EIS for a series of actions that do not qualify as connected, cumulative, or similar, it may need to include in an EA on the first such action discussion of the cumulative effects of reasonably foreseeable future actions. See, e.g., Native Ecosystems Council v. Dombeck (9th Cir.2002).

An agency is more likely to be able to avoid considering cumulative impact in a programmatic EIS if it can convince a court that individual actions are independent and that it is committed to considering cumulative impact at the site-specific stage. *See*, *e.g.*, Salmon River Concerned Citizens v. Robertson (9th Cir.1994). A programmatic EIS may preclude the need for subsequent, site-specific evaluations, but not if its discussion of local conditions is superficial or significant new impacts arise.

The tiering question often arises in connection with efforts by the BLM and the Forest Service to comply with their statutory land use planning responsibilities under FLPMA and the NFMA, respectively. It has long been the practice of agencies to prepare an EIS to accompany a land use plan. The Forest Service in 2005 disavowed that responsibility, even though the NFMA seems to require it. An adequate programmatic EIS at the planning stage may obviate the need for detailed evaluation of implementing decisions. Headwaters, Inc. v. BLM (9th Cir.1990).

See PNRL §§ 10G:11–10G:16.

3. JUDICIAL REVIEW OF EIS ADEQUACY

a. Scope of Review

Judicial review of EIS adequacy tends to be narrower than review of an agency's decision not to prepare an EIS. Most courts reviewing the sufficiency of an EIS apply a "rule of reason"—if the statement contains a reasonably thorough discussion of the likely environmental effects of the proposal and its alternatives, the reviewing court is unlikely to enjoin project implementation. E.g., City of Sausalito v. O'Neill (9th Cir.2004) (reasonably thorough discussion of environmental consequences); Resources Ltd., Inc. v. Robertson (9th Cir.1993). Judicial review is not invariably a pro forma exercise, however. The Forest Service's reliance on stale scientific evidence and unsupported assumptions and its failure to address scientific uncertainty meaningfully led to a remand of the agency's management plan for the northern spotted owl and accompanying EIS in Seattle Audubon Soc'y v. Espy (9th Cir.1993). Vague assurances that adverse environmental consequences will not occur due to unspecified future agency actions are likely to invoke more demanding judicial scrutiny. See, e.g., California v. Block (9th Cir.1982). So is the presence of apparently inflated estimates of a project's economic benefits because they can impair fair consideration of the project's merits by both the agency and the public. NRDC v. United States Forest Serv. (9th Cir.2005); Hughes River Watershed Conservancy v. Glickman (4th Cir.1996).

b. Discussion of Alternatives

The CEQ has described the discussion of the environmental impacts of the proposal and of the alternatives to it considered by the agency as the "heart of the EIS." The preparing agency usually must consider a "no action" alternative. In NRDC v. Hughes (D.D.C.1977), the Interior Department's failure to explain why it proposed to resume coal leasing despite considerable evidence that abundant reserves were already under lease marred the EIS. In NRDC v. Hodel (D.Nev.1985), on the other hand, the district court endorsed the BLM's failure to consider a no grazing alternative because that option was "unthinkable" in light of historic practices. In American Rivers v. FERC (9th Cir.2000), environmental groups argued that the no action alternative for a proposed hydropower facility relicensing was non-issuance of the license, but the court held that no action under the circumstances was continued operation under the terms and conditions of the original license.

An attack on the adequacy of an EIS that includes an assessment of the no action option is usually difficult to sustain, unless the challenger can convince the court that a superficial discussion of alternatives reflects an inappropriate agency predisposal toward the project. *California v. Block*, supra, is illustrative. The Forest Service prepared a programmatic EIS on wilderness designation proposals, but the Ninth Circuit enjoined release of the disputed areas to multiple use management because the agency did not appear to take seriously the possibility of characterizing anything more than one-third of the lands assessed as wilderness. In Northwest Resource Info. Ctr., Inc. v. NMFS (9th Cir.1995), on the other hand, an EIS analyzing alternatives for improving river flow to protect salmon was adequate even though it afforded cursory attention to eliminating an existing program for transporting juvenile salmon around dams.

An agency's failure to consider an alternative suggested in comments on a draft EIS may render the final EIS suspect. Dubois v. United States Dep't of Agric. (1st Cir.1996); Fund for Animals v. Norton (D.D.C.2003) (failure to consider elimination of trail grooming, despite knowledge of its adverse effects on wildlife). Other courts have stated, however, that NEPA does not require consideration of alternatives that do not achieve the agency's purposes in making the proposal. E.g., Colorado Envtl. Coalition v. Dombeck (10th Cir.1999) (Forest Service need not consider alternatives to proposal to add terrain to ski area that would not have increased skiable terrain); Friends of Southeast's Future v. Morrison (9th Cir.1998) (Forest Service need not consider no action alternative to logging because it would not satisfy timber demands); Pit River Tribe v. BLM (E.D. Cal.2004). One court held that agencies need not consider environmentally damaging alternatives to an action whose purpose is to enhance environmental protection of federal lands and resources. Kootenai Tribe v. Veneman (9th Cir.2002) (rejecting attack on Forest Service's failure to consider alternatives to roadless area protection rule that would not have imposed a near-prohibition on road construction).

See PNRL § 10G:23.

c. Supplemental EISs

The CEQ regulations require the land management agencies to supplement previously prepared EISs if they make substantial changes to the proposed action that are relevant to environmental concerns. In Marsh v. Oregon Natural Resources Council (S.Ct.1989), the Supreme Court ruled that supplementation is also necessary if, due to a change in circumstances or the availability of new information, the original EIS is not adequate to assess the impact of the project. In *Headwaters*, supra, the court refused to require supplementation of a regional EIS to consider the effects of timber sales on the northern spotted owl. The BLM's regional EIS and site-specific EA provided adequate treatment of the threats posed by the sales. But in Portland Audubon Soc'y v. Babbitt (9th Cir.1993), the same court held that the BLM's decision not to prepare a supplemental EIS to consider previously unavailable information concerning the effects of timber management plans on the long-range survival of the owl was arbitrary. Unlike *Headwaters*, which involved the effect of a site-specific sale, the plaintiffs in *Portland Audubon* challenged the agency's failure to supplement the EISs accompanying timber management plans that controlled a variety of land use decisions. New information raising the threat of species extinction in a large area if the BLM carried out its timber sale program required a supplemental EIS. Agencies need only supplement an EIS if "there remains 'major Federal action' to occur." Norton v. Southern Utah Wilderness Alliance (S.Ct.2004).

Although agencies may use procedures (such as supplemental environmental reports) that fall short of the full procedural rigor of a supplemental EIS to determine whether new information or changed circumstances exist, they may not use those short cuts to substitute for a supplemental EIS if they find that significant new information does exist. Idaho Sporting Congress v. Alexander (9th Cir.2000). Legal as opposed to factual changes may not require supplementation, and flexibility to address changed circumstances that is built into the agency's proposal may avoid the need to supplement an EIS. ONRC v. U.S. Forest Serv. (W.D. Wash.1999).

See PNRL § 10G:24

d. Injunctive Relief

If a court finds that a land management agency has violated NEPA, it is not automatically required to enjoin the proposed action pending statutory compliance. In *Kleppe v. Sierra Club*, supra, the Supreme Court indicated that the reviewing court must engage in a balancing of the equities, comparing the harms that would be suffered by the parties in the presence and absence of injunctive relief. In *Save the Yaak*, supra, the Ninth Circuit stated that environmental injury is likely to be irreparable because, by its nature, it can seldom be adequately remedied by money damages and is often permanent or long-term. Accordingly, when such injury is likely, "the balance of harms will usually favor the issuance of an injunction to protect the environment." See also Amoco Prod. Co. v. Village of Gambell (S.Ct.1987). State agencies also may be enjoined if their actions are "intertwined" with those of federal agencies. Laub v. United States Dep't of Interior (9th Cir.2003).

Despite the Supreme Court's narrow construction of NEPA, there is little question that the statute has had an enormous influence on public land management during the last 25 years. NEPA itself does not dictate that a land management agency adapt its actions to minimize environmental harm. It does require consideration of environmental consequences, however, and public disclosure of the results of the evaluation process. Environmental assessment, moreover, is an integral part of the land use planning process, which has become an increasingly important influence on public natural resource allocation.

See PNRL § 10G:25.

CHAPTER FIVE

THE WATER RESOURCE

Water is the most important public natural resource because all other uses and life itself are dependent on water quantity and quality. Most questions of water entitlement are decided pursuant to state law. Indeed, water law is a separate though related area unto itself, and it is outlined in David Getches' excellent *Water Law in a Nutshell 3d*. This Nutshell's treatment of the law governing water allocation largely is limited to the ways in which federal law and federal interests intersect with state water rights systems. The first section is concerned with federal rights to take and use water. Section B cursorily describes the federally initiated and financed systems for development of water resources. The final section discusses the broader topic of watershed management.

A. THE ACQUISITION OF WATER RIGHTS ON THE PUBLIC LANDS

Water law defines legal rights to a limited, moving, and largely renewable resource. Those rights are by nature "usufructuary," something less than a fee simple interest, because they usually are dependent on climate and conditions and are terminable upon non-use. States have adopted two radically different systems for allocating water, largely because of climatic and physical differences between the eastern and western states. In some respects, federal water law is superimposed over state systems and in other respects it is subordinate to them.

Under English common law, each owner of land adjacent to a watercourse automatically acquired the right to continued flow of the stream, subject to reasonable use by other riparian owners. In the eastern states, the riparian "natural flow" notion was adopted, but modified to accommodate a greater variety of human uses. The eastern states, of course, have generous rainfall and consequent abundant water resources.

The western states (and territories) rejected the riparian doctrine because it was thought to be unsuitable for the arid and semi-arid West. The "Colorado" or "prior appropriation" doctrine adopted in its place was meant to reward and provide stability to water development for economic purposes. It divorces water rights from riparian land ownership and instead institutes a "first in time" test: the first person to divert water out of a stream and put it to a beneficial use (early defined as municipal, industrial, or agricultural) acquired a right to continue such diversion at the same place at the same time of the year and in the same volumes for as long as the water was devoted to the beneficial use.

Prior appropriation differs from the riparian doctrine in several major respects. First, there is no deficit sharing in times of drought; the senior user receives his full allocation before junior users receive any water. Second, the natural flow theory is entirely discarded; appropriators can and do totally dry up the stream. Third, no nexus between the watercourse and the water use is necessary; diverters may transport the water to wherever the use may be. The last principle enabled miners to transport water by elaborate systems of ditches and canals for use at mine sites where water was lacking. One result of prior appropriation is that more than 90 percent of all water beyond the 100th meridian is used for irrigated agriculture. Another result is that considerable damage has been wreaked upon water dependent ecosystems in the West.

The picture of water allocation in the West is much more complicated than the preceding paragraphs make it sound. First, the states of the High Plains and along the Pacific Coast have adopted mixed or hybrid allocation systems with elements of both prior appropriation and riparianism. Second, adjudication of water rights over the years has produced delicate interactive series of dependent rights, a system on which the participants have long relied and accepted. Third, state water law in the West has changed greatly and that process of change continues. New water entitlements require an administrative finding that the diversion is in the public interest. Transfer rules have been altered. Many states have eschewed the diversion requirement when the state itself acquires minimum instream flow rights for protection of fish and wildlife. Most important, the federal government, as both a sovereign and a landowner, is forcing other changes.

Before the admission of the western states to the Union, the United States could have imposed whatever water use or allocation system it desired, but Congress did not do so. Instead, Congress in the Mining Act of 1866 decreed that all water rights recognized and protected under local law "shall be maintained and protected," even on the public lands. 14 Stat. 253, § 9. Eleven years later, it enacted the 1877 Desert Lands Act (DLA), 43 U.S.C.A. §§ 321–329, to encourage homesteading of the arid public lands of the west. After requiring DLA claimants to irrigate their claims, Congress provided that:

the water of all lakes, rivers and other sources of water supply upon the public lands and not navigable, shall remain and be held free for the appropriation and use of the public for irrigation, mining and manufacturing purposes subject to existing rights.

This language appears to create a federal rule of appropriation for the public lands, but the Supreme Court later construed the words as effecting "a severance of all waters upon the public domain, not theretofore appropriated, from the land itself." "For since 'Congress cannot enforce either [the prior appropriation or riparian rights] rule upon any state,' Kansas v. Colorado, 206 U.S. 46, 94, the full power of choice must remain with the state." California Oregon Power Co. v. Beaver Portland Cement Co. (S.Ct.1935).

In matters of water rights allocation, therefore, state powers were paramount and largely still are. But from an early time, the Supreme Court recognized that limitations on state discretion were necessary to safeguard federal regulatory and property interests. The congressional power over interstate commerce was protected by decreeing that all navigable waters were subject to a servitude by which the United States could maintain uninterrupted navigability without liability. United States v. Rio Grande Dam & Irrigation Co. (S.Ct.1899). Additionally, the Court arrogated unto itself the power to formulate a federal common law to allocate interstate waters by equitable apportionment when the states failed to agree and Congress failed to resolve the dispute. Kansas v. Colorado (S.Ct.1907).

More to the present point is the doctrine of federal implied reserved water rights, also known as the *Winters* doctrine. The Court in Winters v. United States (S.Ct.1908), held that the United States, when it reserved a tract as an Indian reservation without mentioning water use, also impliedly reserved sufficient unappropriated water to serve the reservation's purpose—in this case, to provide the tribe with agricultural self-sufficiency. The *Winters* doctrine provoked western opposition because the Indians' rights were senior to all post-reservation diverters, they were essentially unquantified in that the tribe was entitled to amounts reasonably necessary for both present and future water needs, and they did not require diversion or application to a beneficial use.

Winters was long thought to be limited to tribal reservations. In FPC v. Oregon (S.Ct.1955), however, the Supreme Court distinguished "reserved" federal lands from the public domain and suggested that *Winters* applied to all federal lands reserved for particular purposes. That suggestion became law in Arizona v. California (S.Ct.1963); the Court summarily ruled that the United States impliedly intended to reserve water "sufficient for the future requirements" of national forests, recreation areas, and wildlife refuges established either by legislation or executive order.

The Court further extended the scope of *Winters* in Cappaert v. United States (S.Ct.1976). A rancher pumped groundwater from the same hydrologic system that a species of fish needed for its continued existence. Chief Justice Burger for a unanimous Court ruled that presidential reservation of Devils Hole as a national monument, in large measure for protection of the pupfish, prior to the rancher's use, also impliedly reserved sufficient unappropriated water to insure the species' continuation. The Court explained that reservation of water rights is empowered by both the Commerce and Property Clauses, which permit federal regulation of navigable streams and of federal lands. The key question is whether the government intended to reserve available water; the Court presumes such intent if that water is necessary to accomplish reservation purposes. For that reason, the amount of water reserved is limited to the minimum that is necessary to serve those purposes. By characterizing the Devil's Hole pool as surface water, the Court avoided deciding whether the *Winters* doctrine applies to groundwater.

Just two years later, a sharply divided Court curtailed the scope of the federal implied reserved water rights doctrine in several important respects. United States v. New Mexico (S.Ct.1978), involved an adjudication of water rights in the Mimbres River in New Mexico. The state opposed the Forest Service's request for an implied right to sufficient water for stockwatering and "aesthetic, environmental, recreational or 'fish' purposes" in the Gila National Forest. The Court held, 5–4, that the 1897 Organic Act revealed a congressional intent to reserve the national forests primarily for timber supply and watershed purposes, even though the statute recited a third purpose, to "improve and protect the forest within the boundaries." Because any aesthetic or fish and wildlife preservation purposes were at most secondary, they were not entitled to any implied water rights allocation. Evidently in dicta (because the point was not argued), the Court also opined that the 1960 MUSYA, which recited that national forest establishment purposes included recreation and wildlife, did not change the result because those other purposes remained secondary, and reservation of additional water to promote them might diminish the availability of water flow for the primary purposes. Essentially, the Court insisted on evidence of explicit congressional intent to reserve water instead of inquiring whether an implied reservation was necessary to protect the forests and the purposes for which they were reserved. Justice Powell's dissent thought that the 1897 Congress was somewhat more broad-minded than the majority gave it credit for.

In the wake of *New Mexico*, courts generally have construed federal implied reserved water rights narrowly, e.g., United States v. Idaho (Idaho 2001), but a variety of questions remain to be answered. One court determined that because BLM public lands are only withdrawn and have not been formally ''reserved,'' no water rights accrue to BLM holdings unless a particular tract has been specially reserved for a purpose requiring water. Sierra Club v. Watt (D.C.Cir.1981). That rationale is at best shallow, failing to recognize that FLPMA's dedication of the BLM public lands to certain purposes is the functional equivalent of a reservation. See PNRL § 5:36. The Colorado Supreme Court in United States v. City and County of Denver (Colo.1982), ruled against a federal reserved right to support recreation in Dinosaur National Monument (and against a variety of other federal water claims) because the Monument was reserved to preserve objects of historic and scientific interest rather than for recreational use. That decision, however, appears to afford the state's prior appropriation system a primacy to which it is not entitled under Supreme Court precedents.

Nevertheless, other developments indicate that the federal implied water rights doctrine is alive and well. The court in United States v. Jesse (Colo. 1987), ruled that the Forest Service stated a claim for a water right for minimum instream flow to maintain efficient stream channels as an aspect of "secur[ing] favorable conditions of water flows." The Water Court later determined that the United States had not proven its claims because, among other things, it could control instream flow by attaching permit conditions; that opinion rests on questionable premises. And in Sierra Club v. Yeutter (10th Cir.1990), the lower court held (and the appellate court hinted) that wilderness was entitled to additional water rights. The Arizona Supreme Court later determined that federal reserved rights include groundwater, even when the state does not otherwise recognize appropriative groundwater rights. *In re* Gila River System (Ariz.1999). See also *In re* Snake River Basin Adjudication (Idaho 1998).

Congress more often in recent years has directly addressed water rights when creating various conservation areas, and in some cases has instructed the land management agencies to assert the rights reserved, thus avoiding the need for judicially implied rights. So too have various Presidents in creating new national monuments. National wild, scenic, and recreational river segment designations carry with them express federal water rights, although the amounts reserved are limited to those necessary to accomplish statutory purposes. 16 U.S.C.A. § 1284(c).

In many if not most cases, declaration of federal implied reserved water rights makes little practical difference because most federal reservations tend to be at higher altitudes where future upstream diversion opportunities are impractical anyway. In addition, most federal water rights tend to be for nonconsumptive instream flows and therefore do not foreclose downstream consumptive uses. States' objections therefore often are based on sovereignty and political grounds, rather than on any real harm to beneficial users. Recent liberalizations of state water law offer avenues whereby the political friction can be avoided through compliance with state procedures.

The federal implied reserved water rights doctrine and explicit statutory reservations are not the only means by which the federal government may acquire water rights. The United States as a landowner is entitled to all benefits of state law enjoyed by any private landowner. In riparian states, the United States has riparian rights to the same extent as any other riparian owner. In mixed riparian/appropriation states, the same rule obtains. In re Water of Hallett Creek Stream Sys. (Cal.1988). Further, nothing prevents the federal government from obtaining appropriative water rights pursuant to state law. Historically, that course would have been unavailing because the United States typically desired minimum instream flow guarantees and state law required diversion before water rights could vest.

State v. Morros (Nev.1988), illustrates the possibilities of sovereign cooperation. Federal land agencies applied to the state agency for water rights to maintain the level of a lake for recreation and wildlife (the in situ application) and for water rights to accommodate recreation, stockwatering, and wildlife watering. The Nevada Supreme Court dismissed the State Board of Agriculture's protests against grant of the applications. It determined that liberalization of the water laws in Nevada obviated the diversion requirement, that those laws made beneficial uses out of wildlife protection and recreation, and that the federal agencies need not own livestock or wildlife to obtain water rights for them. Significantly, the court thought that granting the diversionless federal water rights was in the public interest.

The United States has waived its immunity to suit in water rights adjudications in state courts. 43 U.S.C.A. § 666(a) (McCarran Amendment). The waiver does not permit a plaintiff to sue the United States alone. The waiver includes federal implied water rights claims. United States v. District Court In and For Eagle County (S.Ct.1971), but it only extends to general stream adjudications, not mere one-on-one disputes, Dugan v. Rank (S.Ct.1963), and does not apply to administrative proceedings. In Orff v. United States (S.Ct.2005), the Supreme Court held that sovereign immunity barred suit by farmers challenging reduced water allocation to protect endangered species. It concluded that the Reclamation Act, 43 U.S.C.A. § 390uu, waives the federal government's sovereign immunity only when the United States is joined in an action between other parties (such as two water districts) and the action requires construction of a reclamation contract and joinder of the United States is necessary.

See PNRL §§ 5:34–5:37.

B. FEDERAL WATER RESOURCES DEVELOPMENT

Although state law usually controls resolution of questions concerning water *rights* and *allocation*, federal law often governs questions of water resources *development*. Since 1902, the federal government has been the dominant developer of water resources nationwide. The western complex of dams and diversions constructed and operated pursuant to the 1902 Reclamation Act, 43 U.S.C.A. §§ 371–616, the western and midwestern systems of flood control dams built and operated by the Army Corps of Engineers, and the river system controls of the Tennessee Valley Authority (inter alia) all are federally financed and constructed. The reclamation programs and projects are directed primarily at assisting irrigated agriculture in the western states, but flood control, recreation, and power production are also important dam building purposes. In United States v. Alpine Land & Reservoir Co. (9th Cir. 1983), the court held that, despite statutory authority to devote reclamation project water to recreation and wildlife enhancement purposes, the Reclamation Act requires that these allocations be subordinated to the agricultural needs of the farmers served by a reclamation project.

The Endangered Species Act, however, may require that allocations of reclamation project water be reduced in order to protect listed aquatic species. See, e.g., Pacific Coast Fed'n of Fishermen's Ass'ns v. United States Bureau of Reclamation (9th Cir. 2005). Further, in Klamath Irrigation Dist. v. United States (Fed.Cl.2005), a group of agricultural landowners and irrigation districts unsuccessfully sued the United States, alleging that the Bureau of Reclamation (BoR)'s decision to terminate water deliveries as a means of reducing threats to endangered fish species amounted to an unconstitutional taking of their water rights. According to the Court of Federal Claims, the plaintiffs did not have a sufficient usufructuary right in the waters of the Klamath Basin project to sustain their takings claim. Cf. Kandra v. United States (D. Or.2001) (rejecting contention that BoR's suspension of water deliveries to maintain water levels necessary to support endangered species amounted to a breach of contract).

Reclamation projects were supposed to pay for themselves through fees for the use of the stored water, but fees have never approached costs. Because of the negative economic returns to the government of subsidized agriculture, and the ecological damage wrought by water projects, the dam building era likely is closed for the immediate future. Any future water development projects will have to run the gauntlets of federal law, including environmental assessment under NEPA.

The Reclamation Act imposes some federal requirements, such as acreage limitations and residency requirements, on water users, but enforcement of these restrictions has been spotty at best. State law governs water allocation questions not directly addressed by federal law. The Reclamation Act provides that nothing in the Act should be construed to affect or interfere with state laws relating to the control, appropriation, use, or distribution of water used in irrigation, or with any vested right acquired under state law. 43 U.S.C.A. § 383. In Ivanhoe Irrigation Dist. v. McCracken (S.Ct.1958), the Supreme Court confirmed that the BoR must comply with state law when it acquires vested interests in water rights, but held that section 383 did not authorize the state to override the Reclamation Act's acreage limitations. Unlike acquisition of water rights, operation of reclamation projects continued to be governed by federal law. In California v. United States (S.Ct.1978), the issue was whether the United States could ignore conditions placed on its state appropriation permit even in the absence of a direct conflict with federal law. The Court held that it could not; state law thus applies to the control, appropriation, use, or distribution of water unless that law conflicts with a specific federal directive.

See PNRL chapter 21B.

Beginning in 1920, the federal government also assumed primary jurisdiction over public and pri-

vate development of watercourses for hydropower
production, Federal Power Act (FPA), as amended,
16 U.S.C.A. §§ 791a–828c, as a facet of federal
control over interstate commerce and navigation.
Gibbons v. Ogden (S.Ct.1824). The Electric Con-
sumers Protection Act of 1986 reformed federal
licensing procedures to insure more careful consideration of environmental values, including the protection and enhancement of fish and wildlife. But cf.
Brady v. FERC (D.C. Cir.2005) (stating that the
ECPA amendments do not give environmental factors "preemptive force"). Congress amended the
FPA in the Energy Policy Act (EPA) of 2005. The
amendments provide that a license applicant and
any party to a licensing proceeding is entitled to a
trial-type hearing on any disputed issues of material
fact relating to any conditions or prescriptions developed by the Departments of Agriculture, Interi-
or, or Commerce for inclusion in a hydropower
license issued under the FPA. 16 U.S.C.A. § 797(e).

Despite a savings clause in the FPA similar to
section 8 of the Reclamation Act, federal law in the
hydropower licensing sphere overrides contrary
state law. In California v. FERC (S.Ct.1990), the
Supreme Court distinguished *California v. United
States*, supra, and held that minimum instream flow
requirements included in a federal hydropower license preempted similar but more restrictive state
requirements that were designed to protect fish
spawning habitats. Subsequently, the Ninth Circuit
barred a state agency from requiring a federal licen-
see to conduct studies and submit reports on the

environmental effects of its operations as a condition for issuance of an operating permit. Sayles Hydro Assoc. v. Maughan (9th Cir.1993).

One of the most ambitious federal water resources development programs is the system of dams in the Columbia River basin in the Pacific Northwest. The 31 major dams in the area provide cheap hydropower, but they have also contributed heavily to the decline of salmon runs in the region. Switching emphasis from power production to conservation, Congress in 1980 decreed that regional planning henceforward would aim at a more balanced mix of resource uses by placing fish and wildlife concerns on an equal footing with power production. Pacific Northwest Electric Power Planning and Conservation Act, 16 U.S.C.A. §§ 838–839h. The Act authorized the creation of an interstate Conservation Planning Council, which is responsible for developing a Columbia River Basin Fish and Wildlife Program for regional conservation and electric power production, to be implemented by the Bonneville Power Administration, the Corps of Engineers, the BoR, and the Federal Energy Regulatory Commission. In Northwest Resource Info. Ctr., Inc. v. Northwest Power Planning Council (9th Cir.1994), the court agreed with environmental group contentions that, in developing its salmon protection program, the Council failed to provide an adequate explanation for its rejection of the river flow recommendations of the fish and wildlife agencies and to afford appropriate deference to fishery managers. The court also concluded that Congress did not mandate the use of cost-benefit analysis by the Council, and that a fish and wildlife protective measure cannot be rejected solely because it will result in power losses and economic costs. It further found that the application of cost-benefit analysis could thwart fish and wildlife enhancement objectives because it would require the Council to ignore non-economic values which Congress sought to promote, such as "equity, ecology, conservation, and culture." In 1986, Congress enacted the Columbia River Gorge National Scenic Area Act, 16 U.S.C.A. §§ 544–544p, which decreed a massive land use planning and control process for the designated area.

The federal government and federal law also affect water rights allocation in other ways, notably environmental protection, that essentially amount to forms of federal water rights. The dredge-and-fill permit provisions of the Clean Water Act, 33 U.S.C.A. § 1344, for instance, forbid private parties from altering wetlands without federal permission, which in theory is to be given only grudgingly. Several courts likewise have ruled against diverters whose diversions would harm listed endangered or threatened species. Riverside Irrigation Dist. v. Andrews (10th Cir.1985); United States v. Glenn–Colusa Irrigation Dist. (E.D.Cal.1992). The court in the latter case ruled that enforcement of the ESA overrides state water rights.

Perfection of a water right on federal land under state law may be problematic, because, in many cases, the federal land management agency may be able to deny or condition access to the diversion point. See Hunter v. United States (9th Cir.1967); Nevada Land Action Ass'n v. U.S. Forest Serv. (9th Cir.1993).

See PNRL chapters 21–21C.

C. WATERSHED MANAGEMENT

In recent years, the realizations have grown that water quality is as important as water quantity, and that water quality cannot be divorced from land use. In modern public land law, land use controls for the purpose of protecting water supplies and the systems dependent on water fit within the general heading of "watershed management." At least since 1897, when Congress defined the purposes for establishing national forests as including "securing favorable conditions of water flows," "watershed" has been a statutorily important aim of public land management. In the 1960 MUSYA, and again in the 1976 FLPMA, Congress listed watershed as a co-equal multiple use to be managed for sustained yield.

The federal land management agencies have seldom directly addressed that command. Watershed instead has been treated as an implicit value without precise definition. Nevertheless, watershed protection considerations, without the label, are having an increasingly important impact on the law. First, federal implied reserved water rights for minimum instream flow have the effect of preserving streams as streams, contributing to the ecological stability of watershed areas. Second, the same can be said for state minimum instream flow mechanisms and for federal in situ rights acquired under state law. Third, the *Jesse* case, supra, recognized the integrity of the system channel as a value inherent in "favorable conditions of water flows." Fourth, federal water resource development programs have become far more sensitive to environmental and watershed quality consequences than previously. Fifth, federal regulatory law, especially the Endangered Species Act, is forcing cessation or alteration of practices harmful to watershed values. A good example of the latter trend is the case of Pacific Rivers Council v. Robertson (D.Or.1993). The Forest Service refused to revise the land use plans for two forests or to consult formally with the National Marine Fisheries Service (NMFS) after the NMFS listed runs of salmon as threatened. Both reviewing courts determined that the refusal violated the ESA, required the Forest Service to reinitiate consultation, and enjoined all new activities in the watersheds which could have adverse effects on the listed species. The Ninth Circuit went further, reversing the district court's refusal to enjoin ongoing and announced timber, range, and road projects that may affect the salmon as a means of preserving the status quo pending consultation. See section 9B(2).

The court in Northwest Indian Cemetery Protective Ass'n v. Peterson (9th Cir.1985), reached a somewhat similar result on Clean Water Act grounds. The Forest Service's proposed construction of a road and consequent timber harvesting would have increased siltation in streams beyond the level specified as acceptable by state law. The federal agency argued that it would comply with the CWA by using "best management practices" (BMPs), but the Ninth Circuit ruled that compliance with these practices would not necessarily suffice. BMPs are merely a means to achieve substantive, state-issued water quality standards. In this case, the standard required reduced siltation, and the Ninth Circuit affirmed the district court's finding that implementation of the Forest Service projects would cause a violation of the standard. Other opinions concur. Cf. Dubois v. United States Dep't of Agric. (1st Cir.1996) (transfer of water from one stream to another as a result of operation of artificial snowmaking system in national forest ski area required CWA permit). But another court held that the Forest Service was not required to apply for a permit before it contracted for logging and road construction by others that would result in the discharge of pollutants. Newton County Wildlife Ass'n v. Rogers (8th Cir.1998). Cf. ONRC v. Dombeck (9th Cir.1998) (state certification that discharge will not violate CWA requirements is only necessary for point source discharges, not to runoff from activities like cattle grazing).

The federal land management agencies may have to procure discharge permits under the Clean Water Act before spraying pesticides on the land under their jurisdiction, even if the pesticides have been registered by EPA under the Federal Insecticide, Fungicide, and Rodenticide Act (FIFRA). See, e.g., League of Wilderness Defenders/Blue Mountains Biodiversity Project v. Forsgren (9th Cir.2002). See also Headwaters, Inc. v. Talent Irrigation Dist. (9th Cir.2001). In Fairhurst v. Hagener (9th Cir.2005), however, the court concluded that the direct application of pesticides to waters of the United States for the purpose of eliminating pests in accordance with an EPA-approved FIFRA label without leaving excess amounts of the pesticide does not amount to the discharge of a pollutant because, in such a situation, the pesticides do not constitute chemical waste. EPA has taken the position that the application of a pesticide to, over, or near waters of the United States consistent with FIFRA does not constitute the discharge of a pollutant subject to the Clean Water Act's permit requirements, at least under certain circumstances. See 70 Fed. Reg. 5093 (2005).

See PNRL chapter 21, § 11A:2.

CHAPTER SIX

THE MINERAL RESOURCE

Although the United States experimented with leasing lead mines in the early 19th century, Congress did not enact any laws for the general disposition of mineral resources until 1866. By that time, prospectors had occupied the California gold fields and created mining boom towns in many parts of the West. Mineral extraction from the federal public lands has been economically significant at least since 1848, and, for a century, many thought it to be the highest, best, and most preferred use of those lands. Recent debates have centered around the appropriate degree of regulation to prevent adverse environmental effects and the appropriate degree of economic return to the government by those extracting public mineral resources.

The law as it has evolved in this country distinguishes sharply between "locatable" (or "hardrock") minerals, "leasable" (fuel and fertilizer) minerals, and "saleable" (common) minerals. Citizens may obtain rights to the former by locating valuable deposits of hardrock minerals on open public lands pursuant to the General Mining Law (GML) of 1872, 30 U.S.C.A. §§ 22–45. Leases for exploitation of non-hardrock minerals may be obtained from the government under the terms of

149

several statutes, notably the Mineral Leasing Act of 1920, as amended, 30 U.S.C.A. §§ 181–287. If adopted, recent proposals for reform of the GML would make it more like a leasing law; in any event, as section A(8) illustrates, courts have been transforming hardrock law in that direction for a generation. The government may sell common varieties minerals competitively under the Mineral Materials Act, 30 U.S.C.A. §§ 601–604.

A. HARDROCK MINERALS: THE GENERAL MINING LAW OF 1872

Congress consolidated 1866 and 1870 mining legislation into the General Mining Law of 1872, 30 U.S.C.A. §§ 22–45. The GML essentially declares that whoever discovers and develops a valuable mineral deposit on unwithdrawn public lands is entitled to mine that deposit without charge; that miner also can obtain fee title to the surface for a token charge. Historically, hardrock miners needed no federal permit to prospect and mine. The GML is relatively short, succinct, and, in many particulars, ambiguous. Hardrock mining law consequently is now more in the nature of common law created by accretions of judicial and administrative opinions than it is a question of statutory interpretation.

The seemingly simple location system process encompasses several series of steps and problems that must be considered individually. The public lands must be open to prospecting; the mineral discovered must be one within the ambit of the GML; the prospector must diligently prospect before discovery; the claim must be "located"; and the deposit must be both "discovered" and sufficiently "valuable" for the miner to acquire a valid unpatented claim. Thereafter, the locator should perform assessment work or pay fees; and patenting of the claim requires yet further steps and assessments. See generally PNRL chapter 25; Rocky Mountain Mineral Law Foundation, *American Law of Mining 2d* (1984); John D. Leshy, *The Mining Law: A Study in Perpetual Motion* (1987).

1. LANDS OPEN TO PROSPECTING

In 1872, most federal lands were open to homesteading; the GML authorized another method for disposition of the more valuable mineral lands. The past century has seen waves of withdrawals and reservations that in the aggregate have reduced lands available to locators by several orders of magnitude. In lieu settlements, Alaska state selections, small scale grants, land exchanges, land use planning, and Native claims will further reduce the lands available for location. Among the federally owned lands that are off-limits to new locations for hardrock mineral development are:

— national parks, wilderness areas, and parts of wild river corridors;

— acquired lands;

— wildlife refuges, to the extent that the Secretary has not reopened them;

— special purpose withdrawals of lands in any management system;

— lands subject to valid preexisting location claims; and

— lands so designated by Congress or the executive.

In 1922, the Supreme Court stated that "[o]nly where the United States has indicated that the lands are held for disposal under the land laws does the [GML] apply." Oklahoma v. Texas (S.Ct.1922). That no longer is the case: much of the national forest and BLM public land systems remain open to location even though closed to other forms of disposition. But land use planning will result in removal from mineral location of areas devoted to other uses within these systems.

See PNRL §§ 25:4–25:7.

2.   LOCATABLE MINERALS

All substances that are neither animal nor vegetable are mineral, but the 1872 Congress did not intend the word to have so broad a meaning. Coal has never been locatable, and Congress has removed a variety of concededly valuable substances from the operation of the location mechanism. As to the remaining hardrock substances, the test, such as it is, is that the substance "must also be the type of valuable mineral that the 1872 Congress intended to make the basis of a valid claim." Andrus v. Charlestone Stone Prod. Co. (S.Ct.1978). According to the Court, water does not qualify. Because the 1872 legislative history is less than informative, the determination largely depends on stare decisis. Courts have found that peat, stalagmites, fossils, etc. are not minerals for GML purposes, although guano and non-metallic minerals such as diamonds do qualify. By statute, sand, gravel, building stone, pumice, and other "common varieties" are not locatable unless the deposit "has some property giving it distinct and special value." 30 U.S.C.A. § 611. Common varieties instead may be sold. Id.

See PNRL § 25:15.

3. PROSPECTOR'S RIGHTS BEFORE DISCOVERY: *PEDIS POSSESSIO*

Until actual discovery of a valuable mineral deposit, the prospector is protected only by the tenuous doctrine of *pedis possessio*, or "foot possession." Consistent with the law of the mining camps, the Mining Law states that discovery must precede location, 30 U.S.C.A. § 23, but the Supreme Court in Union Oil Co. v. Smith (S.Ct.1919), ruled that the order of time in which these acts occur is not essential to acquisition of an exclusive possessory right. This holding essentially ratified the common practice of staking a claim first and exploring later. Under the nonstatutory right of possession afforded by *pedis possessio*, miners therefore can locate claims whenever and wherever they choose, and their occupation is protected from claimjumpers because such protection is a "necessity." *Union Oil* indicated that while *pedis possessio* affords the exclusive right to occupy the surface for mineral exploration purposes, that protection is sharply limited: "such possession may be maintained only by continued actual occupancy by a qualified locator . . . engaged in persistent and diligent prosecution of work looking to the discovery of a mineral."

Those requirements are wholly impractical for many types of modern mining operations which require very large land areas for efficient exploration and extraction of low grade ores. One court liberalized the doctrine by extending it to area claims without occupancy and development of every claim. MacGuire v. Sturgis (D.Wyo.1971). Most courts require fairly strict compliance with *pedis possessio* requisites on a claim-by-claim basis, however. Thus, in Geomet Exploration, Ltd. v. Lucky McUranium Corp. (Ariz.1979), the court ruled in favor of the second locator who entered with knowledge of the prior locations because the first locator did not (and could not) occupy and explore all 200 of its claims at once. It refused to replace the actual occupancy requirement of *pedis possessio* with a requirement of constructive possession as a means of protecting a potential locator of contiguous, unoccupied claims against a subsequent entrant who remained in possession while searching for minerals. While it accepted the first locator's argument that only those who enter in good faith are entitled to the protections of *pedis possessio*, it ruled that mere knowledge of a previous claim in and of itself does not demonstrate bad faith.

See PNRL § 25:9.

4. LOCATION

"Location" of a claim requires compliance with both federal and state procedural requirements. States usually require some form of marking on the ground, posting at the discovery site, development work to determine the character and extent of the deposit; and recordation in a county office. See, e.g., Wilderness Soc'y v. Dombeck (9th Cir.1999). Most states no longer adhere to the environmentally damaging requirement of sinking a discovery shaft. Prospectors may locate as many claims as they choose. Miners need not maintain markers following valid location to avoid claim forfeiture. Marking the boundaries of a claim on the ground does not always limit the claimant to those boundaries; the Court in Erhardt v. Boaro (S.Ct.1885), ruled that the locator has a certain amount of time in which to "swing" the claim around the axis of the discovery point to follow the vein.

The GML limits a "lode" claim to 1500 feet in length or 300 feet on each side of the middle of the vein, and requires that the end lines be parallel. Placer claims, on the other hand, must conform to the extent practicable to survey lines and are limited to 20 acres, but associations of persons can claim up to 160 acres, 30 U.S.C.A. §§ 35–36. Lodes differ from placers in that the former are aggregations of mineral in place (such as veins) while placer means deposits not in place, such as gold nuggets in a stream. It can be extremely difficult to tell the difference in many situations, but erroneous identification of a lode as a placer, or vice versa, can invalidate the claim. E.g., Webb v. Lujan (9th Cir. 1992). Thus, miners often must locate the claim twice, once as a lode and once as a placer, and the placer claim location must be first in time to avoid being deemed an abandonment of a previously located lode claim. 30 U.S.C.A. § 37. This is just one of several wholly counterproductive aspects of the mineral location system; the industry would prefer to abolish this distinction, but it fears that any congressional tampering with the system will lead to other results less beneficial to miners.

Miners may also locate "mill sites" of five acres each to use for refining operations. As of 2005, claimants are not limited to one mill site per mining claim.

Before the adoption of FLPMA, recordation of mining claims was governed solely by state law. Since 1976, all claimants must file with the BLM notices of intent to hold the claim with the federal government. Failure to file is "conclusively" presumed to be an abandonment. 43 U.S.C.A. § 1744(c). This retroactive procedural requirement was intended to eliminate stale mining claims and provide the land management agencies with information on the current status of claims. The courts have upheld the constitutionality of the filing requirements, concluding that they did not amount to a taking. United States v. Locke (S.Ct.1985); Topaz Beryllium Co. v. United States (10th Cir.1981). See section 3E. The BLM regularly cancels mining locations for lack of or untimely filing. By 1994, the recordation and allied requirements had reduced outstanding mineral location claims from perhaps 10 million or so to less than one million. With the advent of claim maintenance fees of $100 per claim annually, the number of location claims has since further declined considerably. By 2000, only 235,-000 claims were active on BLM lands.

See PNRL § 25:13.

5.   DISCOVERY OF A VALUABLE MINERAL DEPOSIT

The most important question in American hardrock mining law is whether the mineral deposit in question is sufficiently "valuable." Until the point at which the locator has actually uncovered a deposit that meets the value standard, the prospector has only fragile *pedis possessio* rights; after such discovery, however, the miner has a valid "unpatented" claim that qualifies as a true property right.

Over the years, three semantic tests of value have been prominent. The first, the prudent man test, was stated in Castle v. Womble (L.D. 1894), an administrative contest between a homesteader and a locator. The Acting Secretary ultimately ruled that belief and speculation as to whether a claim could be developed are irrelevant: "the requirement relating to discovery refers to present facts, and not to the probabilities of the future." *Castle* indicated that minerals have sufficient value to give rise to an unpatented claim in the following circumstances: "where minerals have been found and the evidence is of such a character that a person of ordinary prudence would be justified in the further expenditure of his labor and means, with a reasonable prospect of success, in developing a valuable mine, the requirements of the statute have been met." Even though it referred to a "valuable mine," the *Castle v. Womble* formulation, soon adopted by courts, was widely believed to rest as much on good faith as on quantitative measurement of the discovery.

The Interior Department in the 1960s constricted the formulation by requiring "profitability," and the Supreme Court upheld the Department's redefinition in United States v. Coleman (S.Ct.1968), a case involving common building stone. The profitability or marketability test requires the miner to show that the deposit can be extracted, removed, and, marketed at a profit. The Supreme Court in *Coleman* opined that the new test complemented the *Castle* "prudent man" test because it is "an admirable effort to identify with greater precision and objectivity the factors relevant to a determination that a mineral deposit is 'valuable.' " In other words, if the mining venture appeared to be an economic loser, no prudent person would undertake it. Further, the marketability test sheds light on the claimant's intention, because one who holds an uneconomic claim may well be doing so for nonmining purposes, contrary to the purposes of the GML.

Application of the *Coleman* profitability test is fraught with difficulties. If, as is the usual case, no actual mining operations have been undertaken, then the whole endeavor is an exercise in speculation. The test is applied as of the date of a patent application, the date that a contest is initiated against an unpatented claim, or the date the land is withdrawn from location. A change of circumstances between the time of location and application of the test thus can vitiate the claim. Bales v. Ruch (E.D. Cal.1981). Courts and agencies agree that the claimant must demonstrate that compliance with relevant environmental protection standards will not cause the operation to lose money, and that the test must be applied claim-by-claim. Beyond that, the inquiry is highly fact-specific, and the legal guidelines are fuzzy. It is clear, however, that the vast majority of mining locators have not made the requisite discovery, which is why most do not even apply for a patent.

A third test, occasionally used by some courts, is the comparative value test, which purports to determine whether mining or some other use is more valuable on national forest areas. The Interior Department long disclaimed any difference between tests depending on land classification. In re Pacific Coast Molybdenum Co. (IBLA 1983). But in United States v. United Mining Co. (IBLA 1998), the Interior Secretary ruled that a comparative test was appropriate for Building Stone Act cases and strongly suggested that comparative values should be considered for GML location claims. Yet another test is used for pre–1920 oil shale claims; the Court in Andrus v. Shell Oil Corp. (S.Ct.1980), ruled that present profitability is not relevant to such claims (which have never yet been profitable).

Section 26 of the GML gives the locator of a senior unpatented mining claim the right to follow the vein or lode beyond the boundaries of the claim under the claim of a junior locator, but not to enter upon the surface of a claim possessed by someone else. Extralateral rights also attach to patented claims, so one owner may be able to mine beneath the land of another without liability by following the vein. Because the GML requires that the end lines of a claim be parallel, non-parallel end lines will eliminate extralateral rights.

See PNRL §§ 25:15–25:20.

6. ASSESSMENT WORK

Until 1992, the GML required the locator of a valid unpatented mining claim to perform at least $100 worth of "assessment work" each year. 30 U.S.C.A. § 28. This requirement was intended to assure maximum development of the resource and prevent a locator from holding multiple claims but developing only a few. Exploration work did not count toward the assessment work requirement. Failure to do the assessment work did not make the claim void or voidable; rather, it opened the claimed area to relocation by another prospector. Later resumption of assessment work in the absence of relocation would reinstate the validity of the claim against the world. If the mineral or the tract had been withdrawn from location in the interim, however, the claim was invalid because the United States became an automatic rival locator. Hickel v. Oil Shale Corp. (S.Ct.1970). In Cliffs Synfuel Corp. v. Norton (10th Cir.2002), the court held that claimants' failure to comply with GML assessment requirements for 46 years resulted in default of their claims to the benefit of the United states, notwithstanding resumption of assessment work thereafter. The claimants' "token" assessment work after the lapse did not amount to the substantial compliance with the assessment work requirements necessary to avoid loss of the claims.

Congress in 1992 mostly substituted a $100 "holding fee" (later called a claim maintenance fee) for the assessment work requirement, with exceptions for small claimants. 30 U.S.C.A. §§ 28f–28k, as amended. Failure to pay "shall conclusively constitute a forfeiture" of the claim. Id. § 28g. The fee is adjustable for inflation. Constitutional challenges to the fee failed. E.g., Kunkes v. United States (Fed. Cir.1996).

See PNRL §§ 25:21–25:23.

7. PATENTING MINING CLAIMS

If a locator discovers a valuable mineral deposit, correctly locates the claim(s), and does $500 worth of assessment work, the locator upon application is entitled to receive, for nominal payment, fee simple title to the surface and minerals of the claim. 30 U.S.C.A. §§ 29, 37. In a few cases, such as wilderness areas, patents are limited to the mineral estate. 16 U.S.C.A. § 1133(d)(3).

In South Dakota v. Andrus (8th Cir.1980), the state sought to enjoin issuance of a patent pending preparation of an EIS under NEPA. The court held that patenting was a mere "ministerial" act once the applicant complied with all statutory requirements. Consequently, because the Secretary had no discretion in the matter, DoI had not taken any "action" and no environmental evaluation was necessary. Even if issuance of the patent constituted an action, it was not major because the granting of the patent did not enable the applicant to do anything; mining operations could not begin without further administrative permission. The holding is open to question because the title transfer will free the locator from federal administrative regulations. Other cases arguably are contrary, as the following section explains.

Patenting of location claims went off on a bumpy road in the 1990s. Courts ruled that patent applications vested no right to the patent until finally approved. Swanson v. Babbitt (9th Cir.1993). See also United States v. Shumway (9th Cir.1999) (issuance of first half mineral entry certificate provided "title of the locator" only if the patent applicant fully complied with the mining laws). The Secretary's actions and inaction aimed at delaying patent consideration and issuance also were upheld. Independence Mining Co. v. Babbitt (9th Cir.1997). Congress has placed a moratorium on patenting since

1993. See Mt. Emmons Mining Co. v. Babbitt (10th Cir.1997).

See PNRL § 25:24.

8.   INROADS ON THE RIGHT OF THE MINING CLAIMANT

For a century, American hardrock mining law encompassed only questions of property rights and relative private entitlements. Balancing the relative values of land uses or guarding against unfortunate environmental or other consequences simply were not relevant. The minerals industries insisted that mining was a statutorily preferred use that was exempt from any regulatory controls.

All this has changed dramatically in the last generation. Fewer lands are open for prospecting; claim validation is more difficult; non-mineral surface uses of mining claims are better policed; the federal land management agency regulations promulgated to ameliorate harmful mining consequences have been upheld; and the assumed absoluteness of property interests in public land mining claims has been severely eroded. Some of these changes are the products of statutory amendments, but many also result from evolving societal attitudes that no longer regard hardrock mining as the highest and best land use.

The GML recites that mineral locators have "the exclusive right of possession and enjoyment of all the surface included within the lines of their locations." 30 U.S.C.A. § 26. When it became common and then acceptable to locate before actual discovery, the location system was amenable to a variety of abuses, notably use of mineral claims for non-mining purposes. That was the situation in United States v. Rizzinelli (D. Idaho 1910): a locator used an unpatented claim as the site for his saloon— evidently a common practice of the day. The court found that non-mineral uses were enjoinable because the statute meant "exclusive right of possession *for prospecting and mining purposes*," not for any purposes. The court characterized the claimant's interest in the claim as "a distinct but qualified property right" in the claim. The United States holds "paramount" title before patenting and has the right to protect its interest against wasteful and unlawful use. Authorizing the locator to engage in uses other than those incident to mining operations would subvert the congressional purpose by turning the GML into a general land disposition statute.

Abuses of the location system continued. Perhaps the most notorious was the effort of Ralph Cameron, a United States Senator from Arizona, to locate claims on the main trail leading into the Grand Canyon and to charge tourists access fees. Many years of litigation ensued before the Supreme Court agreed that this was a wrongful appropriation. Cameron v. United States (S.Ct.1920). Congress in 1955 responded to similar problems of abuse by enacting the Surface Resources Act (SRA), 30 U.S.C.A. § 612. This law provides that post–1955 claims are subject to the rights of the United States to manage surface resources on claims and to the right of the government and "its permittees, and licensees" to use the surface for access so long as that use does not materially interfere with mining operations. In United States v. Richardson (9th Cir.1979), the court, under the authority of the 1955 SRA, entered an injunction against prospecting practices that unreasonably damaged surface resources and the environment.

In United States v. Curtis–Nevada Mines, Inc. (9th Cir.1980), the locator (apparently using his 203 mining claims as a private hunting preserve) tried to bar access to and across the located area to various recreationists. He argued that recreation was not a surface use amenable to government management and that the statutory reference to permittees and licensees meant only persons with an official written permit from the government. The Ninth Circuit rejected both contentions and enjoined Curtis from barring access. As to the first argument, the court determined that the purposes of the SRA included freer access to pursue recreation and thus that "other surface resources" include recreational uses. The other argument failed because, according to the court, all citizens long had had an implied license to use federal lands for recreation unless specifically restricted, so all citizens automatically are licensees for recreational purposes. The SRA was meant to open up the federal lands to more varied uses, but restricting access to the surface of unpatented claims to permit holders "would greatly restrict and inhibit the use of a major portion of the public domain." The claimant has remedies available if public use actively disturbs mining operations, including a suit to enjoin the public use responsible for the interference and application for a patent which, if granted, would result in the conveyance of a fee simple.

In the foregoing instances, the United States challenged the miner's practice without challenging the validity of the mining claim. The latter type of challenge historically has been rare, in part because a determination of invalidity did not prevent the locator from relocating the claim, ostensibly on a different mineral, immediately thereafter. Only when the mineral or the land had been withdrawn from location availability in the interim does claim invalidation actually eject the locator. In *Cameron*, supra, and in United States v. Zweifel (10th Cir. 1975), the locators of facially fraudulent claims argued that the government must first initiate a (lengthy and expensive) administrative contest before bringing ejectment actions because claimants are precluded from suing until after administrative proceedings have run their course. The courts held to the contrary because one purpose of the mining laws is to keep the lands open to qualified locators, and further proceedings would "needlessly prolong" the period of clouded title. In *Cameron*, the Supreme Court buttressed its holding by reference to the Interior Department's general supervisory power over the federal lands.

When the government commences an action to invalidate a claim, it has the initial burden of establishing prima facie invalidity; when that burden is met, the claimant has the ultimate burden of proving compliance with all statutory requirements. The latter also is true of patent application proceedings. Inferences will not suffice, United States v. E.K. Lehmann & Assocs. of Montana, Inc. (IBLA 2004). The GML does not specify a time limit for seeking judicial review of a decision by the Interior Department voiding a claim or denying a patent application. Modern authority requires that a judicial challenge to mining claim invalidation be brought within the general federal statute of limitations period of six years. Wind River Mining Corp. v. United States (9th Cir.1991), applying 28 U.S.C.A. §§ 2401(a).

All of the foregoing instances were ad hoc problems dealt with in a more or less ad hoc manner. From 1872 to 1974, the federal agencies had no general guidelines for ameliorating or controlling damage from prospecting and mining operations. The Forest Service in the latter year, acting under the aegis of the 1897 Organic Act, promulgated regulations "to minimize adverse environmental impacts" from mining. The agency carefully disclaimed any intention to manage mineral resources or deny locators any rights they possessed. Instead, the regulations required locators to give notice before commencing surface-disturbing activities and, if the operation's effects would be "significant," to file a plan of mining operations with the Forest Service for approval. The plan had to include surface environmental protective and reclamation measures, accompanied by a bond to cover the costs of damage or completing inadequate reclamation. The regulations do not specify the ultimate penalties for noncompliance, which are now governed by separate, generic enforcement regulations. The BLM followed with even weaker regulations several years later.

Miners long had argued that location claims were immune to any sort of administrative regulation. The courts unanimously have upheld the Forest Service mining regulations, however, implicitly in dozens of cases and explicitly in United States v. Weiss (9th Cir.1981). The *Weiss* court found ample authority to support the regulations in the Organic Act provision vesting in the Forest Service the power to "make provision for the protection against destruction by fire and depredations ... and ... make such rules and regulations as will insure the objects of such reservations, namely, to regulate their occupancy and use and to preserve the forests thereon from destruction." 16 U.S.C.A. § 551. All Forest Service users must comply with those regulations. Id. § 478. The long lack of regulation does not give miners any sort of prescriptive freedom from regulation; the government has the power to protect its fee title and its reversionary interest in the possessory interest of the locator. But the *Weiss* court also declared that Forest Service regulatory power is not open-ended:

> While prospecting, locating, and developing of mineral resources in the national forests may not be prohibited or so unreasonably circumscribed as to amount to a prohibition, the Secretary may

adopt reasonable rules and regulations which do not impermissibly encroach upon the right to the use and enjoyment of placer claims for mining purposes.

So far, the Forest Service mining regulations have met that test of reasonableness. Most cases involve failure to apply for mining plan approval, and courts have held that such approval is a precondition to undertaking operations. E.g., United States v. Goldfield Deep Mines Co. (9th Cir.1981). United States v. Doremus (9th Cir.1989), involved a challenge to plan provisions. Defendants obtained approval of their mining operations plans but the Forest Service imposed several conditions for environmental protection. They were convicted of violating those conditions. On appeal, they argued that their actions were authorized by the GML and therefore were not prohibited by the regulations. The court dispensed with this notion, citing the 1955 SRA, and held that the regulations applied. A provision of the regulations disclaiming any intention to preclude activities authorized by the GML merely recognized the reasonableness limitations on the agency's regulatory authority noted in *Weiss*. Defendants then argued that the regulations as applied were invalid because the prohibited activities were reasonably incident to their mining operation. The Ninth Circuit agreed with the lower court that the approved mining plan itself is the determination of what methods are reasonable in the circumstances. Thus, the proper course for defendants was to appeal the plan conditions initially, not to challenge their validity after violating them. Essentially, by failing to appeal, the defendants did not exhaust their administrative remedies and forfeited the reasonableness argument.

In Clouser v. Espy (9th Cir.1994), the court upheld a drastic provision of a mining operations plan dictated by the Forest Service. Among many other rulings, the Ninth Circuit panel determined that a prohibition against motorized access to the claim pending a finding of claim validity was reasonable and that motorized access was not essential to the mining of another claim. The key evidence was the fact that the Forest Service had hauled in the necessary equipment on horseback.

The BLM mining regulations rest on different statutory foundations, and they generally are less strict than their Forest Service counterparts. BLM regulatory authority over mining was unclear until 1976, when Congress in FLPMA specifically aimed the following broad directive at mining operations: "In managing the public lands the Secretary shall, by regulation or otherwise, take any action necessary to prevent unnecessary or undue degradation of the public lands." 43 U.S.C.A. § 1732(b).

The BLM regulations as amended in 2000 defined unnecessary and undue degradation to include more than just disturbance greater than the normal result of prudent operation: it also included violation of expanded environmental and operational performance standards. The new Administration in 2001 deleted many such standards and opined that "undue" was surplusage. The *Mineral Policy Center* opinion in 2003 rejected the Department of Interior interpretation, holding that "undue" was independent of "unnecessary" and that Congress intended to prevent unnecessary as well as undue degradation, but otherwise affirming BLM power to make case-by-case determinations. Mineral Policy Ctr. v. Norton (D.D.C.2003).

Like the Forest Service regulations, BLM mining regulations avoid addressing the question whether the agency can forbid mining altogether by refusing to approve an applicant's otherwise suitable plan of operations. 43 C.F.R. § 3809.1. A somewhat affirmative answer to that question emerges obliquely from the opinion in Sierra Club v. Penfold (9th Cir.1988). The BLM regulations divide mining operations into three groups: "plan" mines are those that will disturb more than five acres in a year; "notice" mines involve less than five acres disturbance per year; and "casual" mines cause only negligible disturbance. A casual miner need not even notify the agency; a notice miner must inform the BLM of operation commencement but need not obtain approval; and a plan miner must submit a mining plan of operations for BLM approval. The first issue in *Penfold* was whether the BLM's review of notice mines amounts to the kind of federal action that triggers NEPA evaluation requirements. The court held, on somewhat tenuous grounds, that BLM review of notice mine notices did not require any environmental evaluation because failure to decide was inaction, not the action necessary for

triggering NEPA. Plaintiff in *Penfold* also alleged
that the agency must prepare EAs or EISs on the
cumulative effects of placer plan mines on water
quality and recreational use in specific watersheds.
The appellate court agreed and affirmed an injunction against approval of plan mines operations in
those watersheds pending preparation of adequate
EISs. The lower court properly retained jurisdiction
to pass on the adequacy of the environmental assessment, rejecting the agency's claim that such
evaluation instead should occur in the administrative appeals process through approval of a particular plan of operations.

The implicit holding of *Penfold* is that, no matter
how the miners' rights are defined, their enjoyment
can be postponed until the agency has complied
with the law. In this case, the law required a form
of analysis prior to deciding whether or not to
approve submitted plans. Because NEPA only applies to discretionary decisions, the BLM then necessarily has discretion to deny as well as to approve.
Several cases in the Forest Service context apparently concur. In Havasupai Tribe v. United States
(D.Ariz.1990), the district court reasoned that, although the Forest Service "cannot categorically
deny an otherwise reasonable plan of operations," it
is authorized "to deny an unreasonable plan of
operations or a plan otherwise prohibited by law."
The court offered as an example of the latter situation the presence of an endangered species at a
mine site location. Mineral development of unpat-

ented claims on the federal lands is also subject to regulation under the federal pollution control laws.

See PNRL §§ 25:25–25:37.

B. MINERAL LEASING

Congress enacted the Mineral Leasing Act, 30 U.S.C.A. §§ 181–287, in 1920. That Act removes oil, gas, coal, shale oil, and four fertilizer minerals from the location system and provides for their disposition by lease from the government. Coal never was locatable. The Teapot Dome scandal, uncovered just a few years after MLA enactment, had the effect of forcing the Interior Department to be very cautious in leasing for decades. The leasing model was later used by Congress for disposition of minerals from acquired lands, for offshore oil and gas, and for geothermal resources. In recent years, with 1976 and 1987 amendments to the MLA, essentially separate leasing systems for the major fuel minerals have evolved. This section therefore treats the leasable minerals separately.

Still, all of the federal mineral leasing systems share some similarities, and those similar attributes distinguish leasing from hardrock mineral location. A prospective lessee cannot unilaterally establish a prior right to prospecting, development, or production; the government must first make the area available. Unlike location, leasing results in economic returns to the federal government in the form of rents, royalties, and bonuses. The United States retains far more power to control and condition leasehold development as contrasted with location claims. Diligent development requirements also tend to be far more stringent in the leasing context. The lease itself is a form of contract, the provisions of which can be used for environmental protection and other societal goals. In essence, leasing gives the land management agencies far more discretion than does location. But leases are contracts for which the United States may be liable for breach. Mobil Oil Exploration and Producing Southeast, Inc. v. United States (S.Ct.2000) (awarding restitution to oil companies for breach of outer continental shelf lease contracts).

Until recently, most leasing law distinguished between areas of known or likely mineral occurrence and areas of unknown potential. Leases in the former situation had to be "competitive," that is, subject to competitive bidding, while leases to the latter areas were noncompetitive, that is, granted automatically, and on very favorable terms, to the first qualified applicant. That distinction has now vanished with a few exceptions, such as for several minor minerals, and most leasing of consequence requires at least some form of competitive bidding.

The royalty rate, the lease duration, the diligence requirements, and the maximum permissible acreage under lease vary by mineral. Production in paying quantities usually keeps a lease alive indefinitely, but violation of the law or of lease conditions can terminate the lessee's interest. The Interior Department, generally through the BLM, oversees leasing on all systems, including the national forests. The BLM typically does not issue leases over the objection of the surface management agency, even where that agency does not have a statutory veto.

1. COAL (AND CHEMICAL MINERALS)

The United States owns vast coal reserves in the West. Western coal tends to be lower in sulfur content and in BTU output than eastern coal. By 1970, the federal government had leased more than 16 billion tons of coal to private entities, but production from the federal coal fields was declining; most of the coal leases were held for speculation. From the early 1970s until the present, legal developments and market conditions have conspired to thwart most new coal leasing.

From 1920 to the early 1970s, coal leases could be obtained easily by the "preference right" mechanism provided for in the 1920 MLA. The Federal Coal Leasing Act Amendments (FCLAA) of 1976 amended the MLA in several significant ways, requiring, among other things, intensive planning prior to competitive coal lease sales. Since 1976, most of the legal controversies arising out of federal coal leasing have involved the transition from the old to the new leasing system. Because tens of billions of tons of coal were leased before 1976, this section begins by describing preference right leasing and the problems it engendered. It then takes up the post–1976 coal leasing processes, as most recently amended by the Energy Policy Act of 2005. The final subsection summarizes pertinent parts of the Surface Mining Control and Reclamation Act (SMCRA) of 1977, the provisions of which are integral to the federal coal leasing regime.

Under the pre–1976 preference right leasing scheme, coal explorers applied for prospecting permits, which were routinely granted. Upon discovery of coal deposits, prospecting permittees could apply for noncompetitive preference right leases. The Interior Department issued these leases upon a determination that the applicant had located "commercial quantities" of coal, and the agency seldom exercised its right to impose environmental protective conditions in leases. In areas of known coal occurrence, leasing was ostensibly competitive but in fact competition was largely absent. Preference right leases were highly advantageous for lessees in their duration, royalty, bonus, and due diligence requirements.

Because widespread speculation was subverting the aims of the coal leasing statute, the Interior Department in 1971 informally imposed a moratorium on coal leases and prospecting permits. By 1973, when the Interior Department formalized the moratorium, 183 applications for preference right leases to 12 billion tons of coal were pending, as were a number of applications for prospecting permits. The validity of the original moratorium was upheld in Krueger v. Morton (D.C.Cir.1976). During the decade-long moratorium, the Department changed its definition of "commercial quantities" from roughly, "a lot of coal," to, roughly, a valuable, paying, profitable deposit of coal after all costs, including costs of environmental compliance, are taken into account. The new definition resembled the *Coleman* profitability test applicable to hardrock mining under the GML.

While the 1971–81 moratorium was in effect, the Department studied plans for development of federal coal resources, located primarily in the Northern Great Plains, and began promulgation of an EIS on its nationwide coal leasing program. Environmentalists claimed that the BLM was required to prepare an EIS on coal development in the four-state region studied by the agency in addition to the national and local EISs. The Supreme Court ultimately rejected that challenge, holding that EISs were required only when the agency makes a formal "proposal," which had not occurred in this instance. Kleppe v. Sierra Club (S.Ct.1976). See section 4E. The following year, however, a lower court determined that the nationwide coal leasing EIS was deficient and enjoined all further leasing and developmental activities, thus extending the moratorium into the Reagan Administration. NRDC v. Hughes (D.D.C.1977). In particular, the court took issue with the Department's failure to consider the "no action" alternative. In 1993, the same court blocked the Department's attempt to resume leasing because of noncompliance with an Executive Order requiring all federal agencies to minimize destruction of wetlands. NWF v. Babbitt (D.D.C. 1993).

The decade of the moratorium was dominated by questions of private entitlement generated by the transition from preference right to competitive leasing. Those questions were complicated by the Interior Department's redefinition of commercial quantities, the new societal impulse toward better environmental quality, and the adoption of SMCRA in 1977. The first question was whether a person who had submitted an application for a prospecting permit (now abolished, subject to "valid existing rights") had acquired any species of protectable right or interest which survived the transition. The courts ruled no. E.g., American Nuclear Corp. v. Andrus (D.Wyo.1977). The courts next considered whether the holder of a prospecting permit who had submitted an application for a preference right lease before the moratorium was entitled to lease issuance even though noncompetitive leasing also was outlawed under the 1976 FCLAA. The court in NRDC v. Berklund (D.C.Cir.1979), answered this question: yes, sort of. The environmentalist plaintiffs sued for a declaration that environmental costs had to be factored into the commercial quantities definition, that NEPA required that issuance of any major leases be accompanied by an EIS, and that the Department had the discretion to deny preference right lease applications even if the applicant had made the requisite discovery. The Department agreed to the first two demands, and the court rejected the third. It held that the statute requires issuance of a preference right lease when the permittee has established the presence of commercial quantities of coal. Still, said the court, the Interior Department retains a great deal of discretion over the pre–1976 coal leasing process: the new commercial quantities definition reflected in the agency's regulations "accommodates the cost of protecting the environment, as do lease terms and mining plans under the Department's supervision." The required NEPA analysis also will shape the government's approval or disapproval of mining plans. The lessee thus has a definite property right to lease issuance upon compliance with the statute, but that interest is subject to intensive regulation.

Other coal transition cases raised closer questions. In the first *Utah Int'l* case, Utah Int'l, Inc. v. Andrus (D. Utah 1979), the permittee submitted an application for a preference right lease, and the U.S. Geological Survey determined (under the old test) that commercial quantities were present when the moratorium was imposed. The court rejected plaintiff's claim to lease entitlement under the old test because the BLM had never formally adopted the Survey's findings or decided to grant the lease. Accordingly, the agency could reexamine the commercial quantities question using the new, stricter test. In the second case of the same name, Utah Int'l, Inc. v. Andrus (D.Colo.1980), the facts were roughly the same except that the IBLA had made a final determination favorable to the applicant. Thus, said the Colorado District Court, the *NRDC v. Berklund* test had been met and the permittee was entitled to the lease without reassessment under the post–1976 commercial quantities test. The intermediate situation of prospecting permittees seeking permit extensions was the issue in Peterson v. Department of the Interior (D. Utah 1981). The BLM held the applications in abeyance for seven years after submission before denying them. The court ruled that the permittees lacked substantive rights because administrative delay cannot create a valid existing right. But the permittees had the procedural right to have their applications considered by the BLM under the law in effect when submitted, rather than under the revised commercial quantities test.

Due to the passage of time, the problem of the appropriate treatment of applications pending as of the date of the FCLAA's elimination of the preference right leasing system essentially is ended. The related problem of converting old coal leases to post–1976 standards, however, could continue for some time. The pre-FCLAA leases were of indeterminate duration, subject only to renegotiation at 20–year intervals, and had highly favorable (i.e., very low) royalty rates and no diligence requirements. The 1976 FCLAA imposed diligence requirements (minimum amounts to be mined at specified intervals), increased royalty rates, and provided for renegotiation of terms at ten-year intervals. 30 U.S.C.A. § 207(a). The holders of pre-FCLAA leases argued that lease readjustment to conform to the new statute would improperly interfere with vested rights to continuation of existing lease terms, but attempts by the Department to transpose the new requirements onto the old lessees have met mostly with success in a series of cases.

The first such case, Rosebud Coal Sales Co. v. Andrus (10th Cir.1982), established that the FCLAA provided the Interior Department with an option to renegotiate upon expiration of the original lease term; if the Secretary neglected to exercise that option in a timely manner, he waived his right to so do. See also Valley Camp of Utah, Inc. v. Babbitt (10th Cir.1994) (invalidating royalty readjustment for sublessee for failure to provide timely notice). In later cases, however, the courts ruled that notice of renegotiation given before the twenty-year anniversary date suffices to exercise the option even if the renegotiated terms are not completed until after that date. Then, in Trapper Mining, Inc. v. Lujan (10th Cir.1991), the court determined that the FCLAA ten-year readjustment opportunity automatically applied to the renegotiation of leases the twenty-year anniversary of which occurred after 1976. That is, when the BLM failed to renegotiate Trapper's 1958 and 1959 leases in 1978 and 1979, thereby automatically extending the leases until 1988 and 1989 pursuant to section 207(a), the Department was next entitled to readjust at the end of that ten-year extension, instead of in 1998 and 1999.

Renegotiation may have severe substantive effects on coal lessees whose leases predate 1976. In FMC Wyoming Corp. v. Hodel (10th Cir.1987), the court affirmed the BLM determination that the Secretary under the FCLAA was required to impose a royalty rate adjustment; for surface-mined coal the new minimum rate of 12 ½ percent was many multiples of the old rate. The lessee argued unsuccessfully that the statute requires the Department to examine individual circumstances to determine a reasonable rate, even if that rate was less than 12½ percent. In Coastal States Energy Co. v. Hodel (10th Cir.1987), however, the court found that underground coal was entitled to different royalty treatment under the 1976 amendments. The Secretary had erred by imposing an eight percent across-the-board royalty when Congress made that number a ceiling, subject to case-by-case exemptions. Other new regulatory and financial conditions also may properly be imposed on lessees during renegotiation. Western Energy Co. v. United States Dep't of the Interior (9th Cir.1991); Western Fuels–Utah, Inc. v. Lujan (D.C. Cir.1990). In both cases, the courts rejected the claim that readjustment constituted a compensable taking.

See PNRL §§ 22:4–22:17.

Issuance of new coal leases since 1976 has been rare due to a variety of factors. Procedural requirements for coal leasing under the FCLAA, notably imposition of detailed land use planning processes, have become far stricter. Substantive requirements under a variety of statutes, notably the 1977 SMCRA, also are now far more rigorous. In addition, market conditions (i.e., the low prices of oil and gas) until recently have mostly been unfavorable. The few major coal lease sales initiated by Secretary Watt in the 1980s usually came to grief.

Consequently, the main federal coal leasing activities for a generation have been processing old lease applications and conducting relatively small maintenance or bypass lease sales. The renewed emphasis on increased domestic energy production in the Bush/Norton Administration has not appreciably changed that situation.

The Surface Mining Control and Reclamation Act of 1977 (SMCRA), 30 U.S.C.A. §§ 1201–1328, is directed primarily at coal strip-mining on both public and private lands. SMCRA requires the Interior Secretary to apply to surface mining on the federal lands all of the statute's general regulatory standards, such as reclamation (restoration to preexisting condition) for mined lands, and consider any unique characteristics of particular federal lands. No mining may occur on federal lands without a permit, which must require compliance with a resource recovery and protection plan. In Hodel v. Virginia Surface Mining and Reclamation Ass'n, Inc. (S.Ct.1981), and a companion case, the Supreme Court ruled that the Act neither usurped state authority unduly nor effected a taking of property on its face. See also Stearns Co., Ltd. v. United States (Fed. Cir.2005) (holding that application of SMCRA to mineral property was not a physical taking and that regulatory taking claim was not ripe for review because company had failed to seek a compatibility determination from the Secretary).

SMCRA requires the Interior Secretary to determine whether any federal lands are unsuitable for surface mining and to withdraw such areas or im-

pose appropriate conditions on leasing. 30 U.S.C.A.
§ 1272(b). Under BLM regulations, this review is
conducted principally through the land use planning process by each surface management agency.
Subject to valid existing rights, SMCRA outlaws
mining in parks, refuges, wilderness areas, and wild
river segments. Mining may not proceed in the
national forests unless the Secretary finds that it
would not be incompatible with significant recreational, timber, economic, or other values. Id.
§ 1272(e). In NWF v. Hodel (D.C. Cir.1988), the
court held that the statute bars the agency from
using economic ability to reclaim as the sole criterion for compatibility. The BLM's determination not
to include a "wetlands unsuitability criterion" as a
coal planning screen was rejected as arbitrary in
NWF v. Babbitt (D.D.C. 1993). The court in Utah,
Int'l, Inc. v. Department of the Interior (D. Utah
1982), ruled that federal lessees had an insufficient
property interest to entitle them to all due process
trappings in their challenge to an unsuitability determination. The court also held that the determination did not take the property of the plaintiff,
which had not received permission to mine before
the determination. The Department has had diffi-
culty defining valid existing rights. See, e.g., In re
Permanent Surface Mining Regulation Litigation
(D.D.C.1985); section 6C(2). In 1999, a federal district court held that mountaintop removal mining,
which involves removal of entire coal seams by
removing substantially all of the overburden and
creating a level plateau or gently rolling contour,

violates SMCRA because of its adverse effects on water flow, stream quality, fish migration, and related environmental values. The Third Circuit reversed and vacated that decision, however, on the ground that the plaintiffs' citizen suit under SMCRA to enjoin the West Virginia environmental agency from issuing further SMCRA permits for mountaintop mining was barred by the Eleventh Amendment. Bragg v. West Virginia Coal Ass'n (4th Cir.2001).

See PNRL §§ 22:33–22:47.

Coal leasing since 1976 also has been stymied by environmental requirements in other laws, including NEPA, the Clean Water Act, the ESA, and the FCLAA. The Fort Union coal lease sale was abandoned after a congressional committee objected. See NWF v. Watt (D.D.C.1983). The only major sale to be completed (and some aspects of it remained in litigation a decade later) was the Powder River Basin Sale in 1982. Part of the sale was enjoined for NEPA noncompliance and later abandoned. Northern Cheyenne Tribe v. Hodel (9th Cir.1988). Other plaintiffs challenged the sale on the grounds that the planning preceding the sale was flawed and that the Department failed to obtain fair market value as section 201(a)(1) of the FCLAA demands. The plaintiffs did not appeal the lower court's finding that the land use planning was adequate. An independent Commission had determined that the last-minute finagling by the Department was a causal factor in the sale netting the government up to $100 million less than fair market value; this evidence was disallowed as after the fact. Instead, the Ninth Circuit affirmed the lower court's determination that flaws in the bidding system were irrelevant so long as the high bid represented FMV (defined as a fair return rather than as maximization of revenues), which it did in this instance (compared with the Department's presale FMV estimates). NWF v. Burford (9th Cir.1989).

See PNRL § 22:20.

2.   OIL AND GAS

Before 1987, most federal oil and gas leasing was noncompetitive; the government issued leases automatically to the first qualified applicant in areas of unknown hydrocarbon occurrence. When an area was newly opened to leasing, either by revocation of a withdrawal or by expiration of an existing lease, the first qualified applicant was the winner of a lottery drawing of all applications filed within a designated period. Only in areas officially described as a "known geological structure" (KGS) were the leases put out to competitive bidding.

The pre–1987 federal oil and gas leasing system had more than its share of problems. The KGS determinations were made by use of unrealistic criteria and were essentially invalidated in Arkla Exploration Co. v. Texas Oil & Gas Corp. (8th Cir.1984), where the court held that KGS determinations must take into account actual competitive interest in the tract. The lottery system was riddled with fraudulent practices and hypertechnical rules.

Returns to the government were low. These problems, among others, convinced Congress in 1987 to revise the oil and gas leasing process fairly thoroughly.

The Federal Onshore Oil and Gas Leasing Reform Act (FOOGLRA), codified mostly at 30 U.S.C.A. §§ 188, 195, 226, requires competitive bidding for all leases as an initial matter, but a degree of noncompetitive leasing is allowed if the leases go unsold at auction. The Act abolished the KGS/non-KGS distinction, and imposed a minimum acceptable bid of $2 per acre. All leases now have ten-year primary terms within which the lessee must obtain production or the lease will expire. Whether to lease at all remains a matter within secretarial discretion. Congress also gave the Forest Service a statutory veto power over leasing in national forests and required the BLM and the Forest Service to regulate surface-disturbing activities.

The Energy Policy Act of 2005 provides that all royalty accruing to the United States under any lease for oil and gas development shall, on demand of the Secretary of the Interior, be paid in-kind. The Secretary may receive oil or gas royalties in-kind only if he or she determines that doing so provides benefits to the United States that are greater than or equal to those that are likely to have been received had royalties been taken in-value. Transportation and processing reimbursements paid to, or deductions claimed by, the lessee are subject to review and audit. The lessee must place royalty production in marketable condition at no cost to the United States. 42 U.S.C.A. § 5902.

Few issues arising under the FOOGLRA have been litigated. Several basic questions that predate 1987 but were not addressed by Congress are still unresolved. The first is the meaning of 30 U.S.C.A. § 209, which instructs the Secretary to give a lessee an extension equal to the period of suspension if the Secretary "in the interest of conservation shall direct ... the suspension of operations and production." One of the few cases on point, Copper Valley Machine Works, Inc. v. Andrus (D.C.Cir.1981), came to a somewhat dubious conclusion.

The Department granted the plaintiff an extension of the primary term of its lease in Alaska but conditioned the extension by disallowing operations during the half of the year when they would cause damage to permafrost. The plaintiff belatedly claimed that it was entitled to yet another extension under the statute because the Secretary effectively suspended its operations for half of the extension period. The D.C. Circuit thought that "conservation" carried its broad modern meaning, and therefore encompassed attempts to avoid environmental harm, even though the 1932 Congress almost certainly used the word in the far narrower oil and gas sense of avoiding economic and physical waste. The court then determined that the Secretary had suspended plaintiff's operations, despite the government's claim that only unanticipated stoppages qualify as suspensions. In so holding, the court ignored the difference between a previously imposed condition and an after-discovered problem necessitating suspension, it ignored the "operations *and* production" language (the plaintiff never obtained production), and it in effect ruled that lease terms in Alaska were automatically doubled if they contained the winter-only condition. Getty Oil v. Clark (D.Wyo.1985), arguably is contrary, holding that no suspension occurs if the event triggering suspension is clearly set forth as a lease condition. A subsequent case arising under the Federal Coal Leasing Act Amendments distinguished *Copper Valley*. Hoyl v. Babbitt (10th Cir.1997).

See PNRL §§ 23:10, 22:28.

The second major unresolved problem is the requisite timing and depth of environmental evaluation of lessee operations. The problem is more critical in the oil and gas context than in other areas because of the unknowns: before actually drilling, no one knows if any oil or gas underlay the leased area, or where, or in what quantities; historically, it is commonly said, only one in ten lessees actually drills, and only one in ten wildcat wells is a producer. Those uncertainties mean that early environmental assessment would necessarily be largely speculative.

Oil and gas leasing on the federal lands is a phased process. The Department chooses the lands to lease, premised on rudimentary planning, and then holds a lease sale auction. The lessees are then required to submit an application for permit to drill (APD) before commencing actual drilling operations. Further administrative permission for further development of a field also is required. The land management agencies favored deferral of environmental assessment until the later stages of the process, when uncertainties were reduced, while environmentalists argued that NEPA evaluation should begin upon lease issuance because the agencies lack sufficient control over lessee activities thereafter to avoid environmental damage.

The leading case to reconcile these conflicting strands is Sierra Club v. Peterson (D.C. Cir.1983). The Department decided to issue leases in an area eligible for wilderness consideration. Some of the leases, located in "highly environmentally sensitive" areas, had "no surface occupancy" (NSO) stipulations, meaning that lessees by contract could take no further steps without further governmental permission. The other leases did not contain such a clause. On appeal, the main question was whether the Department could sell leases without NSO stipulations if it had not first prepared an EIS on the lease sale. The D.C. Circuit determined that without an NSO stipulation, the lease sale itself was a commitment of resources (a go, no-go point) that had to be preceded by an EIS. Thus, unless it undertook a difficult environmental analysis at the lease sale stage, the Department could give a lessee only the exclusive procedural right to seek clearance for further operations, and that clearance would require an EIS if it amounted to major action. Two cases in the Ninth Circuit concurred with *Peterson* right down the line; the court in Bob Marshall Alliance v. Hodel (9th Cir.1988), went even further:

it emphasized that the lessee could acquire no property rights under the NSO stipulation, and it ruled that the agency must consider the no-leasing alternative even when issuing NSO leases because leasing "opens the door to potentially harmful post-leasing activity."

A quasi-contrary view, embraced by the BLM, was embodied in Park County Resource Council, Inc. v. United States Dep't of Agric. (10th Cir.1987). That court apparently held that no EIS is necessary at the lease sale stage because development is problematic and environmental concerns can be addressed at the APD stage. The dissimilarities in the cases, however, render the conflicts in legal holdings more apparent than real. In *Park County*, the BLM and the Forest Service jointly prepared an EIS at the APD stage, after which the lessee drilled a dry hole. The case was complicated by a variety of procedural errors below, and the court seemed to assume that it was dealing with an NSO-type situation. Were the same case as *Peterson* or *Bob Marshall* to arise in the Tenth Circuit, it is submitted that that court more than likely would follow the 9th and D.C. Circuit precedent (of which it apparently was ignorant).

The Forest Service and the BLM have tried to obviate what they see as the problem of conditioning the property rights of lessees on subsequent administrative approval by downplaying NSO stipulations and emphasizing pre-lease planning to select appropriate areas and terms for oil and gas leasing. Their success so far is problematic. In Wyoming

Outdoor Council v. United States Forest Serv. (D.C. Cir.1999), the court deferred to the Forest Service's view that its regulations permit it to issue findings concerning whether leasing has been adequately addressed in a NEPA document and that conditions of surface occupancy have been included as stipulations in leases after the BLM identifies specific parcels, as long as the findings are made before leases are actually issued.

The Energy Policy Act of 2005 reduced the rigor of NEPA procedures as applied to exploration or development of oil and gas on the federal lands. The Act provides that certain actions by the Secretaries of Interior and Agriculture in managing the federal lands will be subject to a rebuttable presumption that the use of a categorical exclusion under NEPA would apply if the activity is conducted pursuant to the Mineral Leasing Act for the purpose of exploration or development of oil or gas. The activities that invoke this rebuttable presumption include, among others, certain individual surface disturbances of less than five acres; drilling an oil or gas well within a developed field for which an approved land use plan or any environmental document prepared pursuant to NEPA analyzed such drilling as a reasonably foreseeable activity; and placement of certain pipelines within an approved right-of-way corridor. 42 U.S.C.A. § 15942(a). The Energy Policy Act of 2005 also directed the Secretaries, as a means of ensuring timely action on oil and gas leases and applications for permits to drill on land otherwise available for leasing, to ensure "expeditious compliance" with § 102(2)(C) of NEPA "and any other applicable environmental and cultural resources laws." The Act also requires the Interior Secretary to develop and implement best management practices to improve the administration of the onshore oil and gas leasing program under the Mineral Leasing Act and ensure timely action on oil and gas leases and APDs on land otherwise available for leasing. Pub. L. No. 109–58, § 362, 119 Stat. 594, 721 (2005).

Another provision of the Energy Policy Act of 2005 directed the Secretary of Agriculture to establish a program to remediate, reclaim, and close orphaned, abandoned, or idled oil and gas wells located on federal lands administered by the federal land management agencies. The program must provide for the recovery of the costs of remediation, reclamation, or closure from persons currently providing a bond or other financial assurance required under state or federal law for an oil or gas well that is orphaned, abandoned, or idled or their sureties or guarantors. Pub. L. No. 109–58, § 349(a), 119 Stat. 594, 709.

When an oil and gas lease sale is voided because of agency failures to follow proper procedures, the courts apparently are split on whether the winning bidders are entitled to relief. In Northern Cheyenne Tribe v. Lujan (D. Mont.1991), the court ruled that the leases were void and the lessees entitled to full reimbursement of their rental and bonus payments. In Bob Marshall Alliance v. Lujan (D. Mont.1992), the court agreed that "the leases must be set aside rather than merely suspended," but denied the lessee's claim for refund of rentals because the lessee "knowingly assumed the business risk of an injunction."

For a decade, the hottest area in federal oil and gas leasing has been coalbed methane (CBM). The bane of coal miners, CBM is a promising source of relatively clean energy, and in its billions of tons of coal, the United States also has many billions of cubic feet of natural gas. The relatively low level of disputes over CBM rights and regulation to date probably will intensify as attention is focused on water resources and environmental quality. See, e.g., Wyoming Outdoor Council v. U.S. Army Corps of Eng'rs (D. Wyo.2005) (remanding the Corps' issuance of a general permit under § 404 of the Clean Water Act for the discharge of dredged or fill material associated with the development of CBM).

Oil shale poses a particular problem. Location claims were made before oil shale became leasable only in 1920. In Andrus v. Shell Oil Corp. (S.Ct. 1980), the Supreme Court ruled that ancient oil shale location claims were not subject to the *Coleman* marketability test. Still, a 46–year lapse in assessment work invalidated pre–1920 shale oil location claims in Cliffs Synfuel Corp. v. Norton (10th Cir.2002).

In the Oil Shale, Tar Sands, and Other Strategic Unconventional Fuels Act of 2005, 42 U.S.C.A. § 15927, Congress declared that it is the policy of the United States that domestic oil shale, tar sands, and other unconventional fuels are "strategically important domestic resources that should be developed to reduce the growing dependence of the United States on politically and economically unstable sources of foreign oil imports." The Act requires the Interior Secretary to complete a programmatic EIS under NEPA for a commercial leasing program for these resources on federal lands, with an emphasis on Colorado, Utah, and Wyoming. If the Secretary finds that sufficient support and interest exist, he or she may conduct a lease sale under the commercial leasing program regulations. The Secretary must issue regulations designating work requirements and milestones to ensure diligent development. The Act authorizes the Secretary to conduct land exchanges to facilitate the recovery of oil shale and tar sands.

See PNRL §§ 23:11–23:27, 24:3–24:7

3. GEOTHERMAL ENERGY

Federal leasing of geothermal resources is a unique area of the law because the resource itself is unique. Geothermal energy is produced by the earth's inner heat, conveyed to the surface through some mineral convection system, usually hot water. The heat, if in commercial quantities, can be used to generate electricity or for forms of direct heating. Geothermal systems constitute "other minerals" for purposes of federal mineral reservations. United States v. Union Oil (9th Cir.1997). See also Rosette, Inc. v. United States (10th Cir.2002).

Congress in 1970 classified geothermal as sui
generis by creating a separate leasing system for it.
Geothermal Steam Act (GSA), 30 U.S.C.A. §§ 1001–
1026. The Act excludes certain areas (parks, recreation areas, and refuges, but not wilderness areas)
from leasing, and it regulates geothermal development that could affect Yellowstone's fragile plumb-
ing. Id. § 1026 note. As most recently amended by
the Energy Policy Act of 2005, the GSA generally
requires that leases be awarded to the highest qualified responsible bidder. Lands subject to a mining
claim for which a plan of operations has been approved by a federal land management agency, however, may be available for noncompetitive leasing to
the mining claim holder. Id. § 1003(b). In addition,
the amended GSA requires the Interior Secretary to
make available for a period of two years for noncompetitive leasing any tract for which a competitive lease is held, but for which the Secretary does
not receive any bids in a competitive lease sale. Id.
§ 1003(c). All future forest plans and BLM resource
management plans for areas with high geothermal
resource potential must consider geothermal leasing
and development. Id. § 1003(d)(1).

A geothermal lease may not cover more than the
acreage that the Secretary determines to be reasonably necessary for the proposed use, and in no
event may it cover more than 5,120 acres (except in
cases involving irregular subdivisions). Id.
§ 1003(g). The primary term of a geothermal lease
is ten years, although the Secretary must extend
that term for five years if the lessee has satisfied

applicable work commitment requirements and made required annual payments. The GSA requires that the Secretary prescribe minimum work requirements for geothermal leases and confirm the existence of producible geothermal resources. In lieu of the minimum work requirements, lessees may make minimum annual payments for a limited period that will not impair diligent development. Minimum work requirements do not apply after the date on which the geothermal resource is utilized under a lease in commercial quantities. Id. § 1005. Lessees may enter unit agreements for the purpose of conserving geothermal resources if the Secretary certifies that such an agreement is necessary or in the public interest. Id. § 1017. All geothermal leases must provide for a royalty on electricity produced using geothermal resources, other than direct use of geothermal resources, and on any byproduct that qualifies as a mineral under the MLA that is derived from production under the lease. Lessees also must pay annual rentals; nonpayment will result in lease termination. Id. § 1004.

See PNRL §§ 24:16–24:28.

C. SPLIT ESTATES: PROBLEMS WHERE MINERAL INTERESTS ARE SEPARATED FROM SURFACE INTERESTS

The foregoing sections of this chapter have assumed that the United States owns the surface and mineral estates of the land in fee simple. That is not always the case. The United States retained mineral estates when granting rights-of-way to railroads, lands to stock-raising homesteaders, and other lands to other interests. At the same time, the United States has acquired the surface estate to some lands, leaving the mineral estate in private or state ownership. As in the private sector, such divided ownership invariably causes disputes over the scope of each party's property rights.

1.   FEDERAL MINERALS UNDER PRIVATE SURFACE

When the United States retained mineral rights, it often did so in broad and unilluminating language. The Stock–Raising Homestead Act of 1916, 43 U.S.C.A. § 299 (repealed 1976), for instance, reserves "all the coal and other minerals." Courts have interpreted this and similar federal reservations liberally.

In United States v. Union Oil Co. (9th Cir.1977), the question was whether "coal and other minerals" included geothermal resources—which, likely, were unknown to legislators in 1916. The court did not ask whether those legislators specifically intended to include geothermal resources within the reservation. Instead, "the substantial question is whether it would further Congress's purposes to interpret the words as carrying this meaning." The court determined that the language was capable of including geothermal steam because all elements of geothermal convection are themselves mineral.

Turning to the basic purposes underlying the SBRHA, the court opined that Congress intended both to provide homesteaders with sufficient land to run ranching operations and to provide separately for mineral disposition pursuant to other laws. "[T]he mineral reservation is to be read broadly in light of the agricultural purpose of the grant itself, and in light of Congress's equally clear purpose to retain subsurface resources, particularly sources of energy, for separate disposition and development in the public interest." See also Rosette v. United States (10th Cir.2002). Cf. Aulston v. United States (10th Cir.1990) (another statute's reservation to the United States of "oil and gas" includes carbon dioxide); Hughes v. MWCA, Inc. (10th Cir.2001) (scoria reserved by S–RHA). The court in Occidental Geothermal, Inc. v. Simmons (N.D.Cal.1982), took the *Union Oil* holding a long step further. It determined that a federal geothermal lessee was entitled to erect a generating plant on the privately owned surface estate. Removal and utilization of the resource are inextricably linked in that long-range transportation of steam results in loss of heat and pressure.

The Supreme Court has addressed the scope of federal mineral reservations several times. The leading case is Watt v. Western Nuclear, Inc. (S.Ct. 1983), but the Court's 5–4 holding is less than crystal clear. Plaintiff surface owner claimed the right to extract sand and gravel, but the BLM ruled that plaintiff trespassed because the United States owned those common minerals under a S–RHA reservation. The majority acknowledged that the word "mineral" was used in many different senses and could not be meant literally. Further, neither the legislative history nor contemporary interpretation shed much light. The Court therefore adapted the broad purpose approach of *Union Oil* and devised this inelegant test as best-suited to achieving the congressional goal of encouraging concurrent development of both surface and subsurface resources: "we interpret the mineral reservation in the Act to include substances that are mineral in character (i.e., that are inorganic), that can be removed from the soil, that can be used for commercial purposes, and that there is no reason to suppose were intended to be included in the surface estate." Gravel qualified because it "can be taken from the soil and used for commercial purposes." The dissent contended that the new formulation "compounds, rather than clarifies, the ambiguity inherent in the term 'minerals.' " In any event, the majority's liberal rendering of the S–RHA reservation includes nearly all valuable mineral substances. The Court distinguished *Western Nuclear* in BedRoc Ltd., LLC v. United States (S.Ct.2004), holding that sand and gravel are not "valuable minerals" reserved to the United States under the Pittman Underground Water Act of 1919. In Amoco Prod. Co. v. Southern Ute Indian Tribe (S.Ct.1999), the Court held that reservations of coal to the government in the Coal Lands Acts of 1909 and 1910 upon issuance of land patents did not include coalbed methane contained in coal.

At common law, mineral estates are "dominant" over surface estates in that the mineral owner has the right to go upon the surface for all purposes reasonably related to mineral exploration and development. Ordinarily, the surface owner is compensated only when any damage to the surface occurred through negligent or unnecessary means. A prominent exception to that rule is the provision in SMCRA that surface owner consent is required before the federal government can issue leases to the subsurface coal estate if the coal is to be stripmined. 30 U.S.C.A. § 1304(c).

2. PRIVATE MINERALS UNDER FEDERAL SURFACE

The situation in which the United States owns the surface over a private mineral estate is encountered less often, but it does occur when the government has reacquired a less than fee interest, as it often did in creating the eastern national forests under the Weeks Act of 1911. When the estates are split in this fashion, a common question is the extent to which the mineral owner can develop at the expense of the values for which the United States acquired the surface.

In Downstate Stone Co. v. United States (7th Cir.1983), the court turned that inquiry into a title question (similar to the questions in *Union Oil* and *Western Nuclear*, supra) and decided in favor of the government. Plaintiff mineral owners wanted to stripmine limestone in a national forest. Because the stripmining would destroy the surface and thus the values for which the government had purchased the surface, the court found that the private grantor had not reserved the limestone. It better suited the legislative purposes of the Weeks Act to so hold. As odd and contrary as this holding may sound, it has ample precedent in private sector split estate law. See, e.g., the discussion in Moser v. United States Steel Corp. (Tex.1984).

Even if the mineral is within the reserved mineral estate, the federal agency has the power to prohibit development, but such a prohibition may amount to a Fifth Amendment taking. The latter inquiry depends on whether the mineral owner has established a valid existing right. See, e.g., 30 U.S.C.A. § 1272(e) (provision of SMCRA prohibiting surface mining on certain federal lands, "subject to valid existing rights"); 30 C.F.R. § 761.5. The cases to date are not definitive. See Stearns Co. Ltd. v. United States (Fed. Cir.2005) (holding that SMCRA regulation of private mineral estate did not amount to a physical taking and that regulatory taking claim was not ripe); Belville Min. Co. v. United States (6th Cir.1993) (upholding administrative determinations that valid existing rights existed in some tracts but not others but passing on the constitutional question); Ramex Mining Corp. v. Watt (6th Cir.1985) (taking claim not ripe for review); Whitney Benefits, Inc. v. United States (Fed. Cir.1991) (taking of private property by statute occurred).

Duncan Energy Co. v. United States Forest Service (8th Cir.1995), arose when the land management agency delayed approving a plan of surface operations to the lessee of the severed mineral owner who was under severe time constraints. The court ruled that federal law preempted the state law that allowed access to the dominant mineral estate owner and that the Forest Service had ample authority to regulate surface use by the mineral lessee. The court cautioned, however, that the agency cannot prohibit mineral development and that its regulation must be "reasonable, and thus, expeditious."

CHAPTER SEVEN

THE TIMBER RESOURCE

The shape of the National Forest System emerged gradually over a half century. In 1891, Congress authorized the President to reserve forested areas from settlement to prevent the waste of timber resources attributable to homesteading and uncontrolled exploitation. Six years later, the Organic Act dictated that the national forests insure favorable water flow conditions and furnish a continuous supply of timber. When jurisdiction over the national forests was transferred from the Interior Department to the Agriculture Department in 1905, the United States Forest Service was established. The 1914 Weeks Act, which authorized federal purchase of cutover forested areas in the East, and the creation of national grasslands on the High Plains during the 1930s, added to the lands contained within the National Forest System.

For most of its history, the Forest Service exercised nearly unfettered discretion over the bulk of the nation's public timber lands. The Supreme Court upheld the agency's authority to license grazing in Light v. United States (S.Ct.1911), and to reduce deer herds in Hunt v. United States (S.Ct. 1928), discussed in Chapter 9 below. Aside from disputes between the Forest Service and its timber contractors, which the government usually won, the Forest Service avoided litigation over management of the national forests for the next forty years. After World War II, however, when reduced private stocks caused increased demand for timber on the federal lands, timber production assumed a higher priority for Forest Service personnel. Objections to aspects of even-aged management, especially clear-cutting, and the designation of wilderness areas within the forests sparked several notable disputes in the late 1960s and 1970s. A series of constraints on Forest Service timber-cutting discretion recommended by a Senate subcommittee in 1972 became law in the 1976 National Forest Management Act (NFMA), 16 U.S.C.A. §§ 1600–1614. Other statutes imposed further limitations on Forest Service authority. Noncompliance with the Endangered Species Act (ESA) (discussed in section 9B) and NEPA (discussed in section 4E), for example, led to a nearly complete halt on timber sales in areas of northern spotted owl habitat. The ESA and other statutes designed to prevent the adverse effects of timber cutting on anadromous fish in the Pacific Northwest wrought similar havoc on other timber production in that area. Cf. Native Ecosystems Council v. Dombeck (9th Cir.2002) (halting a timber sale based on inadequate biological assessment prepared by the Forest Service under the ESA).

In addition to restricting the use of even-aged management techniques, the NFMA created new land and resource planning procedures. Management actions now must proceed in accordance with approved plans. For the most part, the Forest Service completed forest plans between 1985 and 1990. After that time, the courts addressed attacks on the validity of those plans as well as on actions allegedly taken in violation of them. The fate of the first generation of land and resource management plans (LRMPs) will dictate to a large degree the nature of the activities that will occur in the national forests over the next decade.

Courts addressing challenges to actions allegedly inconsistent with plans may refuse to reach the merits of those challenges. The Supreme Court's decision in Ohio Forestry Ass'n v. Sierra Club (S.Ct. 1998), discussed supra at section 4A, prohibits judicial review of land use plans on ripeness grounds until implementation is imminent. In a subsequent decision, the Court held that the district court lacked jurisdiction over a suit to compel the BLM to manage public lands in accordance with analogous plans adopted under the Federal Land Policy and Management Act (FLPMA). In doing so, it characterized the BLM plans as but "a preliminary step in the overall process of managing public lands" and as "a general statement of priorities" that "guides and constrains actions, but does not (at least in the usual case) prescribe them." Norton v. Southern Utah Wilderness Alliance (S.Ct.2004).

The courts have enjoined agency projects based on defects in the LRMP. In Pacific Rivers Council v. Thomas (9th Cir.1994), discussed further in Chapter 9, the court required the Forest Service to reopen a completed land and resource management plan to consider the effect of the plan on the chinook salmon, even though it was not listed as threatened under the ESA until after plan adoption. The Ninth Circuit also enjoined ongoing and announced timber, range, and road projects undertaken pursuant to the plan pending compliance with the ESA.

The courts also have invalidated or delayed individual projects based on inconsistency with LRMP provisions. The manner in which LRMPs can impose substantive constraints on agency discretion is illustrated by Lands Council v. Powell (9th Cir. 2005). The court in *Lands Council* held that a timber harvest approved by the Forest Service as part of a watershed restoration project violated the applicable plan because it did not comply with plan provisions designed to protect fisheries and soil conditions. The agency failed to determine whether the project would result in sediment that could interfere with egg hatching, and it analyzed the impact on soil conditions using unverified predictions generated by a spreadsheet model.

The following section outlines the business aspects of public timber management. Section B discusses the theory and practice of multiple use, sustained yield management, the guiding statutory standard for Forest Service operations, and the instances leading to enactment of the NFMA. The short concluding section takes up parallel legal problems on BLM public lands.

A. TIMBER CONTRACTS

A rider to the NFMA authorizes the Forest Service to sell timber from the national forests at not less than appraised value. 16 U.S.C.A. § 472a(a). Although timber sale contracts between the Forest Service and private loggers usually are interpreted and enforced in accordance with normal rules of contract law, statutory and regulatory provisions can alter those rules in some circumstances.

1. ADVERTISEMENT AND BIDDING

The Forest Service must advertise all sales unless extraordinary conditions exist or the appraised value of the sale is less than $10,000. Advertisements must describe the location and estimated quantities of timber offered for sale. The government also must make available to prospective purchasers and the public a prospectus containing a more complete description of the quality and age class of the timber involved, the method of bidding to be used, and the required payment terms.

The Forest Service's bidding methods must "insure open and fair competition," insure that the government receives not less than the appraised value of timber sold, and consider the economic stability of communities whose economies depend on national forest materials. Id. § 472a(e)(1). The NFMA also authorizes the Agriculture Secretary to eliminate collusive bidding practices. Forest Service regulations require that competitive timber sales be offered through either sealed bids or oral auctions following sealed bids. The agency has favored the former method in the eastern and southern forests, while generally conducting oral auctions for timber sales in the West.

Forest Service regulations give the agency the unqualified power to reject all bids. Before adoption of the NFMA, the courts refused to restrict that authority. In S & S Logging Co. v. Barker (9th Cir.1966), the court dismissed the claim that rejection of the high bid on a timber contract constituted a conspiracy in restraint of trade in violation of the antitrust laws. According to the Ninth Circuit, the Forest Service had "unqualified discretion" to reject all bids "with or without reason." Five years later, in Hi–Ridge Lumber Co. v. United States (9th Cir.1971), the Ninth Circuit confirmed that result, endorsing the Forest Service's decision to reject all bids because the high bidder refused to conform to agency road-building specifications. Further, the court found that, because the judiciary lacks the technical expertise possessed by the agency, there were no standards for judicial review of a decision to reject all bids.

Adoption of the NFMA altered that result. In Prineville Sawmill Co. v. United States (Fed.Cir. 1988), the court overturned as arbitrary and capricious a Forest Service decision to reject all bids. Before soliciting bids, the Forest Service estimates the quantities of the various tree species to be offered. Actual contract payments, however, are calculated based on the actual volume of timber cut rather than the estimates contained in the bid specifications. Prineville submitted a "skewed bid" on an Oregon timber sale. It offered to pay an unusually high amount for a tree species whose volume it believed (correctly) the Forest Service had overestimated. It bid a lower than normal amount on the remaining species, which the Forest Service had estimated more accurately. After awarding the contract to Prineville, the high bidder, the government discovered that Prineville's estimates were more accurate than its own. As a result, the company would be obligated to pay much less than it bid. When the Forest Service decided to reject all bids on the ground that its computational errors vitiated the bidding results, Prineville sued. The court concluded that, despite the technical expertise of the Forest Service, the agency's actions were reviewable for "basic fairness." *Hi-Ridge* was distinguishable because of the subsequent adoption of the NFMA mandate that Forest Service bidding practices "insure open and fair competition." The agency's rejection of the high bid based on "20/20 hindsight" violated this mandate and constituted an abuse of discretion. The government canceled the sale not to insure fair competition, but "simply to get even more money for its timber."

See PNRL §§ 20:27–20:30.

2. CONTRACT TERMS AND DURATION

The length and terms of national forest timber contracts must "promote orderly harvesting" in a manner consistent with the substantive limitations of the NFMA. 16 U.S.C.A. § 472a(c). Successful bidders on Forest Service timber contracts must file a plan of operation, which becomes part of the contract upon the agency's approval. Forest Service utilization standards and harvest practices, which are designed to provide optimal practical use of trees and forest products, must be compatible with multiple use resource management objectives, applicable land and resource management plans, and environmental quality standards. Upon contract completion, purchasers must reestablish vegetative cover to minimize erosion in disturbed areas.

Typically, timber sale contracts may not exceed ten years. Everett Plywood Corporation v. United States (Ct.Cl.1981), involved the government's right to cancel before that time. After Everett, the successful high bidder, began road construction into the contract areas, the Forest Service determined that continued construction would cause extensive soil and watershed damage. The parties to the contract agreed to modify it to reduce both the road construction required and the amount of timber to be harvested. Everett nevertheless reserved the right to seek damages under the original contract, which authorized the government to terminate for a variety of reasons, not including environmental damage. The trial court, relying on the contract law doctrine of frustration of purpose, ruled that the government had not breached. The Court of Claims reversed. The environmental damage was reasonably foreseeable and the government, which designed the logging roads, was in a better position to have predicted it before entering the contract. The Forest Service also could have included a provision authorizing termination in the event of environmental damage. Because it did not, the government bore the risk of such damage and was liable in damages for breach. See also Scott Timber Co. v. United States (Fed. Cir.2003) (holding that contract provisions did not give the United States the unilateral authority to suspend operations to protect threatened species).

Government-induced delays in performance also may result in a finding of breach. The court in Stone Forest Indus., Inc. v. United States (Fed.Cir. 1992), held that the government breached a timber contract when the Forest Service's failure to authorize logging in areas affected by wilderness designation caused the contract to expire before the purchaser could commence logging. In Precision Pine & Timber, Inc. v. United States (Fed.Cl.2001), the court held that timber contract suspensions caused by Forest Service delays in conducting consultations with the FWS under the ESA amounted to a breach of the agency's implied duty not to hinder contract performance. The government may be able to rely on the "sovereign acts doctrine," recognized in United States v. Winstar Corp. (S.Ct. 1996) as a defense to breach. The doctrine provides that the United States is not liable for breach of contract when the government, by virtue of a sovereign act, impairs the performance of a contract to which it is a party.

Forest Service regulations adopted after *Everett Plywood* permit contract cancellation if performance would result in serious environmental degradation or resource damage. In the event of cancellation, the purchaser is entitled to reasonable compensation. Cancellation upon application of the purchaser is appropriate if the value of the remaining timber is materially diminished because of catastrophic damage or if cancellation is advantageous to the government. 36 C.F.R. § 223.116.

The courts have been reluctant to allow timber contractors to invoke contractual *force majeure* clauses or impossibility or frustration of purpose as defenses for breach. See, e.g., Seaboard Lumber Co. v. United States (Fed. Cir.2002) (change in federal monetary policies that contributed to collapse of timber market). If the timber contractor can prove breach by the government, it may be entitled to recover lost profits, provided it can show that the breach was a substantial factor in causing the lost profits and that they were foreseeable and reasonably certain in amount. Precision Pine & Timber, Inc. v. United States (Fed.Cl.2004). In Scott Timber Co. v. United States (Fed.Cl.2005), the court held that the contractor failed to show that it would have made a profit but for the breach. The ESA's prohibition on irreversible resource commitments by permit applicants after agency consultation with the FWS has commenced would have precluded the contractor from harvesting timber even if the government had not breached.

See PNRL §§ 20:31–20:44.

B. TRADITIONAL FOREST SERVICE MANAGEMENT

1. THE MULTIPLE–USE, SUSTAINED–YIELD ACT

The concept of multiple use national forest management is derived from the utilitarian philosophy of Gifford Pinchot, the first Chief of the Forest Service. Although the 1897 Organic Act emphasized timber supply, watershed protection, and forest preservation, the Forest Service since its creation managed for a wider variety of uses, including recreation, livestock grazing, and wildlife preservation. The emergence of the wilderness movement prompted loggers, ranchers, and reclamation interests to press for enhanced allocation of forest resources to their needs. When the Forest Service sought guidance, Congress enacted the Multiple–Use, Sustained–Yield Act (MUSYA) of 1960, 16 U.S.C.A. §§ 528–531. The concepts of multiple use and sustained yield continue to govern both the Forest Service and the BLM, whose multiple use mandate is codified in the Federal Land Policy and Management Act of 1976, 43 U.S.C.A. §§ 1701–1784.

The MUSYA enunciates a policy that the national forests be administered for five different purposes— outdoor recreation, range, timber, watershed, and wildlife and fish purposes. The Act directs the Secretary of Agriculture to administer the renewable surface resources of the national forests for multiple use and sustained yield of the products and services obtained from them and to give "due consideration" to the relative values of the various resources in particular areas. The MUSYA defines "multiple use" in part as the management of renewable surface resources so that they are used in the combination that best meets the needs of the American people. Multiple use management, which entails harmonious and coordinated resource management without impairment of the productivity of the land, should reflect periodic adjustments in use to conform to changing needs and conditions. The resulting combination of uses need not necessarily provide the greatest dollar return or the greatest unit output. Sustained yield means the achievement and maintenance in perpetuity of a high-level annual or regular periodic resource output without impairing land productivity. 16 U.S.C.A. § 531.

These statutory provisions notwithstanding, the concept of multiple use is so abstract that its usefulness as a constraint on agency management discretion is questionable. Its meaning tends to conform to the views of the resource user or manager. The scarce judicial interpretations afford broad discretion to the two multiple use agencies. In Sierra Club v. Butz (9th Cir.1973), the district court dismissed the contention that the Forest Service's decision to sell 8.7 billion board feet of timber from the Tongass National Forest in Alaska over a period of fifty years violated the MUSYA. The court found that the Act contemplated that some areas would be unsuited to use of all resources, so that the Forest Service need not afford equal consideration to all potential competing uses. In ordering the sale, the Forest Service properly applied its expertise after considering to some extent all relevant values. On appeal, the Ninth Circuit reversed and remanded in an unreported order. The court interpreted the statutory multiple use mandate as requiring that the agency "informedly and rationally" take the various factors into balance. "The requirement can hardly be satisfied by a showing of knowledge of the consequences and a decision to ignore them." The court remanded to determine whether the Forest Service knew about the ecological consequences of the contract and whether it adequately considered alternatives to the massive timber sale. In a subsequent case, the court in Wind River Multiple–Use Advocates v. Espy (D.Wyo.1993), reached the obvious conclusion that the MUSYA does not contemplate that every acre be managed for every multiple use; Congress recognized that "some land will be used for less than all of the resources."

Despite the Ninth Circuit's invitation to more searching judicial scrutiny of agency decisions for conformity with the key MUSYA mandates, the courts in subsequent decisions by and large have refrained from meaningful review. They have justified minimal review by repeating the mantra, enunciated in Strickland v. Morton (9th Cir.1975), that the statute "breathes discretion at every pore." E.g., Perkins v. Bergland (9th Cir.1979). *Perkins* indicated that multiple use decisions may be reviewed only for irrationality in agency factual determinations, a standard which the court apparently intended to be even more deferential than the Administrative Procedure Act's arbitrary and capricious standard. In Sierra Club v. Marita (E.D.Wis. 1994), the court stated that the "multiple use" language "really just amounts to a statement of principle; it offers no guidance on how to assess the particular management activity at issue."

The Forest Service and the BLM insist that the multiple use, sustained yield statutes impose few if any substantive limitations on their managerial discretion. But the mandates of both the MUSYA and FLPMA are not devoid of substantive content. One of these authors has argued that:

> They demand an equality of resource treatment, and they forbid practices that detract from the future productivity of the land. They demand thought and foresight, and they prohibit economic optimization of single resources. The larger statutory context also requires a broader management viewpoint than that heretofore evidenced. Most significantly, the multiple use legislation requires, implicitly and explicitly [in the case of FLPMA], land use planning that will govern and make predictable (and also "legal") subsequent individual resource allocations.

George Cameron Coggins, *Of Succotash Syndromes and Vacuous Platitudes: The Meaning of "Multiple Use, Sustained Yield" for Public Land Management (Part I)*, 53 U. Colo. L. Rev. 229, 279–80 (1982). At least two courts have agreed that Congress rejected economic optimality as the governing criterion. Texas Comm. on Natural Resources v. Bergland (5th Cir.1978); Sierra Club v. Lyng (E.D.Tex.1988). For the most part, however, limitations on Forest Service discretion in managing national forest resources have been derived from other statutes, if at all. The practical importance of multiple use concepts continues to decline as land use planning and zoning and other factors require tracts to be managed for one or more dominant uses.

See PNRL chapter 16, § 20:64.

2. THE WATERSHED: CLEARCUTTING, *MONONGAHELA*, AND THE NFMA

Timber can be harvested through either even-aged management or selective cutting. One of the three types of even-aged management, clearcutting, entails complete removal of timber from an area. The second, seed tree harvesting, differs only in that a few large trees per acre are left to provide seed for natural regeneration. Shelterwood or shade tree cutting, the third method, leaves more trees in place to provide filtered sunlight for young trees. Both the second and third types result in even-aged forests because the trees originally left standing are typically removed in an early second harvest. Selective cutting, which involves removal of individual trees or small groups and gradual harvesting, produces a more diversified forest.

The advantages of clearcutting are primarily economic, although this method also can produce environmental benefits by, for example, reducing road construction or preventing the spread of insects or disease. Clearcutting eliminates the cost of marking trees and reduces the administrative costs of preparing sales. Even-aged management is also justified as necessary for the regeneration of tree species that cannot grow without direct sunlight. But clearcutting and the other even-aged management techniques take an environmental toll. Clearcut areas tend to be eyesores for years or decades. Even-aged management can adversely affect wildlife dependent on old growth trees. It can diminish soil productivity by removing fallen trees that harbor nitrogen-fixing bacteria and increase water pollution by facilitating soil erosion and raising water temperatures by removing shade trees.

When demand for timber increased after World War II, the Forest Service resorted to clearcutting with increased frequency. Growing public resentment was reflected in documents such as the Bolle Report on timber harvesting practices in the Bitteroot National Forest in Montana. The Report condemned prevailing even-aged management methods for ignoring the economics of regeneration, related forest values, and local concerns that the agency was permitting exploitation of timber resources for non-local benefit. The Report also concluded that the Forest Service was violating multiple use principles.

Matters came to a head when a coalition of environmental organizations challenged the validity of several relatively small clearcuts in the Monongahela National Forest in West Virginia. In West Virginia Div., Izaak Walton League v. Butz (4th Cir. 1975), the court held that the 1897 Organic Act prohibited clearcutting. That practice transgressed the statutory mandate to designate, appraise, and sell only "dead, matured or large growth of trees." 16 U.S.C.A. § 476 (repealed 1976). The court agreed with the plaintiffs that "large growth of trees" referred to the size of individual trees rather than a sizeable grouping of trees, and that maturity should be measured in physiological rather than economic terms. Clearcutting was also inconsistent with the requirement to mark trees individually before harvesting. The Forest Service argued that the MUSYA repealed the Organic Act limitations on harvesting and constituted a congressional ratification of even-aged management practices, but the court found no evidence in the legislative history to support the claim. Shortly after the *Monongahela* decision, an Alaska district court also enjoined performance of a timber contract that envisioned clearcutting. Zieske v. Butz (D. Alaska 1975). The two decisions threatened the entire timber harvest program in the national forests. Congress responded by enacting the NFMA in 1976.

See PNRL §§ 10F:29, 20:2.

C. MODERN FOREST MANAGEMENT

1.   FEDERAL TIMBER POLICY

The national forests include about eighteen percent of commercial timber land, but the Forest Service has jurisdiction over almost half of the nation's inventory of softwood timber, which is the primary source of construction timber. The Forest Service attempts to protect streams from fallen timber, minimize soil erosion and damage to remaining stands attributable to the removal of cut timber, and insure that limbs and stumps are disposed of properly. Nevertheless, Forest Service programmed timber sales, including those that authorize even-aged management, and road construction activities with potential adverse environmental effects, continue to generate political and legal controversy. So does the practice, especially in the Rocky Mountains, of subsidizing the timber industry with below-cost sales.

These disputes often center around the procedural and substantive constraints on Forest Service discretion found in several statutes, including the Endangered Species Act (ESA) and the Clean Water Act (CWA). Chapter 9 discusses the effect on timber sales of the discovery of northern spotted owls in the national forests of the Pacific Northwest. Courts also have enjoined the Forest Service under the ESA from authorizing clearcutting in the habitat of the red-cockaded woodpecker. Sierra Club v. Lyng (E.D.Tex.1988). In Northwest Indian Cemetery Protective Ass'n v. Peterson (9th Cir.1986), the court found that construction of a timber harvesting road in the vicinity of a wilderness study area would violate the CWA by contravening water quality standards issued by the state. In Oregon Natural Resources Council v. Lyng (9th Cir.1989), however, the Ninth Circuit refused to enjoin a timber sale on the basis of alleged noncompliance with the CWA. It held that proper implementation of state-approved best management practices constitutes presumptive compliance with state water quality standards.

See PNRL §§ 20:10–20:11.

Two of the most important sources of legal constraints on timber sales in the national forests are NEPA and the NFMA. The remainder of this section is devoted to analysis of those limitations.

2. THE NATIONAL ENVIRONMENTAL POLICY ACT

Until the mid–1980s, the Forest Service avoided serious disruptions in its timber sales programs from lawsuits based on alleged noncompliance with NEPA. In Kettle Range Conservation Group v. Berglund (E.D.Wash.1979), for example, the court dismissed the claim that the agency had to prepare an EIS for an individual timber sale, because it had already prepared one for the planning unit of which it was a part. Similarly, the court in Sierra Club v. Block (D.Or.1982), refused to require an EIS in connection with a proposal to build a road near a wilderness area that would open a roadless area to logging because an earlier EIS had discussed the general consequences of roadbuilding in the area. In National Wildlife Fed'n v. Coston (9th Cir.1985), the Forest Service adopted a Capital Investment Road and Bridge Program (CIP) that formalized procedures for allocating agency funds for road and bridge construction without preparing an EIS. The

Ninth Circuit held that NEPA did not require an EIS because the CIP was not a proposal for legislation or major federal action. Rather, it was a means of funding actions already proposed for which both programmatic and site-specific EISs had been prepared. EIS preparation therefore would be redundant.

An early case in which the Forest Service was unable to avoid EIS preparation on the basis of a prior programmatic statement was National Wildlife Fed'n v. United States Forest Serv. (D.Or.1984). The Forest Service had prepared an EIS on a Timber Resource Plan (TRP) that set ten-year harvest levels and objectives for an entire forest. The court held that the EIS on the TRP did not justify nonpreparation of an EIS on a subsequently prepared "Action Plan" that set the parameters for timber sales within a particular district. Further, the agency's plan to prepare site-specific EISs for each timber sale did not displace the necessity for an EIS on the Action Plan because neither the programmatic EIS nor the site-specific EISs would assess the cumulative impact of all harvesting in and around the district.

The Forest Service's timber production activities have since been disrupted in a variety of other contexts because of its failure to prepare an EIS or its preparation of inadequate statements. In Save the Yaak Comm. v. Block (9th Cir.1988), the Ninth Circuit enjoined road construction into a beetle-infested area for salvage harvesting because the Forest Service prepared no EIS on the entire road and its EA was not filed until two years after the decision to build. In the same year, the Ninth Circuit also enjoined a series of proposed timber sales in the absence of a forest-wide EIS. The environmental assessments relied on by the agency were insufficient because they failed to address cumulative impacts and raised substantial questions about unknown risks. Sierra Club v. United States Forest Serv. (9th Cir.1988). In Save Our Ecosystems v. Clark (9th Cir.1984), the Forest Service unsuccessfully sought to rely on the Environmental Protection Agency's registration of herbicides under federal pesticide legislation as a justification for not analyzing under NEPA the potential adverse health and environmental effects of a proposed vegetation control program.

The court in NRDC v. United States Forest Serv. (9th Cir.2005), held that the Forest Service violated NEPA on three different grounds in revising the timber harvesting portion of a LRMP. The Forest Service commissioned a report by two economists to project the market demand for timber from the forest. In calculating the allowable sale quantity (ASQ) for the forest, the agency misread the economists' report and used a figure for the ASQ that was twice as high as it should have been. The court held that the discussion of the ASQ in the EIS violated NEPA because it was based on misleading information and thus prevented both agency decisionmakers and the public from making well-informed and reasoned decisions. The court also held that the use of the erroneous demand projection led the Forest Service to ignore reasonable alternatives with lesser environmental costs, such as setting the ASQ equal to the true demand. Finally, the court found that the Forest Service failed to assess in a single EIS the cumulative effects on wildlife viability of federal, state, and private timber harvests in the vicinity of the forest. The court in *Native Ecosystems Council v. Dombeck*, supra, also found inadequate an EIS's discussion of the cumulative impacts of a timber sale and related LRMP amendments.

Noncompliance with both NEPA and the ESA combined to thwart timber sales in northern spotted owl habitat. The ESA issues are discussed in section 9B. In Seattle Audubon Soc'y v. Espy (9th Cir.1993), the court affirmed an injunction on timber sales in part because the EIS failed to address scientific uncertainties or to analyze the impact of a decrease in spotted owl viability on other old-growth dependent species. The Forest Service convinced the Fifth Circuit to overturn a NEPA-based injunction on even-aged management techniques in the Texas national forests in Sierra Club v. Espy (5th Cir.1994).

Before 2005, the Forest Service's planning regulations required the preparation of an EIS for plan adoption or revision. In that year, the Forest Service issued amended planning regulations, which are discussed below. The 2005 regulations authorize the categorical exclusion from NEPA procedures of the adoption or revision of LRMPs based on the agency's assertion that the plan itself typically will not have environmental effects. NEPA compliance is still required at the project or activity stage.

The cases concerning NEPA compliance in the context of timber production in the national forests are too fact-specific to permit easy generalization. The cases indicate, however, that the agency risks disruption of timber sale plans when it fails to assess the cumulative impacts of related timber sales and road-building activity. Preparation of a broad EIS is unlikely to excuse subsequent failure to analyze potential adverse effects if the earlier document does not address the site-specific consequences of timber harvesting. Finally, the courts seem most inclined to insist on rigorous compliance with NEPA when the agency's actions are also alleged to violate the substantive provisions of other statutes, such as the ESA or the CWA.

See PNRL §§ 20:20–20:23.

3. FOREST PLANNING

a. Introduction to Planning Processes

The 1974 Forest and Rangeland Renewable Resources Planning Act (RPA) required the Forest Service to develop long-range, systemwide plans. The RPA's national planning system requirements coexist with the localized planning efforts required by the NFMA. Under the RPA, the Forest Service must prepare an assessment once every ten years of the renewable resources throughout the national forests, a program once every five years proposing long-range planning objectives for all Forest Service activities, and annual reports evaluating actual forest activities in relation to program objectives.

The RPA program provides the framework for the more specific, forest-by-forest plans demanded by the NFMA, although RPA goals are not binding on forest planners. After the Forest Service issues planning regulations that conform to the substantive requirements of the NFMA, local planners devise unit plans in accordance with the regulations and multiple use, sustained yield principles. Management decisions (such as timber contracts, grazing leases, and camping permits) must conform to the plan. The NFMA requires that permits, contracts, and other instruments for use of the forests "be consistent with" land and resource management plans (LRMPs). 16 U.S.C.A. § 1604(i). Compare Native Ecosystems Council v. United States Forest Serv. (9th Cir.2005) (Forest Service violated LRMP by using improper methodology to calculate impact of timber sale on elk hiding cover); Northwoods Wilderness Recovery v. United States Forest Serv. (6th Cir.2003) (change of mix of timber harvest methods violated LRMP), with Pit River Tribe v. BLM (E.D. Cal.2004) (finding no violation of plan requirement to protect access to Native American religious and cultural sites). Site-specific decisions taken pursuant to an invalid plan provision also may be deemed invalid. See, e.g., Idaho Sporting Cong. v. Rittenhouse (9th Cir.2002) (violation of requirement that wildlife habitat be managed to maintain viable populations of native species). The NFMA requires revision of preexisting permits inconsistent with LRMPs, subject to valid existing rights.

The Forest Service issued its first comprehensive planning regulations under the NFMA in 1982. At the end of the Clinton Administration, the Forest Service overhauled those regulations, but the Forest Service repealed those regulations in their entirety and replaced them with yet another new version in 2005. 70 Fed.Reg. 1023 (2005). The 2005 regulations stress the "strategic" and "adaptive" nature of planning and afford more discretion to officials adopting plans for individual units of the National Forest System. The regulations provide that plans will not contain final decisions approving projects or activities except in "extraordinary circumstances." The regulations require that each plan be composed of five elements: desired conditions, objectives, nonbinding technical and scientific guidelines, suitability of areas, and special areas. The 2005 regulations make sustainability of the multiple uses of the national forests the overall goal of NFMA planning, but emphasize social and economic as well as ecological sustainability. The 2000 regulations had established ecological sustainability as the first priority of forest planning. The 2005 regulations presume that lands are available for multiple uses and provide that land use plans will identify suitable uses that best fit the local situation.

b. Substantive Constraints on Timber Harvest Planning

Planning for timber production in the national forests requires the Forest Service to decide initially what land is suitable for timber production. The agency must then calculate the amount of timber to be harvested from this inventory of suitable land. Finally, planners must determine the appropriate methods (such as clearcutting or selective cutting) for harvesting this allowable cut. Although the greatest impetus for enactment of the NFMA was the *Monongahela* court's injunction against clearcutting, the statute constrains agency choices with respect to each of these three decisions.

The NFMA requires the Forest Service to identify lands that are either physically or economically unsuitable for timber production. Harvesting is inappropriate if it would cause irreversible damage to soil, slope, or watershed conditions or adversely affect water quality conditions or fish habitat. The statute also bars timber production on lands that could not be adequately restocked within five years of harvest. Planners must exclude from the inventory lands "not suited for timber production, considering physical, economic, and other pertinent conditions to the extent feasible." 16 U.S.C.A. § 1604(k).

In one of the earliest and most comprehensive judicial assessments of LRMPs, the district court in the *Rio Grande LRMP* case reviewed the Forest Service's planning regulations to determine whether they conformed to various provisions of the NFMA, including the unsuitability limitations. Citizens for Envtl. Quality v. United States (D.Colo. 1989). It concluded that the plan violated the Act because it failed to identify the technology that would prevent timber harvesting under the plan from causing irreversible damage to soil or watersheds. The court also remanded the plan to the agency on the basis of the inadequacy of its economic suitability analysis. In particular, the Forest Service failed to justify increasing the level of unprofitable timber sales. Further, the agency failed to justify placing more emphasis on predetermined timber production goals than on other factors in determining suitability under section 1604(k). By allowing these goals to restrict artificially the alternatives considered to those that would increase timber production, the Forest Service engaged in a "result-biased decision making process."

The court in the *Rio Grande LRMP* case engaged in unusually rigorous scrutiny of the administrative record. Perhaps more typical is the view, expressed in Sierra Club v. Robertson (S.D. Ohio 1994), that the Forest Service has broad discretion to balance the various factors relating to economic suitability and may engage in cost-benefit analysis designed to exclude from timber production lands that do not provide cost-efficient means of meeting plan objectives. The Ninth Circuit has held that the NFMA does not prohibit below-cost timber sales. Thomas v. Peterson (9th Cir.1985). The plaintiff in *Thomas* argued that a proposed timber road was not economical because the value of the timber to which it would provide access was less than the cost of the road. The court disagreed, deferring to the Forest Service's position that, in measuring economic benefits, the agency could consider benefits other than timber access, including motorized recreation, firewood gathering, and local access.

The NFMA also limits the timber inventory by requiring that, to the degree practicable, LRMPs provide for diversity of plant and animal communities. One court found this requirement so vague that it could not discern in it any substantive command to consider any particular creature. Krichbaum v. Kelley (W.D.Va.1994). The court also concluded that naturally occurring forest ecosystems are not the sole yardstick by which to measure diversity. Other courts have characterized diversity as a goal rather than a planning requirement, and concluded that the agency has broad discretion in fashioning a plan that meets the diversity standard. Oregon Natural Resources Council v. Lowe (D.Or. 1993).

An extensive analysis of the diversity requirement occurred in connection with review of two LRMPs for northern Wisconsin forests. The court rejected the plaintiffs' contention that the Forest Service improperly ignored the principles of conservation biology, which supported setting aside large areas of undisturbed habitat to prevent fragmentation of the forest and restricted access to existing habitats. Instead, the LRMP proposed the creation of numerous smaller, undisturbed areas based on the assumption that an adequate mixture of tree species and age-classes necessarily would yield a diversity of habitats, and therefore of biological communities. Deferring to the agency's expertise (a common practice in the early cases construing the diversity requirement), the court accepted the premise that diversity of habitats insures diversity of species. Sierra Club v. Marita (Chequamegon) (7th Cir.1995); Sierra Club v. Marita (Nicolet) (7th Cir.1995). See also Colorado Envtl. Coalition v. Dombeck (10th Cir.1999) (population data not available).

Before the adoption of the 2005 planning regulations, the Forest Service took the position that consideration of the effects of timber harvests on designated "management indicator species" (MIS) or "focal species" could serve as a proxy for compliance with the diversity requirement. The courts endorsed this position in some cases but not others. In Inland Empire Pub. Lands Council v. United States Forest Serv. (9th Cir.1996), the environmental plaintiffs claimed that the agency violated the NFMA's diversity requirement by failing to examine the population dynamics of the species in the area to be affected by timber sales or the effect of the proposed sales on the species' ability to travel between different patches of forest. The court disagreed, deferring instead to the Forest Service's position that a species would remain viable as long as the percentage of each type of habitat (such as nesting and feeding) remaining after the sales would be greater than the percentage required for the species to survive.

In another case, however, a court found that the agency had violated the NFMA by engaging in an incomplete assessment of the cumulative effects of a shelterwood logging project on MIS. The Forest Service studied the effects of logging on the old growth habitat for the MIS, instead of monitoring MIS population trends. The court invalidated this "proxy on proxy" assessment method because the record indicated that the timber stand management reporting system that the Forest Service used to calculate old growth was inaccurate. *Lands Council v. Powell*, supra. Cf. Utah Envtl. Cong. v. Bosworth (10th Cir.2004) (holding that Forest Service may not substitute habitat analysis for actual, quantitative population data for MIS).

The 2005 planning regulations rely primarily on protection of ecosystems and the pursuit of ecological sustainability to maintain the diversity of plant and animal communities and do not require analysis of ecosystem diversity at multiple temporal or spatial scales. The Forest Service removed from the 2005 regulations the previous requirement to provide for viable populations of plant and animal species because of its determination that ensuring species viability is not always possible. Likewise, the 2005 regulations do not include requirements for monitoring MIS because it found the MIS concept to be "flawed." The Forest Service will nevertheless identify species of concern and the regulations do not preclude population monitoring.

In establishing the harvest schedule, the Forest Service may not allow cutting unless stands of trees generally have reached the culmination of mean annual increment of growth. The NFMA requires the agency to limit timber sales from each forest to a quantity equal to or less than the amount that can be removed annually in perpetuity on a sustained-yield basis. 16 U.S.C.A. § 1611(a). This constraint will slow down the liquidation of old-growth forests and basically codifies the agency's preexisting strategy of limiting harvests to non-declining even-flow levels.

The NFMA reflects a compromise on the appropriateness of continued resort to even-aged management techniques. The statute ratified existing contracts that authorized clearcutting. The Forest Service generally may not select a cutting method solely on the basis of economic or gross production optimality. 16 U.S.C.A. § 1604(g)(3)(E)(iv). In Allegheny Defense Project, Inc. v. United States Forest Serv. (3d Cir.2005), the court rejected the claim that the Forest Service's decision to allow a shelterwood cut violated this provision. It concluded that the agency based its decision on the projected environmental as well as economic benefits of the project.

Before authorizing additional clearcuts, the Forest Service must conduct an interdisciplinary review of the potential environmental, biological, aesthetic, engineering, and economic impacts on each advertised sale area and determine that clearcutting is the optimal method for meeting the objectives of the LRMP. The statute permits even-aged management only if clearcut areas are shaped and blended to the extent practicable with the natural terrain and carried out in a manner consistent with the protection of soil, watershed, fish, wildlife, recreation, and aesthetic resources and with timber regeneration. 16 U.S.C.A. § 1604(g)(3)(F). In Sierra Club v. Espy (E.D.Tex.1993), the district court temporarily enjoined clearcutting in the Texas national forests. It concluded that Congress intended clearcutting to be limited to exceptional cases, that it could be undertaken only when consistent with full resource protection, and that the monoculture created by clearcutting is inconsistent with the NFMA's biodiversity mandate. On appeal, the Fifth Circuit vacated the injunction. The district court "erected too high a barrier to even-aged management" because, despite Congress' wariness toward clearcutting, it authorized its use as long as the Forest Service closely examines its effects on forest resources. The appellate court deferred to the agency's choice because it considered alternative harvesting methods, sought to protect old-growth ecosystems, and addressed wildlife habitat concerns. Sierra Club v. Espy (5th Cir.1994).

The *Sierra Club* case came back to the Fifth Circuit in 1999 with a different result. The court found that the Forest Service violated the NFMA because even-aged management was causing substantial and permanent damage to the soil and sedimentation of streams, and because the agency neglected to monitor and inventory fully. Sierra Club v. Peterson (5th Cir.1999). That decision was subsequently reversed, however, for lack of justiciable final agency action. Sierra Club v. Peterson (5th Cir.2000).

See PNRL §§ 10F:30–10F:50, 20:12–20:18.

4. TIMBER MANAGEMENT ON THE BLM LANDS

Timber production is much less important on the BLM lands than in the national forests because, with the exception of the Oregon and California (O & C) lands discussed below, relatively little marketable timber grows on those lands. The BLM is not subject to the NFMA, but its timber-related decisions are subject to the procedural requirements of NEPA and to the substantive provisions of statutes that include the CWA, the ESA, and FLPMA. The CWA requires that the BLM assure that its timber sales comply with state water quality standards. See *Northwest Indian Cemetery Protective Ass'n*, supra. The ESA and NEPA have combined to halt BLM timber production in the habitat of the northern spotted owl in much the same manner that the Forest Service has run afoul of these laws. The importance of NEPA compliance is illustrated by Portland Audubon Soc'y v. Babbitt (9th Cir.1993). The court held that because the BLM's timber management plans did not adequately address the impact of proposed sales on the spotted owl, the agency had to supplement the EISs that accompanied those plans. In the interim, no timber sales with land-altering operations could proceed.

Because of the broad discretion that it affords the agency, the multiple use mandate of FLPMA has not imposed significant limitations on BLM timber production efforts. An Oregon district court held that "[o]nce BLM did a valid multiple use analysis for [public domain] lands, it could favor timber harvest objectives over other multiple use values." Headwaters, Inc. v. BLM (D.Or.1988). The Ninth Circuit later held that, as long as a timber sale is consistent with multiple use principles on a regional basis, FLPMA does not require an additional site-specific assessment. Headwaters, Inc. v. BLM (9th Cir.1990). The court stated that the multiple use mandate does not require accommodation of all uses on every tract.

The richest timber lands under the BLM's jurisdiction are about 3 million acres of land conveyed by the United States for construction of the Oregon & California Railroad and subsequently returned to federal ownership. Congress enacted the O & C Act in 1937 to govern management of these lands. The Act requires that the BLM manage the O & C lands

for permanent forest production, and [that] the timber therefrom shall be sold, cut, and removed in conformity with the principal [sic] of sustained yield for the purpose of providing a permanent source of timber supply, protecting watersheds, regulating stream flow, and contributing to the economic stability of local communities and industries, and providing recreational facilities.

43 U.S.C.A. § 1181a. Although the multiple use
provisions of FLPMA also apply to the O & C lands,
FLPMA itself provides that the O & C Act prevails
in the event of a conflict.

The weight to be given to each of the objectives
set forth in the O & C Act is not completely settled.
The Ninth Circuit in *Headwaters* repudiated the
notion that the phrase "forest production" in section 1181a encompasses not only timber production
but also conservation values such as preservation of
the habitat of endangered or threatened species.
Both the statute and its legislative history, the
court reasoned, envision timber production as a
dominant use. It is possible that in the event of a
conflict between the timber production and watershed protection goals of section 1181a, a court will
deem the dominance accorded timber production in
Headwaters to be less absolute.

One of the *Northern Spotted Owl* cases involved
the relationship between the O & C Act and NEPA.
The O & C Act requires the BLM to determine the
annual productive capacity of the O & C lands and
to sell annually at least one-half billion board feet of
timber, the annual sustained yield capacity, or the
amount that can be sold at reasonable prices in a
normal market. The BLM argued before the district
court in *Portland Audubon Soc'y*, supra, that, to the
extent that an EIS evaluating the impact of timber
production on the owl would prevent the BLM from
offering for sale 500 million board feet per year, the
O & C Act overrides NEPA. The court agreed with
the plaintiff's argument to the contrary; the agency

has the discretion to offer less than that amount based on its obligations under other environmental laws. As long as the BLM's obligations under NEPA and the O & C Act were not irreconcilable, it had to comply with both to the best of its ability. The Ninth Circuit affirmed on this point. Portland Audubon Soc'y v. Babbitt (9th Cir.1993).

See PNRL §§ 20:46–20:63.

CHAPTER EIGHT

THE RANGE RESOURCE

Allocation of grass and other forage on the federal public lands often raises emotional responses out of all proportion to the economic value of the resource. Although roughly 260 million acres of BLM and Forest Service land are used for livestock grazing, those lands provide only about two percent of the livestock feed in the United States. The heat from public land grazing discussions is generated primarily by three factors: the federal range is in lousy shape, ecologically; the primary cause of range deterioration is overgrazing by cows and sheep in a heavily subsidized, exclusive allocation system; and the ranchers defend with passion their "way of life" in the rural West. The last factor was largely responsible for the abortive Sagebrush Rebellion of the late 1970s. See section 4C(2). The current controversies surrounding the range resource cannot be fully understood without knowledge of the peculiar history behind them.

A. PRE–FLPMA GRAZING: THE COMMON LAW AND THE TAYLOR GRAZING ACT

Settlement in the semi-arid areas of the West typically followed a pattern whereby a rancher and his employees would homestead the lands controlling water sources and then use the surrounding public lands for grazing the rancher's livestock. Congress, in the Unlawful Inclosures Act of 1887, 43 U.S.C.A. §§ 1061–1066, decreed that no one could fence off the public lands or otherwise deny anyone access to them. See section 2E(1). Even though the cattle ranchers and nomadic sheepherders using the public lands technically were trespassers, the Supreme Court ruled in 1890 that Congress by its silent acquiescence in their use had bestowed an implicit license on grazing users. Buford v. Houtz (S.Ct.1890). The upshot was the classic "commons" situation: every range user had an incentive to get the grass before someone else did, and the resulting overgrazing severely harmed the productivity of the rangelands. Judicial attempts to prevent large ranchers from monopolizing public land forage were largely futile.

Regulation came slowly to the range. Reservation of areas as national parks and wildlife refuges brought with it some degree of control, and eventually elimination, of some livestock grazing. Using authority vested in it by the 1897 Organic Act, the Forest Service controlled grazing by requiring permits based on the concept of grazing carrying capacity. The Supreme Court in 1911 upheld the program, United States v. Grimaud (S.Ct.1911), and the productivity of the national forests increased as a result. The then-vast public domain remained unregulated, however, causing range wars and further range deterioration.

The watershed event for public land livestock grazing was enactment of the Taylor Grazing Act (TGA) of 1934, 43 U.S.C.A. §§ 315–315r, "pending final disposition." The Act authorized the Interior Department to allocate grazing privileges by a preference permit system. Within a few years, the agency closed virtually the entire public domain by withdrawing the lands into grazing districts. Implementation of the new regulatory program was dominated by beneficiary ranchers through grazing advisory boards. The TGA gave preference to adjacent land and water owners in allotting rights to forage; the initial allocations were made (by the boards and confirmed by the BLM's predecessor agency) on the basis of livestock use during 1929–1934, thereby wiping out the nomadic sheepherders and small ranchers whose use in those Depression years had not been extensive.

See PNRL § 19:2.

From the beginning, the rancher-permittees encouraged the belief that they had permanent, vested property rights in their allowed grazing levels, a position initially strengthened by judicial decision. Red Canyon Sheep Co. v. Ickes (D.C. Cir.1938), involved a challenge to a proposed land exchange. The court concluded that, although grazing rights under the Taylor Act "do not fall within the conventional category of vested rights in property," the Act's privilege to graze "will in the ordinary course of administration ... ripen into a permit" whose holder making economic and beneficial use of the public domain was entitled to protection through equitable relief. Permit renewal long was virtually automatic, so long as the permittee kept control of the base property. But the TGA specifically says that a grazing permit does not give the permittee "any right, title, or interest or estate in or to" the permitted lands. 43 U.S.C.A. § 315b. In United States v. Fuller (S.Ct.1973), the Supreme Court forcefully adopted that position, finding it clear that Congress intended that "no compensable property right be created in the permit lands themselves as a result of issuance of the permit." For that reason, the United States did not have to pay for the enhanced value of land condemned by the government that was attributable to a grazing permit. See also Alves v. United States (Fed. Cir.1998) (holding that a grazing preference attached to base property owned by a TGA permit holder is not a compensable property interest).

Fuller established that ranchers holding Forest Service or BLM grazing permits have only a revocable license to use the federal lands for forage. Congress reaffirmed this principle in FLPMA section 1752(h), but, as indicated below, it also provided that when a permit is canceled for public purposes, the permittee is entitled to compensation for the adjusted value of permanent improvements constructed in the federal allotment, up to the value of the terminated portion of the permit. Id. § 1752(g). Even though the rancher has no legal rights vis-a-vis the government, courts will protect a rancher-permittee's interest in the permit from competing permit applicants. McNeil v. Seaton (D.C.Cir.1960).

See PNRL §§ 19:4–19:6.

The Supreme Court's decision in *United States v. Grimaud*, supra, upheld the Forest Service's authority to charge a fee for grazing on the federal lands. The Court endorsed analogous BLM authority in Brooks v. Dewar (S.Ct.1941). Livestock grazing on the BLM and Forest Service lands always has been heavily subsidized, however, because the fee for grazing has been just a small fraction of fair market value. The subsidy enhances the value of base ranches to which the permits appertain and provides a competitive advantage over nonpermittee ranching operations. That subsidy, when capitalized into the purchase price and mortgage value of the base ranch, induces subsidy recipients to resist reductions in grazing allotments, even when such reductions would be economically beneficial to the rancher in the long run. It is not unusual for permittees to transfer their federal grazing privileges for several times the federal grazing fee, although BLM regulations prohibit "subleasing" of a grazing permit without subleasing of the base property.

In 1970, the Public Land Law Review Commission recommended that fair market value govern

both BLM and Forest Service grazing authorizations, and FLPMA endorsed the general principle
that the United States receive fair market value for
the use of public lands and resources. 43 U.S.C.A.
§ 1701(a)(9). Congress in 1978 imposed an interim
fee formula very favorable to ranchers; although
that authorization expired in 1985, the Interior
Department has continued to use that formula.

See PNRL §§ 19:7, 19:15.

Allocation of grazing permits was governed by
section 3 of the TGA, which authorized the Interior
Secretary to issue permits "to such bona fide settlers, residents, and other stock owners as under
rules and regulations are entitled to participate in
the use of the range." The same provision required
that preference be given to those within or near a
district who are landowners engaged in the livestock business, bona fide occupants or settlers, or
owners of water or water rights. The Interior Secretary interpreted the statutory preference to displace
graziers who did not own base property or fee land
in the vicinity of the public lands. E.g., Garcia v.
Andrus (9th Cir.1982). *McNeil*, supra, held that the
Secretary could not reallocate the rangelands from
a rancher who qualified for the preference to one
who did not, but the court also concluded that the
statute afforded the agency the discretion to determine the number of stock to which the preference
entitled a permittee based on factors such as the
orderly use of the public lands, the forage capacity
of the base property, and the availability of water.

BLM regulation of permittee operations under the TGA was minimal. The agency simply acceded to permittee wishes because the ranchers had the political power to resist any reform proposals. The decision in Diamond Ring Ranch, Inc. v. Morton (10th Cir.1976), was notable only because it was the first instance reaching the courts in which the agency suspended grazing privileges for violation of the regulations. The court recognized that the power to modify, suspend, or revoke grazing permits for noncompliance with the statute or with permit terms is an inherent part of the power to issue such permits.

"Trespass" is a word of art in grazing law meaning putting too many animals out to graze, or leaving them on the range too long, in addition to turning them out onto unpermitted areas. In Holland Livestock Ranch v. United States (I) (9th Cir. 1981), the court upheld a BLM regulation establishing a presumption that putting animals in unfenced proximity to federal forage gave rise to a trespass and it affirmed a reduction of grazing privileges and the imposition of punitive damages for repeated violations. The *Holland II* court ruled that the agency must prove some degree of actual trespass, other than relying on presumptions, before assessing trespass damages. Holland Livestock Ranch v. United States (II) (9th Cir.1983). The agency successfully defended its revocation of the ranch's permit on the basis of numerous and substantial trespasses in Holland Livestock Ranch v. United States (III) (D.Nev.1984). Courts have split on the question whether turning the trespassing beasts loose must be done "willfully" to constitute a violation of Forest Service trespass regulations. Compare United States v. Larson (8th Cir.1984) (no), with United States v. Semenza (9th Cir.1987) (yes). See also United States v. Henderson (9th Cir.2001) (holding that the government had to show that a defendant charged with erecting a gate to exclude the general public without the BLM's approval was aware that the conduct was unlawful).

See PNRL § 19:18.

B. MODERN POST–FLPMA PUBLIC RANGELAND MANAGEMENT

The Age of Preservation, described briefly in Chapter 2, has had less effect on rangeland management than on other areas of federal land law, but that effect is not inconsiderable. The changes wrought in the past generation resulted primarily from three relatively new federal laws: NEPA; FLPMA; and the Wild, Free–Roaming Horses and Burros Act of 1971. The near future likely will see increased prominence of other environmental laws, notably the ESA and CWA, on the federal range.

1. THE NATIONAL ENVIRONMENTAL POLICY ACT

An early NEPA case was the original catalyst for more balanced approaches to public rangeland management. In NRDC v. Morton (D.D.C.1974), the court determined that the BLM must prepare EISs on all of its grazing districts individually, even though it was in the process of promulgating a national programmatic impact statement, because the programmatic EIS did not analyze local geographic conditions. The court rejected the ranching interests' contention that NEPA evaluation was unnecessary because the Taylor Grazing Act provided an effective method of protecting the environment. The ranchers also argued that NEPA did not apply because the BLM's licensing program would not significantly affect the environment, but the evidence of continuing range deterioration, especially in riparian areas, convinced the judge that the contrary was true. The environmental plaintiff made the wise tactical choice of not seeking an injunction against grazing while the EIS promulgation process was pending—but that remedy was later used by courts and a DoI ALJ. Pacific Rivers Council v. Robertson (D.Or.1993); Feller v. BLM, No. UT–06–89–02 (1990), UT–06–91–1 (1993). The *Feller* ALJ rejected the BLM's policy of regarding grazing permit renewals as inaction which does not require environmental assessment or notice to affected interests other than permittees. In a later decision in the same litigation, the IBLA affirmed the ALJ conclusion that an area-wide EIS was insufficient to assess the effects of grazing on the allotments in question. NWF v. BLM (IBLA 1997).

The impact statements on BLM public range management brought out into public scrutiny the rather odd system of grass allocation used by the agency as well as the poor conditions of the federal rangeland. By the BLM's own admission, most public grazing allotments were producing less than half of their estimated grass-growing capacity. But any reforms that might have occurred during the 1970s in response to the information supplied by the 144 EISs resulting from *NRDC v. Morton*, supra, came to an abrupt halt in the early 1980s. Secretary James G. Watt declared a moratorium on further reductions of existing grazing levels on the ground that available data were insufficient to show that those levels were causing adverse impact to the range. By this time, Congress had given the BLM expansive new regulatory authority in the 1976 FLPMA.

Congress on occasion has exempted both BLM and Forest Service decisions authorizing grazing on the federal lands from NEPA evaluation. Pub. L. No. 108–447, § 339, 118 Stat. 2209 (2004), for example, created a categorical exclusion from NEPA for certain decisions that continue current grazing management of an allotment.

See PNRL § 19:10.

2. THE FEDERAL LAND POLICY AND MANAGEMENT ACT AND THE PUBLIC RANGELANDS IMPROVEMENT ACT

In 1976, Congress enacted FLPMA, supplying the BLM with its first permanent authority to manage the public lands for multiple use and sustained yield. FLPMA, as amended by the Public Rangelands Improvement Act (PRIA) of 1978, 43 U.S.C.A.

§§ 1901–1908, also contains a title devoted to live-stock grazing. Although Congress viewed with great alarm the erosion, loss of habitat, and declining productivity of the public rangelands, its substantive changes to the particulars of the regulatory scheme were relatively minor. The new legislation continued to display solicitude for ranchers by retaining permit preferences, financing range improvements, and continuing to institutionalize reliance on the industry's advice. The BLM administers the grazing preference system through the Range Code, 43 C.F.R. §§ 4110–4170. The most sweeping FLPMA reform was the command that the BLM engage in formal land use planning for all of its lands, a topic addressed in the next subsection.

In some ways, FLPMA adds to the security of a permittee's tenure. Section 1752(c) gives existing permittees priority to renew permits so long as the lands remain available for livestock and the permittee has obeyed the law and the permit conditions. If the permit is terminated so the lands can be devoted to another purpose, the permittee is entitled to compensation for permanent improvements he or she built and to two years notice. 43 U.S.C.A. § 1752(g). A claim to compensation under § 1752(g) arises only if the government cancels a grazing permit; a mere suspension does not require compensation. Sacramento Grazing Ass'n, Inc. v. United States (Fed.Cl.2005).

On the other hand, FLPMA and PRIA enhance BLM authority to abate abuses, use new regulatory methods, and lower livestock levels to within graz-

ing capacity. The key provision is 43 U.S.C.A.
§ 1752(e):

> The Secretary concerned shall also specify [in the
> permit] the number of animals to be grazed and
> the seasons of use and ... he may reexamine the
> condition of the range at any time and, if he finds
> on reexamination that the condition of the range
> requires adjustment in the amount or other as-
> pect of grazing use, that the permittee or lessee
> shall adjust his use to the extent the Secretary
> concerned deems necessary. Such readjustment
> shall be put into full force and effect on the date
> specified ...

That section must be read in light of the general
structure and purpose of FLPMA, notably the emphasis on multiple use, sustained yield management
and planning. Id. § 1732(a). The decided cases to
date lay down some basic rules concerning the scope
of the agency's authority to change authorized grazing levels to achieve range protection purposes, but
the more vexing and difficult questions have yet to
be decided.

Perkins v. Bergland (9th Cir.1979), has become a
leading case on judicial review in the Ninth Circuit
for no particularly good reason. The Forest Service
severely reduced the grazing privileges of the plaintiffs, who claimed that the reductions constituted
an unlawful revocation of their permit and were in
any event arbitrary and unsupported. The court
quickly dismissed the revocation claim because a
reduction in levels is not a revocation. The govern-

ment argued that the agency's decision was not reviewable because it was "committed to agency discretion by law" under the APA, 5 U.S.C.A. § 701(a)(2), and that, even if it was reviewable, it was neither arbitrary nor an abuse of discretion. The court decided that the validity of the reductions was reviewable because Congress had expressed a preference for judicial review in section 1701(a)(6) of FLPMA (but that policy was not self-executing and was not specifically enacted in the grazing sections of the statute). The standard of review enunciated by the court, however, was so narrow that very few challenges to multiple use decisions can meet it, semantically or practically. Because the MUSYA "breathe[s] discretion at every pore," the district court should review the agency's "factual findings" for irrationality. The plaintiffs could satisfy their burden of proof only by demonstrating that there was "virtually no evidence in the record to support the agency's methodology in gathering and evaluating the data." The court will not choose among competing expert views. Cf. Forest Guardians v. United States Forest Serv. (9th Cir.2003) (deferring to Forest Service decision to allocate 100% of forage to livestock and none to wild ungulates).

The court in Hinsdale Livestock Co. v. United States (D.Mont.1980), ignored *Perkins* and came to diametrically opposed conclusions in somewhat similar circumstances, even though the controlling provision in both cases was section 1752(e) of FLPMA. The BLM reduced the plaintiffs' grazing allotments because drought conditions created an emergency in which continued grazing would result in severe damage to the range. The district court disputed the agency's finding that an emergency existed, discounting the testimony of the government's experts. It also held that the eviction of the plaintiffs from their allotments amounted to a deprivation of due process. *Hinsdale* may be disregarded as aberrational in nearly all of its rulings.

The opinion in McKinley v. United States (D.N.M. 1993), is far better reasoned. The court there looked more deeply into the Forest Service's rationale for reducing grazing on plaintiff's allotment and determined that the poor conditions on the allotment justified the reductions. The court also held that the loss of value to plaintiff's ranch does not constitute a taking.

NRDC v. Hodel (E.D.Cal.1985), called the *Ramirez* case after its author, arose out of Secretary Watt's attempt to radically revise federal land regulation and privatize federal resources. The Interior Department published proposed rules that in essence would have handed over most if not all management discretion to selected permittees under its "Cooperative Management Agreement" program. In the most searching judicial opinion on public range management yet delivered, the court found in favor of plaintiffs on most of their procedural challenges, obviating the need to address some substantive questions. On the most basic issue presented, however, the court emphatically ruled that the BLM cannot abdicate its statutory authority by turning management over to the permittees through CMAs or otherwise.

The government argued in *Ramirez* that the CMA was authorized by the Public Rangeland Improvement Act, 43 U.S.C.A. § 1908, which directed the Secretary to "explore innovative grazing management policies and systems which might provide incentives to improve range conditions." The court indicated that ordinarily it would defer to the Secretary's judgment in implementation of a discretionary statute. It was "blatantly obvious," however, that the Secretary did not rely on section 1908 in issuing the regulations and that the argument was *post hoc* rationalization entitled to no deference. Further, section 1908 did not authorize the agency to create exceptions to FLPMA's grazing permit requirements. Because the CMA represented a permanent system of preferential permit issuance, it conflicted with FLPMA's directive that the Secretary adhere to one of two prescribed methods of permit issuance. The Secretary could issue permits with or without allotment management plans, but in either case, section 1752 of FLPMA required that permits specify at a minimum numbers of livestock, seasons of use, and related conditions. The general performance standards required by the CMA did not suffice. The CMA also violated section 1732(a), which requires that each permit include a revocation or suspension clause. Notwithstanding vague references in the proposed regulations to the BLM's authority to evaluate the range periodically, the agency had "abdicate[d] its authority in favor of secure rancher tenure." The court concluded that:

> Permittees must be kept under a sufficiently real threat of cancellation or modification in order to adequately protect the public lands from overgrazing or other forms of mismanagement. Any other interpretation of Congressional intent is inconsistent with the dominant purposes expressed [in the TGA, PRIA, and FLPMA]. It is for Congress and not defendants to amend the grazing statutes. In the meantime, it is the public policy of the United States that the Secretary and the BLM, not the ranchers, shall retain final control and decisionmaking authority over livestock grazing practices on the public lands.

Finally, the court held that the Interior Secretary violated NEPA by failing to prepare an EIS. The CMA, which presented a "risk of abuses of privilege reminiscent of times past," was a major federal action with significant environmental impact and the agency's determination to the contrary was plainly unreasonable.

To date, public rangeland management has not received the public and judicial attention accorded the Forest Service's timber management. Consequently, many environmental laws and safeguards that have become common in other areas of modern public land law are still primitive on or absent from the federal range. Regardless of the balance of political power, this state of affairs seems destined to change. Such change may be foretokened by several

1990s controversies. In the first, law professor Joe Feller from Arizona State challenged the BLM's policy of renewing range permits without environmental review, application of environmental standards, or review for consistency with land use plans. Early ALJ and IBLA decisions were favorable to Feller's position, finding, for example, that NEPA requires site-specific EISs before issuance of permits that will have significant environmental consequences, that FLPMA requires a cost-benefit analysis to justify permit renewal, that the BLM must consider all multiple uses in setting stocking rates, and that forage utilization limits must be consistent with land use plans. IBLA affirmed in 1997. NWF v. BLM (IBLA 1997).

Another possible harbinger of change is the case of Pacific Rivers Council v. Robertson (D.Or.1993). The Forest Service prepared land use plans (LRMPs) for two national forests in Oregon. Plaintiffs claimed that the plans and their preparation violated the ESA with respect to salmon species listed after plan promulgation. The court determined that the failure of the Forest Service to reinitiate consultation violated the ESA (see section 9B(2)) and enjoined all new or "additional timber sales, range activities/grazing permits," inter alia. On appeal, the Ninth Circuit affirmed the finding that a violation had occurred, but it broadened the injunction to include "ongoing and announced timber, range, and road projects." Taken together with the possible prominence of BLM land use planning discussed immediately below, this ruling could portend more meaningful judicial review of the BLM's compliance with statutory and regulatory mandates to factor environmental considerations into range allocation and management decisions on an ongoing basis.

See PNRL §§ 19:9, 19:19–19:21.

3. LAND USE PLANNING ON THE BLM PUBLIC LANDS

Required, formal land use planning has not had nearly as dramatic an impact on the BLM public lands as it has had on the national forests, in large part because the Ninth Circuit in effect approved the agency's failure to plan in a systematic fashion. The agency had no pre-FLPMA planning experience of any note, and the FLPMA planning provisions are more hortatory and opaque than those in the NFMA. The agency historically has resisted any action that would detract from its "flexibility," meaning the freedom to decide similar questions differently. Because FLPMA makes land use plan provisions binding on subsequent management actions, 43 U.S.C.A. § 1732(b); Northern Plains Res. Council, Inc. v. BLM (D. Mont.2003), the BLM has given formal planning a relatively low priority in the three decades it has been required.

a. Judicial Review

Fairly early on, courts decided that BLM planning products were reviewable for procedures utilized and for substantive contents. American Motorcyclist

Ass'n v. Watt (AMA I) (C.D.Cal.1981); American Motorcyclist Ass'n v. Watt (AMA II) (C.D.Cal.1982). In the wake of the Supreme Court's decision in *Ohio Forestry*, supra section 4A, holding that Forest Service land use plans are not ripe for review until implemented (in most cases), the conclusions of the *American Motorcyclist* cases are now questionable. Review will be available when the agency makes individual decisions to execute the plan.

The BLM's failure to implement a plan, however, may not be reviewable. In Norton v. Southern Utah Wilderness Alliance (S.Ct.2004), the Supreme Court held that a suit to compel agency action "unlawfully withheld" under section 706(1) of the APA is reviewable only if the agency fails to take a discrete action that it is required to take. The district court in that case lacked jurisdiction over a claim that the BLM violated its obligation under FLPMA to prevent the impairment of wilderness study areas by allowing ORV use that degraded those areas. The Court found that "general deficiencies in compliance," such as the one alleged, lack the specificity required to support review under section 706(1). The plaintiff also claimed that the BLM failed to comply with a land use plan provision stating that ORV use in wilderness study areas "will be monitored and closed if warranted." The Court concluded that this statement did not make the alleged failure reviewable under section 706(1), "at least absent clear indication of binding commitment in the terms of the plan." It described FLPMA resource management plans as "a preliminary step in the overall process of managing public lands" and as "a statement of priorities" that "guides and constrains actions, but does not (at least in the usual case) prescribe them." The Court even found implementation of plan contents to be implicitly subject to budgetary constraints. The Court therefore held that the plan provisions at issue did not amount to legally binding commitments enforceable under § 706(1). Finally, the Court refused to require supplementation of the EIS the BLM prepared on the plan because supplementation is required only if there remains federal agency action to occur. Although the initial plan approval was a major federal action requiring an EIS, that action was completed when the BLM approved the plan. As a result, there was no longer an ongoing major federal action that could require supplementation.

Even when BLM land use plans are reviewable, they will not be reviewable for very much. The statute lacks both procedural and substantive standards, particularly when compared with the NFMA. Although FLPMA section 1712 mandates the development of land use plans for the public lands, the requirements in section 1712(c) that the BLM observe multiple use, sustained yield management principles, use a systematic, interdisciplinary approach, consider present and potential uses of the public lands, and compare long-and short-term benefits impose few constraints on the broad discretion vested in the agency by the rest of the statute. The only real measurable substantive requirements emanating from section 1712(c) are to "give priority to the designation and protection of areas of critical environmental concern" (ACECs) and to enforce all federal and state pollution laws. The breadth of the agency's discretion to designate ACECs will make it relatively difficult to challenge plans even on the basis of the first of these two requirements. The regulations are scarcely more illuminating.

It is possible that the courts will discern primitive, loose standards by which to review BLM compliance with section 1712(c). Moreover, the BLM ignores FLPMA's rudimentary planning requirements entirely at its peril. In *Ramirez*, supra, the district court threw out on procedural grounds the agency's attempt to avoid the statutory requirement that it manage the public lands "in accordance with land use plans developed ... under section 1712." 43 U.S.C.A. § 1732(a). The CMA program contravened this requirement by failing to provide for cancellation or suspension of permits inconsistent with land use plans and by making consistency between plans and permits discretionary rather than mandatory.

A central issue in NRDC v. Hodel (D.Nev.1985), involved what elements the BLM must include in a land use plan under FLPMA. The BLM promulgated a plan for the Reno area in Nevada. Although the area concededly was overgrazed, the planners could not recommend grazing level reductions because of Secretary Watt's moratorium on such actions. Consequently, the plan was merely a vague statement of good intentions to do some unspecified things in the indefinite future, and the accompanying EIS was similarly vacuous. It called for maintenance of existing grazing levels for about five years, followed by necessary adjustments at some unspecified future time. The plaintiffs argued that, instead of prescribing specific, on-the-ground management actions to improve the condition of the range, the plan merely distinguished between existing allotments that required improvements in ecological conditions and those that did not.

The reviewing court was well aware of the alleged deficiencies, agreeing that the plan proposed did not schedule any specific corrective measures. But the court was highly loathe to become a "rangemaster" by engaging in deep or detailed review. Instead, it found each of the alleged flaws insufficient in itself to warrant an injunction and steadfastly refused to consider the Plan/EIS as a whole in light of the identified problems. The crux of the opinion appeared in these paragraphs:

The real question posed . . . is what are BLM land use plans supposed to look like? That is, what kind of detail must the [plan] contain to qualify as a legitimate land use plan required by Congress? FLPMA and PRIA refer to the importance of land use planning in several places. . . . But nowhere in the statutes did Congress describe in detail what sort of information must be studied in a land use plan.

. . . It is therefore a reasonable assumption that Congress intended the BLM to continue its practice of setting grazing capacity at the permit-

decision stage, and that land use planning ...
deal with broader issues [such as] long-term resource conflicts, long-term range trends, planning
of range improvements, and concentrating the
BLM's limited resources on certain key areas.

The Reno plan addressed precisely these matters.
The plaintiffs argued that the BLM should have
prepared allotment management plans for each unit
in the Reno area, but the court characterized such
an effort as an "administrative strait-jacket which
eliminates the room for any flexibility to meet
changing conditions." They also argued that the
agency should have established a fixed level of acceptable livestock use for the foreseeable future, but
the court concluded that variability of factors such
as climate made such an endeavor unrealistic. In
the absence of more precise statutory or regulatory
standards, the court discerned no pattern of illegal
or arbitrary conduct. The Ninth Circuit cursorily
affirmed on the *Perkins* rationale that the BLM
"policy decision" to postpone adjustments in grazing levels until the accumulation of additional data
was not irrational. Neither FLPMA nor PRIA required more than "broad objective-oriented land
use plans."

The upshot of the *Reno* case is that the BLM has
discretion under FLPMA to plan when, where, and
how it chooses. Unless that decision is overturned,
the litigation focus will be on allotment-by-allot-
ment decisions, a trend that may well force even
deeper reforms than district-level review of plans,
as section 8B(2) notes. *Reno* notwithstanding, the

BLM has since reduced livestock grazing levels in some areas. The ESA and federal and state pollution control laws may become increasingly important constraints on the virtually unreviewable management discretion resulting from the *Perkins* and *Reno* cases.

See PNRL § 19:8.

b. Contents and Consequences

In 1995, the BLM promulgated range regulations called the Fundamentals of Rangeland Health. The focuses of the new regulations are protection and enhancement of watersheds, ecological processes, water quality, and endangered species. In the promulgation process, the BLM made many other changes, some of which were challenged in court by permittee ranchers. The district court found four regulations invalid, but the Tenth Circuit reversed as to three of the rules. In the Supreme Court (Public Lands Council v. Babbitt (S.Ct.2000)), the ranchers posed the question as one of preexisting rights to minimum levels of grazing, and they argued that "adjudicated forage rights" could not be diminished pursuant to BLM land use plans. The Court largely ignored those arguments (and elided over ripeness questions) in upholding the three challenged regulations. It determined that the Taylor Grazing Act does not create rights to any grazing intensity levels, that the BLM must prepare plans and act according to their terms, and that the new regulations do not cancel preferences but rather changed the terminology. The Court also found adequate authority for the BLM policy of assuming title to range improvements.

The effects of the new Rangeland Health regulations are evident in Idaho Watersheds Project v. Hahn (9th Cir.1999). The BLM determined in October 1997 that "existing grazing management practices or levels of grazing use on public lands are significant factors in failing to achieve the standards," but failed to modify the grazing permits before the 1998 grazing season as required by the new regulation, 43 C.F.R. 4180.2(c). The Ninth Circuit reversed the lower court's refusal to enjoin grazing in the disputed area. Compare Oregon Natural Desert Ass'n v. Singleton (D.Or.1999) (grazing in a wild and scenic river segment permanently enjoined).

4.   THE WILD, FREE–ROAMING HORSES AND BURROS ACT OF 1971

Wild horses and burros compete with domestic cows and sheep for the sparse grass on the federal public lands. For that reason, the feral animals were killed indiscriminately for decades. Congress in 1971, at the urging of millions of elementary school pupils, decided to protect the existing remnant bands of the once wide ranging herds. The Wild, Free–Roaming Horses and Burros Act (WF–RHBA), as amended, 16 U.S.C.A. §§ 1331–1340, forbids the killing, capture, or harassment of the qualifying beasts on BLM or Forest Service (but not NPS or NWR) areas and on private lands when they stray onto them. The states may not authorize killing or mutilation of protected animals by declaring that the horses are privately owned; the BLM is responsible for ownership determinations. American Horse Protection Ass'n (AHPA) v. United States Dep't of Interior (D.C.Cir.1977). The BLM, however, may round up "excess" animals and either give them up for adoption to individuals or kill them. 16 U.S.C.A. § 1333. The "Adopt–A–Horse" program has given rise to a variety of legal problems because many adopters want the animals for commercial purposes. In Animal Protection Inst. v. Hodel (9th Cir.1988), the court enjoined the BLM from allowing adoptions when, as in that case, it knew that adopters intend to sell the horses to rodeos, relegate them to dog food factories, or otherwise make commercial use of them.

The long experience under the WF–RHBA has two related strands. First, the populations of wild horses and burros have risen dramatically from their presumed levels in 1971, making the Act an unanticipated success story in that sense. The second strand is the continuing battle between the ranchers and the agency, who have sought to control or reduce populations, and the organizations, notably the AHPA, that demand they be left in peace to eat and procreate as they will.

Hard and fast rules are hard to come by in this unique niche of modern public land law. It is clear that the agencies have broad discretion in managing feral populations, even though all "management activities shall be at the minimal feasible level." 16

U.S.C.A. § 1333(a). The 1978 amendments stressed quick removal of "excess" animals to prevent destruction of animal habitat. The overpopulation determination cannot be premised on 1971 populations as the norm or the goal. In Dahl v. Clark (D.Nev.1984), the court refused to require the BLM to reduce horse populations in the area of the plaintiffs' grazing allotments to 1971 levels. The statute requires that the determination be made on the basis of optimality in a particular area. Horses are excess under the WF–RHBA if their removal from an area is necessary for the preservation and maintenance of a "thriving ecological balance and multiple-use relationship" in the area. 16 U.S.C.A. § 1332(f). The amended Act authorizes the Secretary to assess whether overpopulation exists on the basis of the current inventory of wild horses and burros, the information contained in land use plans and court-ordered EISs, and any additional information developed in the course of research studies carried out under the WF–RHBA. Id. § 1333(b)(2). The court in AHPA v. Watt (D.C.Cir.1982), interpreted this provision as a congressional directive to the courts to be wary of overturning the BLM's findings of overpopulation on the basis of insufficient information. Consequently, the Secretary need not study all possibilities before rounding up horses to remedy overpopulation situations.

See PNRL §§ 18:28–18:29.

CHAPTER NINE

THE WILDLIFE RESOURCE

During the past century, the emphasis of wildlife law in general shifted from rules governing fishing and hunting to laws designed to maintain and enhance wildlife habitat. During this same period, the federal presence in wildlife allocation, particularly on the federal lands, steadily increased. This presence has taken two forms. First, Congress from 1900 to 1980 adopted a variety of laws to protect particular wildlife species. The Lacey Act of 1900, 16 U.S.C.A. §§ 701, 3371–3378, prohibited interstate transportation of game taken in violation of state law. The Migratory Bird Treaty Act of 1918, id. §§ 703–711, authorized the Interior Department to manage migratory bird populations by, among other things, establishing hunting seasons and regulating methods of taking. Congress sought to preserve bald eagles by enacting the Bald and Golden Eagle Protection Act of 1940, id. §§ 668–668d, which banned killing or molestation of bald and golden eagles without federal permission.

After a thirty-year period of relative congressional quiescence, the Wild and Free–Roaming Horses and Burros Act of 1971, id. §§ 1331–1340, marked the beginning of a more activist federal posture toward wildlife protection both on and off the federal lands.

Within the next decade, Congress enacted a series of laws to protect wildlife and its habitat. The Marine Mammal Protection Act of 1972, id. §§ 1361–1407, declared a moratorium on taking of or commerce in marine mammals. The Endangered Species Act of 1973, id. §§ 1531–1544, imposed duties on federal agencies to avoid jeopardizing and protect the critical habitats of endangered and threatened species and imposed a prohibition on the taking of such species. Congress set limits on state discretion in managing wildlife through the Sikes Act Extension of 1974, id. §§ 670g–670h, the Fisheries Conservation and Management Act of 1976, id. §§ 1801–1822, and the Fish and Wildlife Coordination Act of 1980, id. §§ 2901–2911.

The second means by which Congress has influenced wildlife law is establishment of mechanisms for protecting wildlife habitat. By the end of the nineteenth century, the national parks and national forests maintained large areas of wildlife habitat. In 1903, President Theodore Roosevelt established the first federal bird refuge by proclamation. Congress quickly followed his example by establishing refuges by statute. In 1916, the National Park Service Organic Act, id. § 1, declared wildlife preservation a primary objective of the park system. The Wilderness Act of 1964, id. §§ 1131–1136, and the consolidation of wildlife refuges into the National Wildlife Refuge System in 1966, id. § 668dd, provided additional areas devoted to uses consistent with protection of wildlife and their habitats.

When the constitutionality of this legislation has been challenged, the courts have recognized expansive federal power from a variety of sources to regulate activities affecting wildlife. Although this power is most sweeping in connection with activities on or that affect the federal lands, it is sufficiently broad to cover activities on state-owned or private lands as well. Wildlife management remains primarily a state prerogative, despite this plethora of federal legislation. Congress has seldom chosen to assert exclusive authority to manage wildlife, even on the federal lands.

See PNRL §§ 18:1, 18:5.

A. WILDLIFE AND THE CONSTITUTION

The bases for federal wildlife regulation and corollary constitutional limitations on state control over wildlife have been long debated. In Geer v. Connecticut (S.Ct.1896), the Supreme Court held that the Commerce Clause did not prohibit a state from barring the export of game taken within its borders. Even though such resource hoarding usually contravenes Commerce Clause limitations on state authority, the Court determined that the export ban differed because the state owned wildlife in trust for the people; that ownership allowed the state to prohibit such commerce. The Court soon retreated from this conception of state property rights in wildlife. Cases such as Missouri v. Holland (S.Ct.1920), and Hunt v. United States (S.Ct.1928), upheld federal legislation and regulation of wildlife. In Hughes v. Oklahoma (S.Ct.1979), the Court over-ruled *Geer*. *Hughes* dealt with a challenge under the dormant Commerce Clause to an Oklahoma statute that barred transportation of minnows taken within the state for sale outside the state. The Court held that wildlife was subject to the same rules govern-ing other articles in commerce and that states could not claim ownership of animals which they did not possess or control. *Hughes* does not bar states from regulating commerce in wildlife for the purpose of protecting legitimate state interests, provided less discriminatory regulatory alternatives do not exist. See Maine v. Taylor (S.Ct.1986). The Privileges and Immunities and Equal Protection Clauses impose additional limitations on state attempts to discrimi-nate against nonresidents whose livelihood involves taking wildlife, but not on state discrimination against sport hunters and fishermen. Baldwin v. Montana Fish & Game Comm'n (S.Ct.1978). Minne-sota ex rel. Hatch v. Hoeven (D.N.D.2005), held that the Privileges and Immunities Clause does not protect access to recreational hunting.

The Constitution authorizes Congress to protect wildlife and the habitat necessary to support it in several ways. In addition to limiting state control of wildlife, the Commerce Clause affirmatively author-izes extensive federal regulation. See United States v. Helsley (9th Cir.1979). *Missouri v. Holland*, su-pra, not only undermined the state ownership theo-ry as a justification for regulation of migratory birds, it also upheld the 1918 Migratory Bird Treaty

Act as a legitimate exercise of the treaty power. Eight years later, in *Hunt*, supra, the Supreme Court dismissed Arizona's argument that the federal government was bound by state law in the implementation of a deer kill program designed to abate overpopulation on federal lands. Citing *Camfield*, discussed in sections 3B–C, the Court concluded that "the power of the United States to ... protect its lands and property does not admit of doubt," regardless of contrary state game laws. In Kleppe v. New Mexico (S.Ct.1976), the Court confirmed that the Property Clause authorizes federal preemption of state jurisdiction over wildlife on the federal lands. See section 3B. Lower courts have held that this authority extends to regulation of wildlife off the federal lands, provided there is some connection to those lands. E.g., United States v. Brown (8th Cir.1977). More recently, the courts have ruled that the Commerce Clause was not violated when the Endangered Species Act was applied to projects that threatened the viability of a species found only in one state, GDF Realty Invs., Ltd. v. Norton (5th Cir.2003); Rancho Viejo, L.L.C. v. Norton (D.C. Cir.2003); National Ass'n of Home Builders v. Babbitt (D.C. Cir.1997), or was used to preclude takings of red wolves found on private land. Gibbs v. Babbitt (4th Cir.2000). The courts in theses cases did not agree, however, on the rationale for upholding the ESA's application under the Commerce Clause.

See PNRL §§ 18:3–18:4.

B. ENDANGERED SPECIES PROTECTION

The Endangered Species Act (ESA) of 1973, 16 U.S.C.A. §§ 1531–1543, is the most absolute of the federal statutes designed to protect public natural resources and probably the most stringent wildlife law in the world. Despite three reauthorizations with but minor tinkering since its adoption, it is also the most controversial federal resource law. The economic impact of the ESA has been far-reaching. The failure of the Forest Service and the BLM to protect adequately the northern spotted owl and its habitat resulted in judicial decrees shutting down the timber industry in wide areas of the Pacific Northwest, despite appropriations legislation that temporarily precluded judicial challenges to timber sales in spotted owl habitat. See Robertson v. Seattle Audubon Soc'y (S.Ct.1992). Efforts to protect the severely depleted stocks of salmon and other anadromous fish in the same region later caused similar disruptions in industries such as hydroelectric power generation. E.g., Idaho Dep't of Fish & Game v. NMFS (D. Or.1994). Property rights advocates have charged that implementation of the ESA threatens uncompensated regulatory takings.

The goal of the ESA is the conservation of endangered and threatened species and the ecosystems upon which they depend. 16 U.S.C.A. § 1531(b). To achieve that goal, section 7 of the Act imposes a series of duties, procedural and substantive, on all federal agencies. Id. § 1536. Each agency must in-

sure, in consultation with the Fish and Wildlife
Service (FWS) or the National Oceanic and Atmo-
spheric Administration Fisheries (NOAA Fisheries)
(previously known as the National Marine Fisheries
Service (NMFS)), that its actions are not likely to
jeopardize the continued existence of any listed
species or result in the destruction or adverse modification of its critical habitat. The cabinet-level Endangered Species Committee (also known as the
"God Squad") may authorize projects otherwise
barred by this obligation. Id. § 1536(e)-(*o*). In addition, section 7 affirmatively requires each agency to
conserve listed species. Section 9 prohibits any person from, among other things, "taking" any endangered or threatened species, and it defines a "taking" broadly. Id. §§ 1538(a), 1532(19). The ESA
preempts state laws that prevent federal agencies
from protecting species listed under the Act. See
National Audubon Soc'y v. Davis (9th Cir.2002)
(state law prohibiting the use of leghold traps).

The potency of the ESA was illustrated in the
Snail Darter case, TVA v. Hill (S.Ct.1978). When
the Tennessee Valley Authority's Tellico Dam was
nearing completion, scientists discovered a previously unknown species of perch, the snail darter.
Completion and operation of the dam would have
eradicated the only known population of snail dar-
ters and destroyed their critical habitat. The first
question before the Court was whether the TVA
would violate the ESA, which was adopted shortly
after discovery of the fish, if it completed the project. The plain language of section 7 and Congress'

intention to "halt and reverse the trend towards species extinction, whatever the cost," compelled an affirmative answer. The Court also held that continued appropriations for the Tellico Dam after enactment of the ESA did not implicitly repeal the Act as it applied to the dam. The second question was whether injunctive relief was the appropriate remedy. The Court refused the agency's invitation to interpret the statute "reasonably" and fashion a remedy based on "common sense":

> Congress has spoken in the plainest of words, making it abundantly clear that the balance has been struck in favor of affording endangered species the highest of priorities, thereby adopting a policy which it described as "institutionalized caution."

Separation of powers principles required issuance of an injunction prescribed by statute.

The Endangered Species Committee subsequently refused to exempt dam construction from the statute because the value of the continued existence of the snail darter outweighed the dam's dubious economic value. Congress itself later exempted the Tellico Dam, but the discovery of other snail darter populations at other locations defused that controversy.

Protection of endangered and threatened species has been a critical recent focus of public land law litigation. That litigation encompasses four main aspects of ESA interpretation: listing and habitat designation; section 7 consultation; conserving listed species; and the section 9 taking prohibition.

1.   LISTING AND CRITICAL HABITAT DESIGNATION

The ESA requires the FWS to list those species it finds to be endangered or threatened. An endangered species is one that is in danger of extinction throughout all or a significant portion of its range. A species is threatened if it is likely to become endangered within the foreseeable future. 16 U.S.C.A. § 1532(20). The statute affords greater protection to endangered than to threatened species. Instead of prohibiting the taking of the latter, for example, the ESA vests in the Secretary of the Interior the discretion to extend the statutory prohibitions to threatened species of fish or wildlife and to issue whatever regulations are deemed "necessary and advisable to provide for [their] conservation". Id. § 1533(d).

The meaning of the phrase "throughout a significant portion of its range" was at issue in Defenders of Wildlife v. Norton (9th Cir.2001). The Interior Department interpreted the statute to make a species eligible for listing if it faces threats in enough portions of its range that the entire species is or soon will be in danger of extinction. The court invalidated the definition, concluding that a species is extinct throughout a significant portion of its range if there are major geographical areas in which it is no longer viable but once was. Thus, if the area in which the species is expected to survive is much smaller than its historical range, the Secretary must explain any conclusion that the area in which the species can no longer live is not a "significant portion of its range." Another court found a determination by the FWS that the current range of the gray wolf was the only significant portion of its range, even though there are major geographic areas outside the current range where the wolf was once viable but is now endangered, to be inconsistent with the decision in *Defenders of Wildlife v. Norton*. Defenders of Wildlife v. Secretary (D. Or.2005). The FWS's position essentially meant that the viability of one population rendered insignificant all areas of the wolf's historical or current range outside the area containing that population. Such an interpretation rendered the phrase "significant portion of its range" superfluous.

Defenders of Wildlife v. Secretary, supra, also dealt with the ESA's definition of a "species" as including any "distinct population segment" (DPS) of a species of fish or wildlife that interbreeds when mature. The FWS and the NMFS issued a joint policy statement to clarify the meaning of the term DPS. The court held that the FWS improperly applied the policy statement to justify downlisting two DPSs of gray wolf from endangered to threatened. It ruled that the FWS may not downlist a species unless it demonstrates that the factors relevant to listing in section 4(a)(1) support that action. The FWS here improperly extended the boundaries of the wolf's core areas to encompass its entire historical range, even though the wolf's population status had not improved outside the core recovery areas. See also National Ass'n of Home Builders v. Norton (9th Cir.2003) (FWS improperly designated DPS of owls). In National Wildlife Fed'n v. Norton (D. Vt.2005), the court held that the FWS improperly combined two DPSs that contained two admittedly distinct gray wolf populations, based on geography, not biology. According to the court, the ESA prevents the FWS from downlisting or delisting a portion of a population based on geographical area that it previously determined warranted an endangered listing by lumping together a core population with a low to non-existent population outside the area.

Listing and delisting decisions must be based solely on the best scientific and commercial data available; economic considerations are irrelevant to these determinations. E.g., Southwest Ctr. for Biological Diversity v. Babbitt (D.D.C.1996). Litigants have succeeded in forcing the FWS to list species. In Northern Spotted Owl v. Hodel (W.D.Wash.1988), the court found the agency's decision not to list the owl as endangered to be arbitrary because it was unsupported by expert scientific evidence. The court also took issue with the apparent failure of the FWS even to consider whether to list the bird as threatened. The ESA vests in the FWS the discretion to defer responding to a citizen listing petition if it determines that other pending and imminent listing proposals merit a higher priority. Biodiversity Legal Found. v. Babbitt (10th Cir.1998). In Center for Biological Diversity v. Norton (9th Cir.2001), however, the court invalidated the FWS's Petition Management Guidance, which, among other things, improperly equated the FWS's designation of a species as a candidate for listing with a finding that listing is warranted but precluded by pending petitions to list other species.

Efforts to prevent or reverse listings generally have been less successful. In City of Las Vegas v. Lujan (D.C.Cir.1989), the court upheld the emergency listing of the desert tortoise near the Colorado River. Some courts, however, have temporarily reversed listing decisions on the basis of failure to comply with ESA procedures. E.g., Endangered Species Comm. of the Bldg. Ind. Ass'n v. Babbitt (D.D.C.1994). Compare Moden v. FWS (D. Or.2003) (concluding that the FWS acted arbitrarily in denying a petition to delist sucker fish).

In most instances, the ESA requires the FWS to designate critical habitat concurrently with species listing. Critical habitat is the area occupied by the species at the time of listing which is essential to its conservation and which may require special management considerations or protection. 16 U.S.C.A. § 1532(5). Economic considerations are relevant to habitat designation; the FWS may exclude an area on the basis of cost-benefit analysis. In another phase of the northern spotted owl litigation, the FWS failed to designate critical habitat at the time it listed the owl as threatened on the ground that it was not determinable. The district court held that the decision was unsupported by the record and an abuse of discretion; it ordered expeditious critical habitat designation. The court regarded habitat designation as "a central component" of the ESA's mandate to prevent permanent species loss, which may be deferred only in limited circumstances. Northern Spotted Owl v. Lujan (W.D.Wash.1991). These do not include claims that it is fiscally impossible for the FWS to implement the statutory habitat designation mandate, Forest Guardians v. Babbitt (10th Cir.1999), or that designation would be less beneficial to the species than other actions, such as state-run comprehensive management. NRDC v. U.S. Dep't of the Interior (9th Cir.1997). Some courts have invalidated critical habitat designations that were not based upon the best available scientific data. See, e.g., Home Builders Ass'n of N. Calif. v. FWS (E.D. Cal.2003).

The courts have addressed the relationship between decisions to list and to designate critical habitat. In New Mexico Cattle Growers Ass'n v. FWS (10th Cir.2001), the court invalidated the FWS's "incremental baseline approach" to critical habitat designation. Under that approach, the FWS did not consider the economic impact of habitat designation unless it would not occur but for the designation. Any impact that did not satisfy this "but for" test was attributed to a different cause, such as the listing of the species concerned. The Tenth Circuit held that the approach violates the ESA. FWS regulations defined the "jeopardy" standard of § 7(a)(2) in terms virtually identical to those used to define the same section's "adverse modification" standard. Because the regulatory def-

inition of "jeopardy" encompassed the definition of
adverse modification, the baseline approach rendered any economic analysis of critical habitat designation meaningless. The court held that the FWS
must analyze the economic impact of designation,
even if it is attributable coextensively to other
causes, including listing. A district court subsequently disagreed with the Tenth Circuit's "ill ad-
vised" reading of the statute, finding the baseline
approach to be a reasonable method for assessing
the actual costs of habitat designation by comparing
the situation with and without such designation.
Cape Hatteras Access Pres. Alliance v. United
States Dep't of the Interior (D.D.C.2004).

The courts also have addressed the relationship
between the FWS's regulatory definitions of "jeopardy" and "adverse modification" of critical habitat. In Sierra Club v. FWS (5th Cir.2001), the court
ruled that the regulations did not impermissibly
equate the standards for species jeopardy and destruction or adverse modification of critical habitat.
It also concluded, however, that the latter definition
improperly required that an action affect both survival and recovery to trigger the section 7 consultation requirement, and it declared the regulation to
be facially invalid. Consultation is required where
an action affects recovery, even if it does not affect
species survival. Other courts have reached the
same conclusion. See Gifford Pinchot Task Force v.
FWS (9th Cir.2004).

See PNRL §§ 15C:3–15:4.

2. THE SECTION 7 CONSULTATION PROCESS

Section 7 of the ESA precludes federal agencies from taking actions likely to jeopardize the continued existence of listed species or result in the destruction or adverse modification of their critical habitat. Before proceeding with a proposed action, a land management agency must ascertain whether any listed species may be present in the affected area and, if so, whether the species is likely to be affected by the action. The second inquiry takes the form of a biological assessment, which may be incorporated into an EIS or EA prepared under NEPA. If the assessment reveals a likely adverse effect, the proposing agency must formally consult with the FWS. The statute bars the proposing agency from making any irreversible resource commitments during the consultation process that would foreclose reasonable alternative measures with no adverse effects on listed species or critical habitat. 16 U.S.C.A. § 1536(d); NRDC v. Houston (9th Cir. 1998); Pacific Rivers Council v. Thomas (9th Cir. 1994).

At the end of the consultation process, the FWS must issue a biological opinion. In *Idaho Dep't of Fish & Game v. NMFS*, supra, the district court remanded a biological "no jeopardy" opinion concerning the effect of hydropower operations on anadromous fish because the NMFS used an arbitrary baseline to measure the effects of the project and engaged in flawed assumptions concerning worst case risk. Although "the situation literally crie[d] out for a major overhaul," the NMFS improperly endorsed preservation of the status quo. In a later case, a court ordered the NMFS to withdraw a biological opinion on issuance of water quality standards under the Clean Water Act because it based its no jeopardy finding on speculative and unenforceable state commitments to minimize harm to listed species in the future. Northwest Envtl. Advocates v. EPA (D. Or.2003). See also National Wildlife Fed'n v. NMFS (D. Or.2003) (biological opinion on dam operations invalid due to improper reliance on off-site mitigation measures that were not reasonably certain to occur). In Pacific Coast Fed'n v. NMFS (9th Cir.2001), the Ninth Circuit upheld in large part another district court's conclusion that several biological opinions were arbitrary and capricious because the NMFS failed to evaluate the impact of BLM and Forest Service timber sales at the project as well as the watershed level, failed to consider the short-term impacts of the sales, and included the unsupported conclusion that natural vegetation regrowth would adequately mitigate the adverse impact of logging on fish migration.

If a biological opinion concludes that the proposed action would jeopardize a listed species or adversely affect its critical habitat, the action may not proceed unless the FWS suggests alternatives that avoid the problem. Even if the opinion finds that the action would not violate section 7, the FWS may suggest mitigation measures. According to the Ninth Circuit, the action agency need not adopt the recommendations of the FWS or NMFS, although deviation from them risks a finding of statutory violation. Tribal Village of Akutan v. Hodel (9th Cir. 1988). Compliance with a biological opinion does not displace the substantive obligations of the land management agency under other statutes. Substantive obligations under other statutes typically do not trump ESA obligations either, however. Aluminum Co. v. BPA (9th Cir.1999).

The courts require thorough and conscientious compliance with the ESA consultation procedures, just as they rigorously scrutinize compliance by the federal land management agencies with the environmental assessment processes of NEPA. In Thomas v. Peterson (9th Cir.1985), the court reversed the district court's refusal to enjoin construction of a timber road into endangered gray wolf habitat. The Forest Service justified its failure to inquire of the FWS whether any listed species were present in the affected area by characterizing it as a de minimis procedural violation. The Ninth Circuit concluded that a failure to prepare a biological assessment for a project in an area where listed species may be present cannot be considered a de minimis violation. Forest Service affidavits that it had conducted a "sufficient study" were not an adequate substitute for the required consultation procedures. The court also held that an injunction against the project pending compliance was the mandatory remedy.

The issues raised by the application of ESA consultation procedures to segmented activities are similar to those discussed in section 4E in connection with NEPA. The court in Conner v. Burford (9th Cir.1988), rejected the government's argument that evaluation of the effects of onshore oil and gas leasing in the national forests on listed species was required only upon the formulation of specific exploration or production plans, rather than upon lease issuance. Instead, the court required the Forest Service to preclude by lease stipulation any form of substantial development until issuance of a biological opinion. The degree to which the FWS may tier a site-specific biological opinion to a previously prepared programmatic EIS is unclear. See, e.g., NRDC v. Rodgers (E.D. Cal.2005) (interpreting the authority to tier narrowly).

FWS regulations require consultation only if there is "discretionary Federal involvement or control." 50 C.F.R. § 402.03. One court required consultation on the BoR's renewal of water service contracts because the agency has the discretion to alter the term of renewal, if necessary, to comply with the ESA. NRDC v. Houston (9th Cir.1998). Compare Sierra Club v. Babbitt (9th Cir.1995) (consultation not required for the BLM's grant of right-of-way for logging operations before the adoption of the ESA); Forest Guardians v. United States Forest Serv. (D. Ariz.2004) (section 7 did not apply due to absence of remaining discretionary control over easement).

A district court sought to reconcile the Ninth Circuit precedents by stating that consultation is not required if an agency has entered a contract, the contract has been completed at the time litigants seek to require consultation, and there is no ongoing agency action remaining to be taken. National Wildlife Fed'n v. FEMA (W.D. Wash.2004). In that case, the court held that the ESA required FEMA to consult in connection with its implementation of the National Flood Insurance Program because it had the discretion to guide development away from areas containing listed species. In another case, the no jeopardy provision applied to the Corps of Engineers's operation of the river system because the ESA did not preclude the Corps from meeting its duties under the Flood Control Act. That statute afforded the Corps discretion to balance the primary statutory interest in navigation with other interests. In re Operation of the Mo. River Sys. Litig. (8th Cir.2005).

The ESA sometimes requires an agency that has already engaged in consultation to reinitiate consultation based on subsequent developments. In *Pacific Rivers Council*, supra, the court required the Forest Service to reinitiate consultation when the NMFS listed a chinook salmon species after adoption of a land and resource management plan. It also reversed the district court's refusal to enjoin ongoing and announced timber, range, and road projects that could affect the fish. This result was necessary to prevent irreversible resource commitments pending consultation. In Environmental Prot. Info. Ctr. v. Simpson Timber Co. (9th Cir. 2001), however, the court refused to require reinitiation of consultation after a listing of threatened species that might be affected by a previously issued incidental take permit. The FWS did not retain discretionary control over the permit to implement measures beneficial to the newly listed species.

See PNRL §§ 15C:9–15C:15.

3. THE DUTIES TO AVOID HARM AND CONSERVE LISTED SPECIES

It is often difficult to distinguish between the procedural and substantive responsibilities arising under section 7. Agencies must not take action that is "likely to jeopardize" a listed species. The courts have interpreted this prohibition broadly. In *Thomas v. Peterson*, supra, for example, the court enjoined an action because of the potential impact on wolves, even though it was not clear that any members of the species actually inhabited the affected area. According to one court, it is arbitrary for an agency to rely solely on the recommendations of the FWS or the NOAA Fisheries to establish compliance with the substantive requirements of section 7(a)(2). The agency must engage in independent consideration of the sufficiency of reasonable and prudent alternatives contained in a biological opinion. Florida Key Deer v. Brown (S.D. Fla.2005).

Compliance with the no jeopardy duty requires reliance on the best available scientific and commercial data available. Heartwood, Inc. v. United States Forest Serv. (8th Cir.2004) (new studies not necessary when available evidence supported determination of no jeopardy); Selkirk Conservation Alliance v. Forsgren (9th Cir.2003). In *Gifford Pinchot Task*

Force, supra, the issue was whether the FWS could base a finding of no jeopardy on the use of models that predicted the effect of proposed timber harvests on spotted owls. Characterizing the issue as a close one, the court held that the ESA does not prohibit the use of a sound habitat proxy method for conducting jeopardy assessments. Environmental groups argued that habitat is already accounted for in the adverse modification prong of section 7 analysis. The court responded that if habitat proxy is used correctly, it can evaluate habitat that has not been designated as critical habitat, thereby indirectly evaluating the effect of a proposed action outside the critical habitat.

In Defenders of Wildlife v. EPA (9th Cir. 2005), the issue was whether the mandate in section 7(a)(2) that agencies "insure" against jeopardy to species empowers EPA to make decisions to preserve species even if one of its substantive enabling acts does not. EPA argued that it lacked the authority to deny a state's request under the Clean Water Act for delegation of the authority to administer the Act's discharge permit program based on the impact of such a delegation on listed species. The court disagreed, concluding that section 7(a)(2) confers on agencies such as EPA an affirmative authority to protect listed species that "goes beyond that conferred by agencies' own governing statutes." The court interpreted section 7(a)(2) as conferring authority and responsibility on agencies to protect listed species "when the agency engages in an affirmative action that is both within its decisionmaking authority and unconstrained by earlier agency commitments."

Agencies may apply to the Endangered Species Committee, which is chaired by the Interior Secretary, for an exemption from their section 7 obligations. The Secretary must hold a hearing if the agency has participated in good faith in consultation procedures and made a reasonable effort to develop alternatives that would not violate the no jeopardy prohibition. An exemption will issue if at least five members of the Committee agree that there are no reasonable alternatives, project benefits clearly outweigh the benefits of alternatives consistent with species and critical habitat preservation, and the agency has not made irreversible resource commitments. The Committee must condition an exemption on compliance with prescribed mitigation and enhancement measures. Because few agencies have sought exemptions, the scope of the Committee's power to provide them is unclear.

Section 7 also requires the land management agencies to take affirmative steps to conserve listed species. The courts have relied on this ill-defined obligation to remand FWS bird hunting regulations, bar the use of lead shot with the potential to harm bald eagles, and deny water use permits that threatened listed fish species. An agency cannot justify noncompliance on the ground that the action required to comply would violate its primary goals, but it retains discretion to choose the means of compliance. Pyramid Lake Paiute Tribe v. United States Dep't of the Navy (9th Cir.1990). In *Defend-*

ers of Wildlife v. Secretary, supra, the court held that the affirmative conservation duty applies to the FWS, although it also held that the FWS did not violate the duty when it downlisted two DPSs of gray wolf because it had implemented specific and concrete conservation and recovery programs for the wolf.

See PNRL §§ 15C:16–15C:18.

4. THE SECTION 9 PROHIBITION ON TAKINGS

Both federal land managers and users are subject to the prohibition in section 9 of the ESA on the "taking" of listed species. Knowing violators are subject to criminal penalties. In Sweet Home Chapter v. Babbitt (D.C.Cir.1993), the court held that the FWS need not extend the taking prohibition to threatened species on a species-by-species basis. Other courts have barred sports hunting of wolves and grizzly bears on the federal lands as violative of section 9. In Sierra Club v. Clark (8th Cir.1985), the court concluded that the ESA authorizes sport hunting of threatened species only in the rare case in which population pressures within a given ecosystem cannot otherwise be alleviated. In Cold Mountain v. Garber (9th Cir.2004), the court held that the Forest Service did not engage in a taking of bald eagles when it issued a special use permit allowing Montana to operate a facility to test bison for brucellosis because the record did not indicate that the state's violation of permit conditions caused reproductive failure of an eagle nest.

The scope of the section 9 prohibition depends largely on the meaning of "taking." The Act defines that term to include harm or harassment, and FWS regulations define both of these broadly to include significant habitat modification and disruption of normal behavioral patterns. The First Circuit held in American Bald Eagle v. Bhatti (1st Cir.1993), that an activity that creates a mere risk of injury is not a taking. The Ninth Circuit later reached the same result. NWF v. Burlington N. R.R., Inc. (9th Cir.1994).

For many years, there was no definitive answer to the question of whether habitat modification may amount to a taking in violation of section 9. The FWS took the position that it could, and some lower courts agreed. The Supreme Court in Babbitt v. Sweet Home Chapter (S.Ct.1995) ended the argument by deciding, 6–3, that the FWS definitions were within its authority. The regulation is supported by the ordinary meaning of "harm," the purpose of the statute, and the incidental take permit mechanism of the ESA. The taking prohibition operates on private and state lands as well as federal lands.

The ESA authorizes takings otherwise prohibited by the statute that result from but are not the purpose of carrying out an otherwise lawful activity. 16 U.S.C.A. § 1539(a). To take advantage of this exemption, an agency must receive an incidental take statement from the FWS. An individual must procure an incidental take permit, which requires submission of a habitat conservation plan to miti-

gate adverse impact on listed species. Loggerhead
Turtle v. County Council (11th Cir.1998). Exemptions are not available unless the FWS finds that
the permit will not appreciably reduce the likelihood of survival and recovery of the listed species in
the wild. Alaskan Natives engaged in subsistence
use may also be exempt from the takings prohibition. Id. § 1539(d); section 9E(2).

The court in Arizona Cattle Growers Ass'n v.
United States Fish and Wildlife (9th Cir.2001), addressed the relationship between sections 7 and 9 of
the ESA in a situation in which a federal agency
authorizes private action that might result in a
taking. The FWS issued a series of incidental take
statements under section 7(b)(4) after consulting
with the BLM and the Forest Service on the effects
of issuing cattle grazing permits on federal lands.
The permit holders challenged the statements on
the ground that the grazing activities did not result
in any takings. The FWS had argued before the
district court that the term "taking" in section
7(b)(4) should be interpreted more broadly than it
is the section 9 prohibition on takings. In particular, the FWS argued that takings under section
7(b)(4) include situations in which harm to a listed
species is possible or likely in the future due to the
proposed action. The Ninth Circuit rejected the
argument, holding that the definition of a taking is
the same under both sections 7 and 9. The FWS's
interpretation would allow the agency to engage in
widespread land regulation even in the absence of
section 9 liability, contrary to congressional intent.

The court in *Arizona Cattle Growers* also held
that it is arbitrary and capricious for the FWS to
issue an incidental take statement when it has no
rational basis to conclude that a take will occur
incident to an otherwise lawful activity. Applying
this test, several of the FWS's incidental take statements were invalid because there was no evidence
that any listed species existed on the grazing allotments in question. Evidence that a parcel is capable
of supporting a protected species or that small numbers of species "likely" survived in the area was
insufficient to support an incidental take statement,
as was the mere potential for harm. The court also
held that one of the FWS's incidental take statements was invalid, even though endangered species
existed on an allotment to which cattle had access,
because the FWS failed to specify the amount of the
anticipated take or to provide a clear standard for
determining when the authorized take level had
been exceeded. The statement need not include a
numerical limit for the permissible amount of the
take, if it is not practical to provide one, and the
FWS may use ecological conditions linked to the
take of the protected species as a surrogate for
defining the amount of the incidental take. The
take statement in question was invalid, however,
because the description of the ecological conditions
that were to serve as a surrogate for the amount of
the incidental take was too vague.

See PNRL §§ 15C:19–15C:25.

C. THE NATIONAL WILDLIFE REFUGE SYSTEM

Although national wildlife refuges have been established by presidential proclamation and legislation throughout the 20th century, Congress did not enact a single law to govern refuge administration until it passed the National Wildlife Refuge System Administration Act (NWRSAA) of 1966, 16 U.S.C.A. §§ 668dd–668ee. The NWRSAA was designed to protect resident and migratory wildlife populations within the refuges. Some of the refuges that predate the Act, however, were established for grazing domestic livestock as well as wildlife protection. The Interior Secretary's effort in 1975 to transfer jurisdiction over three such units to the BLM was aborted by litigation and legislation. The NWRSAA now vests sole responsibility to administer all units of the refuge system in the FWS. The court in Trustees for Alaska v. Watt (D. Alaska 1981), prevented the Interior Secretary from transferring from the FWS to the U.S. Geological Survey the authority to conduct a study of the Arctic National Wildlife Refuge for the purpose of formulating mineral exploration guidelines.

The National Wildlife Refuge System Improvement Act of 1997, 16 U.S.C. §§ 668dd–668ee, establishes a hierarchy of wildlife refuge uses. All human use must be "compatible" and not "materially interfere with" the System mission or the refuge purpose. The Act divides uses into three tiers. Conservation of wildlife, plants, and habitat is the top tier; all uses must be compatible with wildlife conservation, which must be formally determined. The next highest priority is given to "wildlife dependent recreational uses," which specifically include hunting and fishing along with birdwatching, education, and so forth. These uses are entitled to "enhanced consideration." Inclusion of hunting and fishing as preferred uses ends the controversy over the appropriateness of those activities in refuges. "All other uses" have the lowest priority. These priorities are to be established and enforced through land use planning; no new uses may be allowed until specific compatibility findings are made.

Under the former compatibility standard, the court in New England Naturist Ass'n v. Larsen (D.R.I.1988), upheld the FWS' decision to close a small refuge to all human use to protect threatened species habitat. Another court barred a refuge land exchange on the basis of the damage to wildlife that would have ensued. National Audubon Soc'y v. Hodel (D. Alaska 1984).

Although the outer limits of agency discretion under the 1997 Act have yet to be determined, one court has rejected the contention that the exercise of the FWS's professional judgment is unreviewable. Wyoming v. United States (10th Cir.2002). According to the court, the Act limits FWS discretion by requiring it to develop a conservation plan for each refuge that complies with state policies and objectives to the "maximum extent practicable." The court held that the statute does not afford the FWS unlimited discretion to act in a manner that threatens the well-being of a neighboring state's livestock or game industry.

Special constraints on the discretion of the FWS to authorize "compatible uses" apply to recreational uses of refuges. The Refuge Recreation Act (RRA) of 1962, which was preserved by the NWRSAA, authorizes "appropriate incidental or secondary" recreational use only to the extent that it is "practicable and not inconsistent with ... the primary objectives" of the refuge. Further, the FWS must determine that non-wildlife-related recreational use "will not interfere with" primary refuge purposes. 16 U.S.C.A. § 460k. In Defenders of Wildlife v. Andrus (D.D.C.1978), the plaintiff challenged FWS regulations authorizing recreational boating in the Ruby Lake Refuge, the primary purpose of which was to provide breeding grounds and sanctuary for migratory birds. The court held that the Interior Secretary failed to satisfy his burden of proving that the permitted recreational uses were incidental to and compatible with, and would not interfere with, primary refuge purposes. The court also found that the RRA does not permit the Secretary to balance economic, political, or recreational interests against such purposes. Finally, the court refused to permit past recreational abuses and the consequent deterioration of wildlife resources in the refuge to water down the statutory standard. The same court later invalidated the regulations adopted on remand from the first *Ruby Lake* case because they authorized uses that still interfered with primary refuge purposes. Defenders of Wildlife v. Andrus (D.D.C.1978).

FWS efforts to restrict commercial recreational use of the refuges are likely to receive deferential judicial review. In Niobrara River Ranch, L.L.C. v. Huber (8th Cir.2004), for example, the court upheld the FWS's decision to impose a temporary moratorium on the issuance of licenses for commercial recreational outfitters pending development of a management study on the need to reduce river use.

See PNRL chapter 14A.

Before the NWRSIA, humaneist groups were unable to take advantage of the *Ruby Lake* precedents to bar hunting in the national wildlife refuges. Humane Soc'y v. Lujan (D.D.C.1991). The question was settled by Congress in the NWRSIA: hunting and fishing are preferred uses of refuges.

The NWRSAA bars the FWS from regulating fishing and hunting on lands adjacent to wildlife refuges unless endangered or threatened species are involved. FWS regulation of these activities must be consistent with state law unless the application of that law would be inconsistent with federal management goals. 16 U.S.C.A. § 668dd(c). Treaties protecting wildlife, such as the Migratory Bird Treaty Act (MBTA), and implementing statutes also constrain FWS discretion. The courts have disagreed on whether the MBTA's prohibition on the taking of protected migratory birds applies to federal agencies. Compare Sierra Club v. Martin (11th Cir.1997) (no), with Humane Soc'y of the United States v. Glickman (D.C. Cir.2000) (yes).

The NWRSIA contains a "savings clause," which states that the Act should not be construed as affecting the authority of the states to manage, control, or regulate fish and wildlife under state laws in any area within a national wildlife refuge. 16 U.S.C.A. § 668dd(m). The meaning of this provision was at issue in *Wyoming v. United States*, supra. The state sued the FWS to challenge its decision to block the state's proposal to vaccinate elk in a national refuge that was part of the NWRS to prevent the spread of brucellosis to domestic livestock. The Tenth Circuit held that sovereign immunity barred the state's claim that the FWS's decision was beyond the scope of its authority under the NWRSIA. The court interpreted the savings clause as indicating not that state wildlife policies could override federal prerogatives within a refuge, but instead as a statement that "ordinary principles of conflict preemption" would govern. The court held that the FWS's decision to refuse to permit vaccination of elk within the refuge based on concerns about the safety and efficacy of the program was not, by itself, beyond the FWS's statutory authority. Barring the FWS from making a decision it regarded as necessary to protect the health of wildlife within the refuge would prevent it from fulfilling its mission of consistently managing the refuges as "a national system." The court nevertheless remanded for a determination of whether the FWS's decision to block the state's vaccination program was arbitrary and capricious under the APA. See also National Audubon Soc'y v. Davis (9th Cir.2002) (agreeing with the court in *Wyoming* that the savings clause was not meant "to eviscerate the primacy of federal authority over NWR management" and holding that state law prohibiting federal agencies from using leghold traps was preempted by the NWRSIA).

See PNRL § 18:10.

D. WILDLIFE CONSERVATION AND MANAGEMENT ON OTHER FEDERAL LANDS

1. THE NATIONAL PARK SYSTEM

"Catch and release" fishing is permitted in many park system units, but commercial fishing is banned in maritime park areas designated as wilderness. Alaska Wildlife Alliance v. Jensen (9th Cir.1997). Hunting is not allowed in parks, absent special legislative authorization. The Alaska National Interest Lands Conservation Act (ANILCA), for example, designated several areas as preserves instead of parks so that hunting could continue. In Fund for Animals v. Mainella (D.D.C.2003), the court held that the NPS Organic Act did not bar the NPS from allowing a bear hunt authorized by New Jersey from taking place in a national recreation area where the area's enabling act permitted hunting. Because the Organic Act does not defer to state wildlife law, the Park Service is not constrained by that law. See New Mexico St. Game Comm'n v. Udall (10th Cir.1969). In National Rifle Ass'n v. Potter (D.D.C.1986), the court upheld a Park Service regulation that confined hunting and trapping to areas in which it was mandated by federal law. A ban on hunting on state-owned areas within the parks because of threats to park values has also been upheld. United States v. Brown (8th Cir.1977).

The Park Service's occasional practice of relying on off-park hunting to control park wildlife populations has generated controversy. In Fund for Animals, Inc. v. Lujan (9th Cir.1992), the court refused to enjoin implementation of a plan adopted by the Interior and Agriculture Departments and state wildlife officials to prevent transmission of brucellosis to Montana cattle; the plan authorized hunters to kill bison migrating out of Yellowstone National Park. The plaintiff conservation group failed to demonstrate either irreparable injury or a balance of hardships in its favor. Subsequent litigation over the Yellowstone bison herds resulted in orders upholding NPS Interim Plans for control of the beasts. Greater Yellowstone Coalition v. Babbitt (9th Cir. 1997); Intertribal Bison Coop. v. Babbitt (D. Mont. 1998) (Organic Act does not prohibit killing). See also Davis v. Latschar (D.C. Cir.2000) (upholding Park Service controlled deer harvest to prevent overbrowsing).

The reintroduction of wolves into Yellowstone has engendered considerable opposition from cattle and sheep ranchers on adjacent private land. The Interior Secretary designated the entire wolf population in Wyoming, Montana, and Idaho as "experimental, nonessential" under the ESA, thereby increasing the flexibility of the government in managing the species. Under the agency's plan, wolves outside designated recovery zones were subject to state management and control, and livestock operators would be permitted to kill depredating wolves on grazing allotments on both federal and private lands. After wolf populations increased, the animals would be delisted and revert to animal game status subject to state control. The Ninth and Tenth Circuits rejected challenges by ranchers to the wolf reintroduction, holding that an occasional wolf sighting does not amount to establishment of a population, a situation in which experimental populations of the same species are precluded. Wyoming Farm Bureau v. Babbitt (10th Cir.2000); McKittrick v. United States (9th Cir.1998).

See PNRL §§ 14:3; 18:14.

2. NATIONAL FOREST SYSTEM AND BLM LANDS

As a general matter, the states establish hunting seasons and conditions for Forest System and BLM-administered lands, while the federal agencies are responsible for habitat improvement. The Forest Service has always considered wildlife management and protection as one its principal responsibilities, and the Multiple–Use, Sustained–Yield Act requires that "due consideration" be given to fish and wildlife resources. 16 U.S.C.A. §§ 528–529. The Act disavows any intention to affect the "jurisdiction or responsibilities of the several States with respect to wildlife and fish in the national forests." Id. § 528.

Prior to the adoption of FLPMA, the BLM lacked explicit statutory authorization to manage wildlife, and state hunting and fishing laws governed activity on the public lands. Section 1732(a) of FLPMA now requires management in accordance with multiple use, sustained yield principles. Both the Forest Service and the BLM accordingly must balance wildlife protection with other uses to promote high yields of both commodity and noncommodity resources. Cf. Sierra Club–Black Hills Group v. United States Forest Serv. (10th Cir.2001) (interpreting statute creating wildlife preserve as imposing limits on Forest Service discretion under the NFMA to authorize timber sales).

Section 1732(b) of FLPMA, which applies to both the Forest Service and the BLM, indicates that the statute should not be interpreted as affecting the authority of the states to manage fish and resident wildlife. State regulations typically promote sport hunting and fishing, sometimes at the expense of non-game wildlife species. Section 1732(b) also authorizes the two multiple use agencies to designate areas in which no hunting or fishing will be permitted "for reasons of public safety, administration, or compliance with provisions of applicable law." The legislative history provides little definitive guidance on the scope of this authorization.

The meaning of section 1732(b) was at issue in the fifth *Alaska Wolf Kill* case, Defenders of Wildlife v. Andrus (D.C.Cir.1980). The Alaska Department of Fish and Game, without federal authorization, announced a program to shoot wolves from aircraft on federal lands for the ostensible purpose of increasing moose and caribou populations. After the Interior Department denied their request to prepare an EIS, environmental groups and individuals sued the Department. The district court ordered the agency to take all steps necessary to stop the wolf kills on federal lands pending preparation of an EIS. The appellate court reversed. As indicated in section 4E, the court held that NEPA requires that the federal government engage in an "overt act" before environmental assessment responsibilities apply. Because the Interior Department had not proposed to *do* anything, its failure to stop the state's wolf kill did not require it to prepare an EIS. Cf. Fund for Animals, Inc. v. Thomas (D.C. Cir. 1997) (concluding that Forest Service policy of deferring to states on whether to permit baiting of wild game animals on federal lands was not a major federal action and may not have been an action at all).

The district court had also concluded that, even if NEPA did not otherwise require an EIS in the circumstances, the agency's duty under FLPMA to manage federal lands and resources required it to prohibit major federal actions with significant environmental effects pending EIS preparation. The D.C. Circuit reasoned, however, that even though FLPMA imposed a general planning and management duty, the district court's decision interfered with Congress' allocation to the states of the primary responsibility for managing wildlife programs within their boundaries. Congress could have preempted state management of wildlife on the federal lands, but FLPMA section 1732(b) indicated that it chose not to do so. The statute's "cautious and limited permission to intervene in an area of state responsibility and authority" therefore did not support the conclusion that each state action which the Secretary fails to prevent thereby becomes a federal action for purposes of NEPA.

Had the court in the *Alaska Wolf Kill* case characterized the wolf kill program as habitat manipulation rather than sport hunting, it might have reached a different result. NEPA has been one of the principal bases for challenging resource development on the federal lands that threatens wildlife habitat, although in recent years the ESA has replaced NEPA as the weapon of choice of environmentalists opposed to such development. Courts have relied on the ESA to enjoin proposed dams, roads, and timber harvests, among other activities. Failure to abide by the procedures dictated by these two laws can abort projects with potential adverse effects on wildlife.

In Cabinet Mountains Wilderness v. Peterson (D.C.Cir.1982), the court rejected challenges to the Forest Service's approval of hardrock mining exploration activities in a wilderness area that supported grizzly bears, a threatened species under the ESA. Both the Forest Service and the FWS found that the proposal could adversely affect the bears, but the Forest Service issued a finding of no significant impact and did not prepare an EIS under NEPA. It relied on its adoption of a series of FWS recommendations for mitigating these adverse effects. The court concluded that if a proposal is modified before implementation by adding mitigation measures which compensate for possible adverse effects, the threshold requirement of significant environmental effects is not satisfied and the agency need not prepare an EIS. For essentially the same reasons, the court also held that the Forest Service's approval of exploration activities did not violate its duty under the ESA to avoid action that may jeopardize listed species or their habitat.

In Foundation for N. Am. Wild Sheep v. United States Dep't of Agric. (9th Cir.1982), on the other hand, the court overturned the Forest Service's decision not to draft an EIS when it issued a special use permit to reopen a mining access road through an area used by Desert Bighorn Sheep for lambing and rearing. The agency argued that closure of the road during the period of the year when the sheep used the area for these purposes would sufficiently mitigate the adverse environmental effects of use of the road. The court disagreed, finding that the agency ignored or gave inadequate attention to the anticipated volume of traffic on the road and the sheep's susceptibility to stress-related diseases. The court characterized as unreasonable the Forest Service's conclusion that mitigation would render the road's environmental impact insignificant because it was based on unsupported assumptions and insufficient analysis. Similarly, the court in National Audubon Soc'y v. Hoffman (2d Cir.1997) refused to allow the Forest Service to avoid preparation of an

EIS on road construction and logging operations based on proposed mitigation measures designed to prevent disruption of black bears because there was no assurance that the measures would be effective. Similar efforts to avoid NEPA analysis could prevent the Forest Service or the BLM from implementing individual proposals and broader policies relating to activities such as timber harvesting and grazing.

The federal government not only protects certain species on its lands, it kills others when they threaten human economic interests. The current main target of operations under the Animal Damage Control Act of 1931, 7 U.S.C.A. §§ 426–426b, is the wily, fecund coyote. In Southern Utah Wilderness Alliance v. Thompson (D. Utah 1993), the court upheld the Forest Service's Animal Damage Control program against a variety of challenges. It basically deferred to agency guesses based on rancher self-reporting to determine that a need for control existed. The land management agencies may derive additional authority to engage in predator control under other statutes. In Forest Guardians v. Animal & Plant Health Inspection Serv. (9th Cir.2002), for example, the court deferred to the Forest Service's discretion under the Wilderness Act to kill mountain lions to protect private livestock. The IBLA similarly has upheld predator control programs on a regular basis.

See PNRL §§ 18:17, 18:25–18:27.

3.   SUBSISTENCE USE OF WILDLIFE

The ANILCA affords priority to subsistence use of federal lands and resources, including wildlife, by rural Alaskans to protect and enhance their traditional lifestyle. Although ANILCA authorizes state regulation of subsistence uses of wildlife, the Alaska Supreme Court held that the state's subsistence laws violated the state constitution. McDowell v. Alaska (Alaska 1989). That ruling vested temporary responsibility for subsistence regulation in the FWS.

ANILCA defines subsistence use as "the customary and traditional uses by rural Alaskans of wild, renewable resources for direct personal or family consumption as food, shelter, fuel, clothing, tools, or transportation." 16 U.S.C.A. § 3113. Nonwasteful subsistence uses of fish and wildlife have priority on all public lands in Alaska over all other consumptive uses, unless it is necessary to restrict taking to insure viability of fish or wildlife populations or continued subsistence uses of those populations. ANILCA does not provide subsistence users with a property right in land, however, and subsistence uses must not conflict with conservation of natural and healthy fish and wildlife populations. Id. §§ 3125(1), 3112(1). The federal land management agencies must evaluate the effects of all major land use decisions except offshore oil and gas leasing on subsistence uses. The Ninth Circuit enjoined timber harvest operations because the Forest Service failed to comply with this obligation. City of Tenakee Springs v. Clough (9th Cir.1990). After Congress addressed the situation in the Tongass Timber Reform Act, the court dismissed the litigation. City of Tenakee Springs v. Franzel (9th Cir.1992).

See PNRL §§ 18:18–18:23.

CHAPTER TEN

THE RECREATION RESOURCE

Recreation is not typically viewed as a resource. Yet persons pursuing recreational opportunities impose the single greatest demand on the federal lands. Recreational use of public resources includes sightseeing, hiking, camping, swimming, rafting, off-road vehicle use, skiing, and hunting. Like the more conventional commodity resources such as water, minerals, timber, rangeland, and wildlife, recreation has generated important economic opportunities. Facilitating tourism is the biggest industry in some western states, and many small communities near the federal lands depend on tourism for their existence. Recreation in fact outstrips all commodity resources on the federal lands put together in value. See Laitos & Carr, *The Transformation on the Public Lands*, 26 Ecology L.Q. 140 (1999).

Like the more conventional resources, recreation often conflicts with both commodity and noncommodity resource uses. As a result, commodity resource users often oppose expanded recreational use of the federal lands. Because intensive recreation can degrade the environment, one form of recreation may preclude or diminish the ability to enjoy others. Thus, hikers in the Grand Canyon have long sought to restrict motorized access to the Canyon by air and water. Such conflicts are likely to become even more common as recreational use of the federal lands continues to increase.

Since 1960, Congress has tried in a variety of contexts to increase access to the federal lands for recreational purposes. The organic acts for the principal land management agencies elevate recreational use to a high priority. Recreation is a permissible use on all of the federal land systems, but its prominence differs by system. On one end of the spectrum, low intensity recreation is virtually the only permissible human use in wilderness areas. On the other end, recreation is but one of many legitimate multiple uses on the BLM public lands and in the national forests. Recreation is one of two dominant uses of the national park system and an important secondary use of the national wildlife refuges.

A. ACQUISITION OF RECREATIONAL LANDS

Of the various statutes authorizing the federal government to reacquire land that once was included in the public domain, some have little to do with recreational use of the federal lands. The Weeks Act of 1911, 16 U.S.C.A. § 515, for example, authorizes the Agriculture Secretary to purchase lands within the watersheds of navigable streams to enhance streamflow or timber production. FLPMA authorizes condemnation to secure access to the public lands. 43 U.S.C.A. § 1715(b). Other statutes authorize acquisition to promote recreation. The Refuge Recreation Act of 1962 vests in the Interior Secretary the power to acquire land suitable for fish and wildlife-oriented recreation. 16 U.S.C.A. § 460k–1.

The Land and Water Conservation Fund (LWCF) Act of 1965, 16 U.S.C.A. §§ 460*l*–4 to 460*l*–11, is by far the most important mechanism for adding to the federal recreational land base. The Act is financed by special taxes and earmarked receipts from activities such as offshore oil and gas leasing that are collected into the Fund. Despite a short-lived moratorium on new acquisitions imposed by Interior Secretary Watt in the 1980s and Congress' consistent failure to appropriate monies up to the authorized ceilings, the LWCF has financed the acquisition of approximately three million acres for addition to or expansion of federal land systems available for recreational pursuits. The states have bought an additional two million acres with LWCF grants.

The LWCF Act permitted the federal land management agencies to charge only nominal fees for recreational access to most federal lands. In 2004, however, Congress adopted the Federal Lands Recreation Enhancement Act (FLREA), 16 U.S.C.A. §§ 6801–6814, which repealed portions of the LWCF Act. The FLREA authorizes the agencies to charge fees for recreational use of the federal lands in certain circumstances. In establishing such fees, an agency must ensure that the amount of the fee is commensurate with the benefits and services provided to visitors. It also must consider the aggregate effects of recreation fees on recreation uses and recreation service providers, comparable fees charged elsewhere by nearby private sector operators, and the public policy or management objectives served by the fee. The FLREA distinguishes among four different kinds of recreation fees and establishes different conditions for each kind. Entrance fees are those charged to enter land managed by the NPS or the FWS. Standard amenity fees are those charged for recreational use of lands or waters under the jurisdiction of the BLM, the Forest Service, or the BoR. Additional expanded amenity recreation fees may be charged for use of specific facilities, equipment, or services listed in the statute. The agencies may charge special recreation permit fees for group activities and motorized recreational vehicle use.

The LWCF Act constrains Fund expenditures for both federal and state acquisitions. At least forty percent of Fund disbursements must be devoted to federal land purchases. Lands acquired for the national parks and forests must have value for outdoor recreation, and the Forest Service may not spend more than fifteen percent of its allotment west of the 100th meridian. Property acquired by the states with LWCF grants may not be converted to uses other than public outdoor recreation without the approval of the Secretary of the Interior. The Secretary may not provide such approval unless the proposed conversion is consistent with a statewide outdoor recreation plan. The Secretary also

312 THE RECREATION RESOURCE Ch. 10

must impose conditions on the conversion that are necessary to assure that the state substitutes other recreational property of equivalent value, usefulness, and location. Id. § 460*l*–8(f)(3).

The Secretary's failure to comply with these conditions thwarted a proposed resort development in Friends of Shawangunks, Inc. v. Clark (2d Cir. 1985). A New York–New Jersey interstate park commission used matching federal funds derived from the LWCF to purchase additional acres for a state park and a conservation easement over an adjacent lake. The lands subject to the easement included a nonoperating golf course. Several years later, a national hotel chain purchased some of the land burdened by the easement for the purpose of developing a resort with condominiums, ski facilities, and a golf course. The interstate agency decided to amend the conservation easement to allow the development to proceed. The district court ruled that the proposed development did not constitute a conversion subject to LWCF limitations because the public had no preexisting access to the lands subject to the easement. Accordingly, those lands were not being devoted to "public outdoor recreation uses." The Second Circuit reversed, holding that the statutory phrase encompassed uses not involving the public's actual physical presence on the property. By affording scenic vistas to the public and serving as a buffer zone between the park and developed areas, the burdened lands were providing outdoor recreation to the public. The court relied in part on the statutory objective of conservation, which includes protection of land in its natural state. It also held that amendment of the easement amounted to a conversion to uses other than public outdoor recreation because the proposed development would change both the character of the land protected by the easement and the population having access to it. By approving the amendment, the agency would convey away its right to prevent such changes. The court remanded to determine whether Secretarial approval was nevertheless appropriate.

The court in Sierra Club v. Davies (8th Cir.1992), upheld the Secretary's determination that another project was not a conversion subject to LWCF limitations. A LWCF grant to develop an Arkansas state park's recreational facilities enabled the public to search a diamond-bearing geological formation for minerals. The Interior Department concluded that a proposal to authorize test drilling to determine the feasibility of commercial diamond mining in the park was not a conversion for LWCF purposes because it was merely a temporary non-conforming use. Any subsequent testing or mining activity would require Secretarial approval. The Eighth Circuit deferred to the agency's reasoning because the drilling would not cause permanent damage to the character of the land and, with limited exceptions, would not preclude public access to the park.

See PNRL §§ 10C:42–10C:50, 17:2.1.

B. RECREATION AND THE NATIONAL PARK SYSTEM

For some visitors, the primary attraction of the national parks is the opportunity they provide for access to undisturbed natural beauty. For others, enjoyment of the parks is enhanced by, and may even depend on, the availability of amenities such as hotels, motorized transportation, and ski lifts. If the Park Service caters to the desires of one group, it may diminish the extent to which the other is able to enjoy park visitation. Conflicts between those who seek to minimize man-made intrusions on the often spectacular scenery found in the parks and those who support the provision of recreation-enhancing facilities have proliferated as national park visitation has increased.

The National Park Service Organic Act authorizes the Interior Secretary to foster present enjoyment as well as resource preservation. The Act directs the agency to "promote and regulate" park use in a manner that conforms to the fundamental purpose of the park system, which is "to conserve the scenery and the natural and historic objects and the wild life therein and to provide for the enjoyment of the same in such manner and by such means as will leave them unimpaired for the enjoyment of future generations." 16 U.S.C.A. § 1. Because promotion of park use must "conform to" the purpose of conservation of scenery, wildlife, and other natural objects, resource preservation arguably should trump recreation promotion in the event of an irreconcilable conflict. The mandate to

leave park resources unimpaired for future generations appears to reinforce this theoretical conclusion.

In practice, however, the courts have been loathe
to interfere with the Park Service's discretion in
balancing its duties to facilitate recreation and safeguard park resources. Attempts to overturn agency
efforts to limit recreational activities by commercial
enterprises have failed in most instances. See, e.g.,
Free Enterprise Canoe Renters Ass'n v. Watt (8th
Cir.1983). In Isle Royale Boaters Ass'n v. Norton
(6th Cir.2003), the court upheld a NPS management plan that removed docks for motor boats and
altered trail access and sheltering facilities at other
docks, concluding that the plan was consistent with
the agency's obligation to conserve scenery and
facilitate visitor enjoyment of scenery and wildlife.
The courts have afforded similar deference to the
decisions of the other land management agencies. In
Great Am. Houseboat Co. v. United States (9th
Cir.1986), the court held that a Forest Service regulation did not violate the equal protection clause by
banning commercial but not individual use of
houseboats on a recreational lake to avoid over-
crowding and degradation of the recreational experience.

Conversely, the Park Service has successfully defended recreational policies against the claim that
they were skewed in favor of for-profit concessionaires. In Wilderness Pub. Rights Fund v. Kleppe
(9th Cir.1979), the plaintiffs challenged the Park
Service's allocation of boating and rafting permits

on the Colorado River. By freezing usage at 1972 levels, the agency apportioned 92 percent of the permits to commercial concessionaires who operated guided trips through the Grand Canyon. Only eight percent of the permits were allotted to noncommercial users. The plaintiffs argued that the Park Service should have afforded these users with either a priority over or equal access with commercial users.

The court in *Wilderness Pub. Rights Fund* held that the NPS's allocation was not an arbitrary method of accommodating the interests of the prospective users. It rejected the plaintiffs' argument that the agency violated its statutory duty to grant permits for use of the parks on terms that do not interfere with "free access" by the public to park resources. 16 U.S.C.A. § 3. The court disagreed with the plaintiffs' characterization of the chosen allocation methodology. The dispute was not between recreational and commercial users of the river. Instead, NPS regulations created two categories of recreational users: those who had the skill and equipment to run the river on their own and those who needed professional help. The Park Service recognized its obligation to protect both classes of users. Agency regulations also reserved the right, however, to limit the number of permits issued if necessary to protect ecological and environmental values. Because the NPS concluded that limits on use were essential to protect the river, any attempt to protect the rights of all classes of users would necessarily entail limits on "free access" by some users. The Park Service erred neither in deciding to allocate use nor in its chosen allocation method.

In a few are instances, NPS decisions to authorize more intensive development for recreational purposes have been vulnerable to challenge. In Sierra Club v. Lujan (D.Ariz.1989), the court preliminarily enjoined a proposal to convert rustic cabins into more intrusive facilities on the North Rim of the Grand Canyon because plaintiffs made a sufficient showing that the decision not to prepare an EIS was arbitrary. The court found it likely that, instead of engaging in good faith compliance with NEPA, the Park Service used the EA it had issued to justify entering a concessions contract for construction of a hotel, that the agency did not fairly consider the no action option, and that it did not give sufficient weight to opposition to the project. Because the injunction was based on alleged noncompliance with NEPA procedures, it does not reflect substantive limitations on the discretion of the NPS to balance its recreation promoting and resource conservation mandates.

The Organic Act and the NPS Concessions Policy Act of 1965 authorized the Interior Secretary to contract for recreational services. The latter required that facility development by concessionaires be consistent "to the highest practicable degree" with park system preservation goals. 16 U.S.C.A. § 20. The Supreme Court has interpreted the discretion of the NPS to enter concession contracts broadly. See, e.g., Universal Interpretive Shuttle Corp. v. Washington MATC (S.Ct.1968). The 1965

Act was widely criticized for allowing preferential monopolies and failing to insure a fair return to the government.

Congress in 1998 thoroughly overhauled the system in the National Parks Omnibus Management Act, also known as the National Park Service Concessions Management Act (NPSCMA) of 1998, 16 U.S.C.A. §§ 5951–5983, which repealed the 1965 Act. The NPSCMA limits facility development to the extent "necessary and appropriate for public use," in a manner "consistent to the highest practicable degree with the preservation and conservation" of park values and resources. 16 U.S.C.A. § 5952(1). Concessionaire fees now remain at the park of origin; most preferences are outlawed and competition enhanced; and fair market value is now the standard, among other changes. In City of Sausalito v. O'Neill (9th Cir.2004), the court held that the NPS's plan to develop a former military base did not violate the mandate of the NPSCMA and its implementing regulations that development of visitor services be limited to locations that are consistent with preservation of park resources and values.

An association of concessionaires challenged the NPS's regulations implementing the NPSCMA in Amfac Resorts, L.L.C. v. United States Dep't of the Interior (D.C. Cir.2002). The court rejected the concessionaires' claim that the regulations violated the NPSCMA by allowing a preferential right of renewal only if contracts executed under the 1965 Act expressly so stated. The court upheld other provisions of the regulations, including the provision limiting a leasehold surrender interest to projects costing more than 50 percent of a structure's replacement costs. The D.C. Circuit also held that concession contracts are not service or procurement contracts within the meaning of the Contract Disputes Act, 41 U.S.C.A § 602, but the Supreme Court later held that this issue was not ripe for review. National Park Hospitality Ass'n v. United States Dep't of Interior (S.Ct.2003).

The Organic Act requires the agency to formulate general management plans that describe measures for preserving a unit's resources, the type and intensity of development associated with public use of the unit, commitments for visitor carrying capacities, and potential modifications to unit boundaries. 16 U.S.C.A. § 1a–7(b). Subsequent management actions apparently must be consistent with NPS master plans until the agency waives plan provisions.

Other statutes also may impose planning obligations on the NPS. In Sierra Club v. United States (N.D.Cal.1998), the NPS quickly came up with a plan to replace lodging facilities that had been damaged and destroyed by a flood at a different site nearby, which would require rerouting a road. The court ruled that NPS failure to promulgate a plan earlier as required by the Wild and Scenic Rivers Act gave no right to an injunction and that the WSRA does not prohibit roads in scenic river corridors. The court enjoined the new development, however, on NEPA grounds.

Technological developments have posed an interesting twist on the question of the extent to which the Park Service may authorize commercial use of the national parks. In Edmonds Inst. v. Babbitt (D.D.C.2000), the issue was whether the Park Service could enter a contract to permit bioprospecting of an enzyme found in a thermal pool in Yellowstone National Park. The district court upheld the agreement, denying that the use was "consumptive" in nature and finding it consistent with NPS authorizing legislation.

See PNRL §§ 14:3–14:4, 17:12–17:28.1.

C. NATIONAL RECREATION AREAS AND TRAILS

Opportunities for recreation on the federal lands extend beyond the traditional land system categories. Recently created National Conservation Areas and National Riparian Conservation Areas are meant to accommodate recreation in a manner consistent with resource preservation. Beginning in the 1970s, Congress lumped together excess federal parcels into urban recreation areas to facilitate access by city dwellers to NPS-managed lands, despite the criticism that maintenance of these new areas diverted resources from the traditional western parks and distorted the Park Service's primary preservation mission.

In 1968, Congress enacted the National Trails System Act (NTSA), 16 U.S.C.A. §§ 1241–1251, to "provide for the ever-increasing outdoor recreation needs of an expanding population." Only Congress can designate national scenic or historic trails such as the Appalachian and Lewis and Clark Trails. The land management agencies may create national recreation trails, which tend to be shorter, of local significance, and accessible to urban areas. The NTSA leaves most decisions concerning management and protection of the national trails to agency discretion, and the Act has generated little litigation beyond condemnation actions, with one exception.

That exception relates to the "rails-to-trails" program. The NTSA directs federal agencies to facilitate the conversion of unused railroad rights-of-way into state or locally managed hiking trails. Id. § 1247. Upon conversion, instead of reverting to abutting property owners, the right-of-way becomes a public easement of indefinite duration. In Preseault v. ICC (S.Ct.1990), the Supreme Court avoided deciding whether postponement of the date on which a reversionary interest takes effect as a result of conversion under section 1247 constitutes a compensable taking under the Fifth Amendment. The Court of Appeals for the Federal Circuit subsequently held that it did. Preseault v. United States (Fed. Cir.1996). The fate of a takings claim arising from a rails-to-trails conversion may depend on the nature of the interests conveyed to the railroad and retained by the government at the time of the initial grant to the railroad. See, e.g., Beres v. United States (Fed.Cl.2005). For further discussion, see section 3E(2), supra.

National Recreation Areas (NRAs) encompass a sizable amount of land, federal and nonfederal, for recreational use. The early NRAs were established around large reservoirs created by federally constructed dams such as the Hoover Dam on the lower Colorado River. By the early 1990s, Congress had extended this designation to nearly fifty areas. In the absence of an organic act for NRAs, management of each is governed by the statute that created it. Generally, these statutes create a management standard that resembles the "dominant but not exclusive use" idea reflected in the compatibility test applicable to the national wildlife refuges. See Chapter 9. Section 7 of the Hells Canyon National Recreation Area (HCNRA) Act, for example, directs the Interior Secretary to administer the area in a manner compatible with protection of the rivers within the area, conservation of scenic and wilderness values, preservation of biologically unique features, and maintenance of fish and wildlife habitat. 16 U.S.C.A. § 460gg–4.

Despite the vagueness of the standards that typically apply to management of the NRAs, blatant noncompliance with statutory directives may result in judicial disruption of agency proposals. In Oregon Natural Resources Council v. Lyng (9th Cir.1989), environmental groups sued to enjoin a Forest Service timber sale in the HCNRA. They claimed that the sale of dead and threatened trees in a beetle-infested area violated the statutory requirement that timber sales be limited to areas where harvesting was occurring when the NRA was created. The court held that this limitation applied only to sales that took place before issuance of a comprehensive management plan; the sale at issue occurred four years after the Forest Service promulgated a plan. The plaintiffs also argued that no sales could take place until the Agriculture Secretary issued regulations governing the timing, location, and manner of harvesting. The court agreed, concluding that the statute created a mandatory duty to issue regulations to govern timber harvesting by selective cutting. The court directed the lower court to consider enjoining any portion of the sale that was not already completed.

See PNRL §§ 17:41–17:49.

D. RECREATION ON OTHER FEDERAL LANDS

Recreation on lands administered by the BLM and the Forest Service is subject to the multiple use mandate applicable to those agencies. The source of that mandate for the BLM public lands is FLPMA, while recreation is one of the uses authorized in the national forests pursuant to the MUSYA and the NFMA. Some particular activities, such as skiing, are governed by more specific statutory mandates. For years, the Forest Service authorized recreation concessions for downhill skiing under a dual permit system derived from the agency's authority under the 1897 Organic Act and a 1915 law that authorized the agency to issue permits for recreational facilities. The 1915 statute limited permits to eighty-acre tracts and thirty-year terms, and forbade any permittee from interfering with public enjoyment of the forests. The courts upheld issuance of base eighty-acre permits for the ski lodge and related facilities, and revocable permits under the 1897 Act for the larger adjacent area needed for skiing. Wilson v. Block (D.C. Cir.1983).

Despite these endorsements of the status quo, the ski industry's concern over the revocable nature of the 1897 Act permits prompted Congress to adopt the National Forest Ski Area Act (NFSAA) of 1986. 16 U.S.C.A. § 497b. The Act authorizes the Agriculture Secretary to conform pre–1986 permits to the terms of the NFSAA, but only with the permittee's consent. Conversion provides the permittee with the opportunity to contract for larger tracts and longer, renewable terms than those available under the old system. The NFSAA, however, also vests in the Secretary the power to cancel permits, without compensation, for a variety of reasons, including a determination during planning that the area is needed "for higher public purposes." The Secretary also may modify permits to reflect changed circumstances and impose reasonable terms and conditions and charge a fair market value fee to permittees. Thus, permittees face a difficult choice under the NFSAA: on the one hand, conversion is likely to result in increased regulation and expense, and may result in permit cancellation. On the other hand, failure to convert leaves ski operators with a secure, eighty-acre base permit but only a revocable permit for the bulk of the skiing operation.

Forest Service that corresponds to the NPSCMA, Forest Service permitting and regulation of other commercial recreational facilities are governed by the 1897 and 1915 Acts. Generally, the agency will issue a permit only to proposed uses that fulfill a public need and do not serve a function that can logically be provided on private lands. The extent of the Forest Service's authority to transfer long-term or permanent interests in national forest land to private developers is unsettled, as is the definition of the "property rights" afforded by Forest Service permits to commercial recreation facilities. In United States v. Patzer (10th Cir.1993), the court upheld the FS permit scheme against vagueness challenges. Cf. United States v. Albers (9th Cir.2000) (holding that NPS regulations forbidding parachute "BASE" jumping were not overly vague).

Permits authorizing enjoyment of private cabins, docks, boats, and similar facilities in the national forests apparently create no vested property rights. In *Great Am. Houseboat*, supra, the Ninth Circuit endorsed a change in permit conditions that effectively precluded a time-share operator from using Lake Shasta. In Paulina Lake Historic Cabin Owners Ass'n v. United States Dep't of Agric. (D.Or. 1983), the Forest Service successfully defended its right to take title to and possession of a lodge and cabin after expiration of the permit term. Cf. King v. United States (10th Cir.2002) (treating a Forest Service special use permit as a contract). Other agencies enjoy similarly broad authority.

Attempts by the land management agencies to restrict recreational pursuits involving the expression of ideas or the exercise of religion may invoke heightened judicial scrutiny. See, e.g., United States v. True (9th Cir.1991). The countervailing interests at stake are demonstrated by United States v. Rainbow Family (E.D.Tex.1988). In the first decision, the court declared that regulation of expressive activity on the federal lands (in this case, the national forests) must be "narrowly tailored as to time, place and manner, and serve substantial governmental interests, as well as leave open ample alternative channels of communication." The court struck down Forest Service regulations requiring a special use permit for gatherings such as the one planned by the Rainbow Family, a loose-knit group of persons who met annually to discuss politics and ecology and to worship. The regulations afforded too much discretion to the agency to deny a permit without explanation. In the second case, however, the court acknowledged that the government may seek judicial assistance in preventing irreparable harm or creation of a public nuisance when it promotes a genuine interest such as preserving the public health or safety. Based on the agency's evidence that a past Family gathering had caused outbreaks of bacterial infection, the court required the Family to comply with sanitary standards and site rehabilitation requirements.

Efforts by Native Americans to invoke constitutional protection for their use of the federal lands for religious purposes have not succeeded in court.

In Lyng v. Northwest Indian Cemetery Protective Ass'n (S.Ct.1988), the Supreme Court held that the free exercise clause of the First Amendment did not preclude road construction and timber harvesting in a portion of a national forest the tribes traditionally used for religious purposes. The Court noted that the Indians could continue to visit the affected area, even though it conceded that the activities challenged could have a negative effect on traditional religious practices. It indicated that the result might have been different if the government had precluded access to the area by the tribes. In the same year, the Eighth Circuit upheld the Forest Service's denial of a special use permit to a Native American group that sought to erect a camp with permanent structures in the Black Hills National Forest. United States v. Means (8th Cir.1988). A 1996 Executive Order instructs federal agencies to accommodate sacred site access and use "to the extent practicable."

See PNRL §§ 17:2, 17:29–17:33.

E. OFF–ROAD VEHICLE REGULATION

Americans have a right in the nature of a license to use the federal lands for recreation, but that right is revocable by Congress or a land management agency properly exercising its statutory discretion. See PNRL § 17.02. Both the legislature and the agencies are reluctant to impose limits on public recreation, except where off-road vehicles (ORVs) are involved. ORVs such as snowmobiles, dune buggies, jeeps, and motorcycles have caused considerable damage to all types of ecosystems, from the California deserts to the Alaskan tundra. ORV use on the federal lands sometimes provokes the opposition of commercial users such as ranchers. But conflicts between ORV users and nonmotorized recreational users, deprived of the solitude they seek by the noise of internal combustion engines, are far more common.

1.   ORV USE ON THE BLM PUBLIC LANDS

Executive Order No. 11644, issued by President Nixon in 1972, imposed the first significant restrictions on ORVs on the federal lands. The Order directed the land management agencies to justify opening an area to ORV use, but BLM regulations diluted the Order's protections by leaving areas open unless specifically closed. In NWF v. Morton (D.D.C.1975), the court remanded the regulations to the BLM on the ground that they authorized consideration of factors not included in the Order and failed to mandate appropriate evaluation of environmental impact. Although the BLM issued regulations on remand that closely tracked the criteria for ORV use contained in the Executive Order, inadequate enforcement resources prevented the agency from imposing significant restrictions on ORV use.

The controversy over ORV use on the BLM lands came to a head in the California Desert Conservation Area (CDCA). When it created the CDCA out of BLM desert areas in section 1781 of FLPMA, Congress directed the BLM to formulate a multiple use, sustained yield management plan for the area. Describing resources in the CDCA as "extremely fragile, easily scarred, and slowly healed," Congress nevertheless specified that the area should be available for outdoor recreational uses, "including the use, where appropriate, of [ORVs]." In American Motorcyclist Ass'n v. Watt (C.D.Cal.1982), environmentalists convinced the court to enjoin the BLM from approving ORV use until it revised the CDCA plan. The court found that the plan criteria for selecting approved routes for ORV travel were inconsistent with the BLM's general ORV regulations. The regulations required the agency to minimize environmental damage, harassment of wildlife, and conflicts between ORV and other recreational uses, but the plan authorized ORV use as long as the selected route would not cause considerable adverse impact. By focusing solely on the latter inquiry, the plan criteria improperly skewed route designation decisions in favor of ORV use.

The CDCA management plan opened the Dove Springs Canyon to ORV use without restriction. After unsuccessful pursuit of administrative remedies, the Sierra Club sought an injunction compelling closure. It argued that continued ORV use violated Executive Order No. 11644, BLM regulations, and FLPMA. The Ninth Circuit in Sierra Club v. Clark (9th Cir.1985), agreed that the plan's designation of part of the CDCA as open for ORV use did not render the BLM's general ORV regulations inapplicable. Those regulations required closure upon a finding that ORVs were causing "considerable adverse effects." The court deferred to the BLM's view that this test required consideration of adverse effects in the context of the entire 12 million-acre CDCA rather than on a parcel-by-parcel basis, and to its finding that the effects in the Canyon did not require closure. Although the court preferred the Sierra Club's interpretation, "which would disallow the virtual sacrifice of a priceless natural area in order to accommodate a special recreational activity," that view conflicted with congressional intent. Given the considerable adverse effects necessarily attributable to unrestricted ORV use, the Club's interpretation would inevitably result in the total prohibition of ORV use. That result would clash with the FLPMA directive to provide for ORV use "where appropriate." 43 U.S.C.A. § 1781(a)(4). The court gave short shrift to other provisions of the statute, which required that multiple use management not result in "permanent impairment of productivity of the land and the quality of the environment," id. § 1702(c), and that the agency prevent "unnecessary and undue degradation" of the public lands. Id. § 1732(b). The same court also upheld the BLM's decision to permit an annual ORV race along a 110–mile route from Barstow to Las Vegas. Sierra Club v. Clark (9th Cir. 1985).

The ORV cases indicate that the BLM has broad discretion to open or close portions of the CDCA to ORV use, provided it complies with regulatory and CDCA plan provisions. Opponents of ORV use in the CDCA increase their chances of minimizing the adverse effects of such use by participating in plan promulgation and amendment.

See PNRL § § 17:8–17:9.

2. ORV USE ON OTHER FEDERAL LAND SYSTEMS

The extent of permissible ORV use varies by federal land system. Wilderness areas by definition are roadless, see section 11D, but the agency responsible for managing such areas may authorize ORV use if it retains sufficient control to avoid permanent damage. Voyageurs Region Nat'l Park Ass'n v. Lujan (8th Cir.1992) (concerning snowmobiles). The court in Northwest Motorcycle Ass'n v. United States Dep't of Agric. (9th Cir.1994), addressed the question whether the Forest Service could create a buffer zone by barring ORVs in a portion of Wenatchee National Forest adjacent to a designated wilderness area. Despite a statutory provision prohibiting the creation of protective perimeters around wilderness areas in Washington, the court upheld the ban. It reasoned that the Forest Service could consider the wilderness classification of the adjacent land as a factor in determining whether to permit ORV use, provided it did not ban this type of recreation solely because of its potential adverse impact on wilderness. Motorized recreation in the national wildlife refuges is disfavored. Unless the FWS finds that ORV use is compatible with wildlife welfare, it is prohibited. Cf. Defenders of Wildlife v. Andrus (D.D.C.1978) (powerboats).

The National Park Service routinely restricts all kinds of vehicle use; motorized access to portions of some of the parks, for example, is restricted to shuttle buses. The courts have adopted a deferential review posture toward NPS decisions on the permissible extent of ORV use. In Conservation Law Found. of New England, Inc. v. Secretary of the Interior (1st Cir.1989), environmentalists challenged the provisions of the management plan for the Cape Cod National Seashore that authorized ORV use along sixteen percent of the beach. The court held that the plan violated neither the Seashore enabling legislation nor Executive Order No. 11644. It deferred to the agency's conclusions that ORV use would not be incompatible with preservation of seashore resources and was an "appropriate" public use, even though the statute did not include ORV use in its list of authorized recreational pursuits. According to the court, the statute did not require the NPS to prohibit any development that would alter the scenery from the condition that existed at the time the area was designated as a national seashore. Similarly, the court deferred to the agency's finding that ORV use that complied with the restrictions set forth in the plan would not adversely affect natural, aesthetic, or scenic values, and therefore that it was consistent with the Executive Order. The court brushed aside the plaintiff's contention that violations of these restrictions were widespread. See also Southern Utah Wilderness Alliance v. National Park Serv. (D. Utah 2005) (upholding NPS ban on motorized access to portions of Canyonlands National Park).

Another case in which recreational and preservational interests clashed over ORV use in the national parks was Southern Utah Wilderness Alliance v. Dabney (10th Cir.2000). The NPS adopted a backcountry management plan for a national park and a national recreation area. The plan allowed ORV use in some areas but not others, depending on the fragility and uniqueness of the natural resources found there. The district court held that, although the plan did not violate Executive Order 11644, it violated the Park Service Organic Act to the extent that it allowed ORV use in areas in which it would permanently impair unique park resources. On appeal, the Tenth Circuit agreed that the Organic Act allows the NPS to balance the potentially conflicting policies of resource conservation and visitor enjoyment in determining whether to allow ORV use. It remanded back to the district court, however, because the lower court had not acknowledged the continuing dispute among the parties over the level of impairment that ORV use would cause. The appellate court directed the lower court to assess whether ORV use would be temporary and minor, as claimed by the NPS, or would amount to the kind of significant, permanent impairment prohibited by the Act.

While the *Dabney* case was pending before the Tenth Circuit, the NPS adopted a new policy that interpreted the Organic Act's requirement that it manage park resources in a manner that leaves them unimpaired for future generations, 16 U.S.C.A. § 1. The policy defined "impairment" as an impact that, in the judgment of the NPS, "would harm the integrity of the park resources or values, including the opportunities that otherwise would be present for the enjoyment of those resources or values." Relying on the new policy, the NPS prohibited ORVs in parts of Canyonlands National Park. Motor vehicle user groups sued, contending that the prohibition violated the Organic Act by depriving the public of the ability to use and enjoy significant portions of the park. The court deferred to the NPS's new definition of impairment, rejecting the argument that the Organic Act requires that the agency equally balance preservation with public use in making management decisions. It found that the overriding purpose of the Act is resource preservation. The court also held that the NPS's decision to close certain areas to motorized access to prevent impairment of a wetlands ecosystem was within the agency's broad discretion. Finally, it held that the agency did not fail to consider the impact on park resources if closure to motor vehicles resulted in an increase in hiking and backpacking. *Southern Utah Wilderness Alliance v. National Park Serv.*, supra.

The use of snowmobiles in the national parks has generated both controversy and litigation. In Mausolf v. Babbitt (8th Cir.1997), the court deferred to the Park Service's decision to ban the use of snowmobiles in a park to avoid adverse effects on wolves listed as threatened under the ESA. But cf. Voyageurs Nat'l Park Ass'n v. Norton (8th Cir.2004) (holding that decision not to renew the same ban was not an abuse of discretion). The controversy over whether to allow snowmobiles in the national parks heated up when, at the end of the Clinton Administration, the NPS issued regulations phasing out the use of snowmobiles in Yellowstone and Grand Teton National Parks. Two years later, the agency decided to allow snowmobiles in the two Parks, subject to restrictions. When environmental groups challenged the new policy, a federal district court vacated and remanded the latest version of the rules, characterizing the NPS's 180 degree reversal of position as "quintessentially arbitrary and capricious." Fund for Animals v. Norton (D.D.C. 2003). The court rejected the agency's argument that the development of cleaner, quieter engines and the requirement that snowmobilers be accompanied by guides justified the reversal, pointing out that, in issuing the earlier regulations, the NPS had taken into account the new engines and that the NPS itself acknowledged that the guide system was flawed.

Before the second set of regulations went into effect, a coalition of snowmobile manufacturers and businesses dependent on tourism in the two parks challenged the earlier ban. A different district court vacated the regulations on the ground that they had been adopted in violation of NEPA and the APA. International Snowmobile Mfrs. Ass'n v. Norton (D. Wyo.2004). The court found that the NPS failed to assess adequately the impacts on noise and air pollution of the snowcoaches that would replace snowmobiles, failed to engage in good faith cooperation with affected states, inadequately considered public comments, and made a "prejudged" or "predetermined" political decision. The Wyoming district court found the ban to be a radical and unexplained departure from the NPS's previous approach of allowing snowmobile use. Even though the court concluded that the NPS properly interpreted the Organic Act to subjugate visitor enjoyment to the agency's conservation obligation, and that its decision to allow visitor access in the winter only through snowcoaches was within its discretion, it attacked the ban as a "wrongheaded decision, based on poor judgment." The NPS eventually issued new regulations on snowmobile use that were very similar to the ones remanded in the *Fund for Animals* case.

The appropriate location and extent of ORV use in the national forests is governed largely by unit-by-unit ORV plans. Forest Service regulations limit restrictions and closures on ORV use to measures of last resort, but authorize those constraints if ORV use will cause considerable adverse effects on forest resources or visitors. In *Northwest Motorcycle Ass'n*, supra, the Forest Service banned ORV use in part of the Wenatchee National Forest to avoid a "user conflict" between ORV users and non-motorized recreational users. The court deferred to the agency's justification for the ban, refusing to second-guess its finding that the conflict existed. Accordingly, both of the multiple use agencies have the power to determine the extent of ORV use within relatively broad statutory constraints.

See PNRL §§ 14:3, 17:3–17:7, 17:10.

F. FEDERAL LIABILITY FOR RECREATIONAL MISHAPS

By enacting the Federal Tort Claims Act (FTCA) in 1946, the federal government waived its sovereign immunity to liability for torts committed by its agents. Specific statutes may preserve immunity in particular circumstances, however. See, e.g., Flood Control Act, 33 U.S.C.A. § 702c (immunizing the United States from liability for damages from floods); Central Green Co. v. United States (S.Ct. 2001). Most asserted tort claims against the United States in public land law arise out of recreational accidents. The government is liable "under circumstances where the United States, if a private person, would be liable to the claimant" for such damage, loss, injury, or death "in accordance with the law of the place where the allegedly tortious act or omission occurred." 28 U.S.C.A. § 1346(b). The FTCA allows recovery only for negligent torts; strict liability and intentional tort claims are precluded. Of the many statutory exceptions to liability, two are particularly relevant to public natural resources law. First, the FTCA incorporates state defenses such as those created by recreational land use statutes. Second, the United States is not liable in tort for the discretionary decisions of its employees. These defenses are sufficiently broad that the government escapes liability in most instances.

Most states have enacted legislation exempting landowners from tort liability to persons allowed to enter the land without fee for recreational purposes, unless the landowner willfully or maliciously fails to guard against a known hazard. These state statutes have prevented recovery against the United States in a plethora of cases. Otteson v. United States (10th Cir.1980), is typical. The plaintiff's decedent was killed in a jeep accident on a Forest Service logging road. The estate argued that the Colorado recreational use statute did not apply because the government, unlike a private landowner, has a duty to open its land to the public for recreational purposes. Because the purpose of the statutory defense is to encourage private landowners to open their land for public recreational use, the plaintiff argued that the defense should not apply to the United States. The court disagreed, relying on United States v. New Mexico (S.Ct.1978), in asserting that recreation is but a "secondary and supplemental purpose" of the national forests.

The state recreational use statutes authorize recovery if the landowner charges a fee for recreational use. At least before the enactment of the FLREA in 2004, most federal land management agencies did not charge admission or user fees. But the Park Service did, and it was therefore not shielded by the exception. Most courts read the fee exception narrowly, requiring that the agency charge for entry or for the activity that resulted in the injury. See, e.g.,

Hardy v. Loon Mountain Recreation Corp. (1st Cir. 2002). The Ninth Circuit, however, has read the fee exception liberally. E.g., Thompson v. United States (9th Cir.1979) (holding that entry fee paid to the sponsor of a motorcycle race on the BLM lands amounted to sufficient "consideration" to vitiate the government's recreational use defense).

The court stretched the meaning of "consideration" to (and probably beyond) the limit in Ducey v. United States (9th Cir.1983). Plaintiff's decedents were killed during a flash flood in a national recreational area. The NPS charged no admission or use fee, but the marina concessionaire, which charged for food, boat slips, and trailer spaces, paid a percentage of its gross income to the government. The court held that the concession agreement implicitly obligated the United States to allow recreational access. As a result, payments to the concessionaire constituted fees for permission to enter. The court also ruled that because the concessionaire was an independent contractor, the government was not liable for its actions under the FTCA.

A plaintiff in a negligence action under the FTCA generally must demonstrate that the government breached a duty whose breach by a private party would have created liability under state law. The FTCA has generated interesting federalism issues, however, that sometimes alter this principle. In Bilderback v. United States (D.Or.1982), for example, the plaintiffs were injured when their car hit a Forest Service pack horse. Under the law of Oregon, where the mishap occurred, livestock may roam at large on open range without liability. The court refused to permit the government to take advantage of this state law defense. It ruled that federal laws governing livestock grazing preempted the state rule on federal lands. Further, the applicable standard of care was derived from federal livestock law rather than state law.

Despite the adoption of the FTCA, the United States remains immune from suit on claims based on a government employee's exercise of or failure to perform a discretionary function. 28 U.S.C.A. § 2680(a). This exception may apply even in suits authorized under other statutes. See, e.g., McMellon v. United States (4th Cir.2004) (Suits in Admiralty Act). The discretionary function exception shields conduct that was not prescribed by statute, regulation, or policy, and that was based on considerations of social, economic, or political policy. United States v. Gaubert (S.Ct.1991). The second part of this test focuses not on the subjective intent of the agency, but on whether the actions taken are susceptible to policy analysis. Elder v. United States (10th Cir. 2002). Discretionary conduct is not confined to the policy or planning level. The exception therefore covers some fairly low-level decisions.

In the rare discretionary function cases that do not involve recreational use of the federal lands, the government has generally prevailed. See, e.g., OSI, Inc. v. United States (11th Cir.2002) (suit for lost property values caused by landfill contamination); Kelly v. United States (9th Cir.2001) (plane crash during mission to drop fire retardant); Barton v.

United States (10th Cir.1979) (government pesticide spraying injured plaintiff's cattle).

Most of the cases involve public recreation. Johnson v. United States (10th Cir.1991), is representative of the decisions that interpret the exception broadly. The court held that the National Park Service's decisions concerning the appropriate extent of regulation of mountain climbing in Grand Teton National Park involved discretion because, in the absence of controlling statutes or regulations, they involved the exercise of judgment or choice. The decisions implicated policy concerns because they required the agency to balance competing considerations related to visitor safety, resource availability, and the appropriate degree of governmental interference in recreational activity. The plaintiff could not pursue claims relating to the manner in which the Park Service conducted rescue operations for basically the same reasons.

Occasionally, the courts have construed the discretionary function exception narrowly. In Summers v. United States (9th Cir.1990), for instance, the court concluded that the Park Service's failure to warn of the dangers to barefoot visitors posed by hot coals in a fire ring was not protected by the discretionary function exception. The decision involved a departure from safety considerations under an established policy rather than the balancing of competing policy concerns.

It is sometimes difficult to reconcile discretionary function exception precedents, particularly involving application of the second part of the *Gaubert* test. Nevertheless, some courts have generalized about the applicability of the discretionary function exception. According to one court, the government is likely to be immune from suit when its decisions (such as a decision not to repair) result from priority-setting demanded by the need to allocate scarce resources. See Mitchell v. United States (3d Cir. 2000). One case stated that three types of decisions tend to be shielded from tort liability under the exception: (1) the proper response to hazards; (2) whether and how to make federal lands safe for visitors; and (3) whether to warn of potential danger. Edwards v. TVA (6th Cir.2001). See also Sharp ex rel. Estate of Sharp v. United States (6th Cir. 2005) (proper response to hazards involves balancing of interests); Oberson v. United States (D. Mont.2004) (design decisions are typically immune from review). Yet another court stated that while decisions regarding the design of government action are likely to be protected by the exception, decisions regarding implementation are not. Ambros–Marcial v. United States (D. Ariz.2005). The exception is not likely to shield the government from liability for decisions to forego routine maintenance based on fiscal reasons. O'Toole v. United States (9th Cir. 2002).

See PNRL §§ 10:4–10:7.

CHAPTER ELEVEN

THE PRESERVATION RESOURCE

"Preservation" is not only a philosophy of public land management that opposes nonrenewable consumptive use of valuable resources on moral as well as utilitarian grounds, it is also a resource unto itself. The feature of exclusivity that characterizes the traditional commodity resources also applies to limited use or non-use of a land area. Congress has adopted statutes, such as the Endangered Species Act discussed in section 9B above, that are designed to preserve selected public resources through regulation of agency and private conduct that may adversely affect the preservation target. Section A of this chapter describes another such law, the Archaeological Resources Protection Act of 1979.

Federal preservation initiatives are usually accomplished through land withdrawal or reservation, two processes described in section 4B above. In the nineteenth century, Congress first mandated federal land and resource preservation by reserving historic battlegrounds such as Gettysburg and national parks such as Yellowstone and Yosemite. The National Park Service Organic Act of 1916 recognized preservation, along with recreation, as the predominant purposes of that federal land system. Section B

343

of this chapter analyzes the authority of the Park Service, as well as the other land management agencies, to abate threats to the integrity of federal lands managed primarily for these purposes that are attributable to activities on adjacent private land and lands administered by other agencies.

Congress has created several federal lands designations whose purpose is primarily preservational. The Wild and Scenic Rivers Act, discussed in section C below, created a system for designating and preserving free-flowing rivers that possess outstanding scenic, recreational, geologic, fish and wildlife, historic, cultural, or similar values. The Wilderness Act of 1964 established a new land system in which preservation is the raison d'etre. The Act, which is the focus of section D of this chapter, defines wilderness as "an area where the earth and its community of life are untrammeled by man, where man himself is a visitor who does not remain." 16 U.S.C.A. § 1131(c). The Act seeks to preclude the intrusion of a permanent human presence into these areas.

The legal tools for preserving federal lands and resources raise a host of intractable questions, many of which are merely touched upon in this chapter. One recurring issue is whether natural resource preservation necessarily entails economic sacrifice. Another is whether the rationale for resource preservation is limited to ecological concerns, or whether anthropocentric considerations should also play a role. Such philosophical issues have shaped past and are likely to affect future decisions concerning the identification of public resources suitable for preservation and the selection of appropriate management techniques for such resources.

A. PRESERVATION OF ARCHAEO-LOGICAL AND HISTORICAL ARTIFACTS

A primary goal of the 1906 Antiquities Act, 16 U.S.C.A. §§ 431–433, was the preservation of ancient Indian ruins and artifacts. In addition to authorizing the withdrawal and reservation as national monuments of lands containing objects of historic, scientific, or scenic significance, the Act prohibits the appropriation, destruction, or excavation of historic or prehistoric ruins or "objects of antiquity" on federal lands without a permit. The *Black Hills* litigation demonstrates that the statute applies well beyond the context of Indian ruins and artifacts. After the United States seized the fossilized remains of a Tyrannosaurus Rex found on an Indian allotment on federal land, the company that had purchased from the allottee the rights to the remains sued to regain custody. The Eighth Circuit held that, even though the fossil is now personal property, it was an "interest in land" at the time of sale for purposes of the Antiquities Act. Accordingly, the sale was void absent the Interior Secretary's approval, which was neither sought nor provided. Black Hills Inst. v. South Dakota School of Mines and Technology (8th Cir.1993).

The effectiveness of the Antiquities Act was hampered by insufficient penalties for violations and by an appellate court holding that the statute was void for vagueness. United States v. Diaz (9th Cir.1974). Fears that the 1906 Act was not adequately protecting archaeological resources on federal lands prompted Congress to enact the Archaeological Resources Protection Act (ARPA) of 1979, 16 U.S.C.A. §§ 470aa–470*ll*. The Ninth Circuit rejected claims that ARPA was unconstitutionally broad and void for vagueness in United States v. Austin (9th Cir. 1990). The criminal defendant's contention that the statutory prohibitions interfered with his "academic freedom" because he was motivated by curiosity in excavating a Native American archaeological site failed to convince the court, particularly because he lacked any affiliation with an academic institution. The statute was not void as applied because Austin had fair notice that the artifacts he unearthed were covered by the Act.

ARPA prohibits any person from excavating, removing, damaging, altering, or defacing archaeological resources located on public or Indian lands, or attempting to engage in any of these activities, without a permit. According to one court, the government need not prove that a defendant charged with violating this prohibition knew he or she was violating the law, but it must show that the defendant knew or had reason to know that the resource at issue was an archaeological resource as defined by ARPA. United States v. Lynch (9th Cir.2000). See also United States v. Quarrell (10th Cir.2002) (government need not prove that defendant knew he or she was excavating on federal land). Public lands are those owned in fee by the United States, except lands on the outer continental shelf. Archaeological resources include "any material remains of past human life or activities which are of archaeological interest" that are at least 100 years old, excluding arrowheads and fossils not found in an archaeological context. 16 U.S.C.A. §§ 470bb(1), 470ee(g). See Bonnichsen v. United States (9th Cir. 2004) (holding that the 8000–9000 year-old remains of the "Kennewick Man" qualified as an archaeological resource). The statute does not apply to resources lawfully possessed before adoption of ARPA. By exempting less than century old artifacts from its definition of "archaeological resource," Congress did not intend to divest itself of title to such resources on federal land. United States v. Shivers (5th Cir.1996). The coins at issue in *Shivers* were owned by the government because they were embedded in the soil pursuant to the law of finds.

Correcting a deficiency in the Antiquities Act, ARPA also bars the sale, purchase, exchange, transportation, or receipt of resources obtained in violation of the Act or of other federal, state, or local laws. In United States v. Gerber (7th Cir.1993), the court ruled that this prohibition covered violation of an Indiana statute that forbade trespass and conversion on private as well as federal or Indian lands.

Permits from federal land managers to excavate archaeological resources on federal or Indian lands are available only if the applicant is qualified, the activity is designed to further knowledge in the public interest and is consistent with land use plans, and the United States will retain ownership of located artifacts. ARPA disclaims any intention to repeal, modify, or impose additional restrictions on activities permitted under laws relating to mining, mineral leasing, and other multiple uses of the public lands. 16 U.S.C.A. § 470kk. Although the meaning of this provision is not entirely clear, it neither imposes liability for the unintentional effects of permitted activities on archaeological resources, see Attakai v. United States (D.Ariz.1990), nor authorizes miners and other land users to steal or destroy artifacts. Cf. San Carlos Apache Tribe v. United States (D. Ariz.2003) (holding that ARPA did not apply to drawdown of lake levels because it did not involve intentional excavation).

Congress designed the Historic Sites Act of 1935, 16 U.S.C.A. §§ 461–469h, to preserve for public use historic sites, buildings, and objects of national significance. The Act requires preservation of historical or archaeological "data" that is at risk due to flooding, federal construction projects, or other federally licensed activities, but it has had little impact on resource development on the federal lands. The National Historic Preservation Act (NHPA) of 1966, 16 U.S.C.A. §§ 470–470w–6, extends federal protection to historic resources that lack national significance. It authorizes the Interior Secretary to maintain a National Register of Historic Places and prohibits federal agencies from approving undertakings that would affect listed properties without prior compliance with NEPA-like evaluation procedures. An undertaking includes federally funded or licensed projects, but not projects subject to state or local regulation administered pursuant to a delegation of authority by a federal agency if the projects are neither funded nor licensed by the federal government. National Mining Ass'n v. Fowler (D.C. Cir.2003). One court held that an oil and gas lease sale is an undertaking, despite the BLM's claim that it is not the point at which the agency decision has the potential to affect historic properties. Montana Wilderness Ass'n v. Fry (D. Mont.2004). Another case upheld a BLM finding that a seismic oil and gas exploration project would have no adverse effects on historic properties. Southern Utah Wilderness Alliance v. Norton (D.D.C.2004).

The Advisory Council on Historic Preservation has the authority to issue binding procedural regulations under the NHPA, but not substantive regulations. Like NEPA, the NHPA lacks substantive bite. Unlike NEPA, however, the NHPA has not generated a significant volume of litigation pertinent to activities on the federal lands. Where the NHPA does apply, noncompliance with its procedures may provide the basis for a court to enjoin an undertaking. See, e.g., Friends of the Atglen–Susquehanna Trail, Inc. v. Surface Transp. Bd. (3d Cir.2001). The courts are split on the question of whether the NHPA creates a private right of action against the government. San Carlos Apache Tribe v. United States (9th Cir.2005) (holding that it does not and describing contrary opinions in other Circuits).

See PNRL chapter 15B.

B. EXTERNAL THREATS

1. EXTERNAL THREATS FROM NON–FEDERAL LANDS

Areas and resources in all of the federal land management systems, but particularly those in the national parks, have become increasingly threatened in recent years by activities occurring on adjacent private lands. The activities posing the greatest threats to the integrity of the parks have included road development, logging, mining, agriculture, energy development, and recreation. Cases construing the Property Clause have largely dispelled doubts about the constitutionality of efforts to regulate activities on private lands to abate such threats. See section 3B. Uncertainty about the adequacy of agency statutory authority and political will to protect public resources from external threats remains.

The decisions in the *Redwood National Park* litigation addressed the scope of the Interior Department's authority to protect park resources against external threats. The Sierra Club sued the Department to force it to protect the Park from damage allegedly attributable to or threatened by logging operations on private land adjacent to the Park. These operations left the Park vulnerable to high winds, landslides, mudslides, and stream siltation which endangered tree roots and aquatic life. The plaintiff claimed that the Department had a judicially enforceable duty to prevent or mitigate damage to the redwoods, but the Department sought dismissal on the ground that the exercise of its discretionary authority to protect Park resources was nonreviewable. Cautioning that the standard of review was narrow, the district court nevertheless held that the agency's discretion was limited and subject to judicial review. Sierra Club v. Department of the Interior (I) (N.D.Cal.1974). The Secretary had a legal duty to use the powers vested in him by the Redwood National Park Act "to afford as full protection as is reasonably possible to the timber, soil, and streams within the boundaries of the park." 16 U.S.C.A. § 79c(e). In addition, the National Park Service Organic Act imposed on the Secretary a general duty in the nature of a public trust to conserve park resources for future generations. Id. § 1. See section 4D.

The next year, after reviewing evidence of the Interior Department's efforts to protect the Park against the adverse effects of logging on adjacent private lands, the district court held that the agency had abused its discretion in refusing to perform the general public trust and specific duties imposed on it. A task force commissioned by the Department suggested, among other things, the imposition of a moratorium on harvesting and the acquisition of a management zone around the threatened area of the Park. The Department adopted none of the recommendations except the execution of cooperative agreements with timber companies, but the court discounted these agreements because they were unenforceable, vague and laden with qualifications, and inadequate in scope given evidence of continuing damage to Park timber, soil, streams, and aesthetics. The court therefore ordered the Department to take various actions such as acquisition of land near the Park. Sierra Club v. Department of the Interior (II) (N.D.Cal.1975). In Sierra Club v. Department of the Interior (III) (N.D.Cal. 1976), the court "purged" the agency of its breach of duty, concluding that it made a good faith attempt to comply with the court's order. That attempt bore little fruit because the Office of Management and Budget disapproved of the Department's request to seek additional statutory authority to regulate activities outside the Park, the timber companies rejected timber harvesting guidelines, and the Justice Department failed to initiate litigation to restrain timber harvesting that imminently endangered the Park, despite the Interior Department's request that it do so. Congress provided relief in 1978, when it authorized the purchase of additional acreage for the Park.

The import of the *Redwood National Park* cases is unclear. In 1980, another district court refused to recognize an independent public trust duty binding on the Interior Secretary outside of the 1916 Organic Act. Sierra Club v. Andrus (D.D.C.1980). The agency's efforts to abate other external threats have met with mixed success. Compare United States v. Moore (S.D. W.Va.1986) (enjoining pesticide spraying on federal and private land within the boundaries of a national river) with United States v. County Bd. of Arlington County (E.D.Va.1979) (failing to stop as a public nuisance construction of buildings that would allegedly interfere with views of the national capital parks).

Specific statutory authorizations to regulate activities giving rise to external threats provide agencies with the best chance of abating those threats. Federal pollution control legislation provides such authority in certain instances. The Clean Air Act, for example, authorizes the imposition of limitations on sources whose emissions "may reasonably be anticipated to cause or contribute to any impairment of visibility" on federal lands in which scenic vistas are an important value. 42 U.S.C.A. § 7491(b)(2).

See PNRL § 14:5.

2. EXTERNAL THREATS FROM FEDERAL LANDS

Congress may specifically direct one federal land management agency to avoid taking or authorizing activities with potential adverse effects on a federal land area under the jurisdiction of another agency. In 1984, for example, Congress banned geothermal leasing on national forest land west of Yellowstone National Park, and it later amended the Geothermal Steam Act to require all leases or drilling permits to condition operations as necessary to protect "significant geothermal features" in NPS units. 30 U.S.C.A. § 1026(c).

Explicit directives of this sort do not always prevent spillover effects from one federal land system to another. The 1956 Colorado River Storage Project Act, 43 U.S.C.A. § 620b, declared the legislature's intention that no dam or reservoir constructed under the Act be within any national park or monument. Despite this provision, the Tenth Circuit refused to require the Interior Secretary to prevent water impounded behind Glen Canyon Dam from spreading into Rainbow Bridge National Monument. Friends of the Earth v. Armstrong (10th Cir.1973). The court held that subsequent appropriations acts funding dam construction had repealed the prohibition by implication. Inexplicably, the court retained jurisdiction so that the plaintiffs could apply for further relief in the event of unexpected structural damage to the Bridge. *FOE* was decided before TVA v. Hill (S.Ct.1978), in which the Supreme Court firmly stated that repeals by implication are disfavored.

Absent legislation specifically directed at accommodating the interests of adjacent federal land systems, the agencies must coordinate activities by themselves or with the intervention of the Justice Department. Processes such as NEPA evaluation and land use planning often require consultation with other agencies but rarely dictate that one agency follow the recommendations of another. Given the differing legal mandates of the land management agencies, it may be difficult for one agency to prevent another from authorizing activities that threaten resources under its jurisdiction.

See PNRL § 14:5.

C. RIVER PRESERVATION

One of the principal purposes of the Wild and Scenic Rivers Act (WSRA) of 1968, 16 U.S.C.A. §§ 1271–1287, is to limit activities on other federal lands that might adversely affect resources in the wild and scenic river area. Several concerns prompted passage. State water law regimes, especially in western states adhering to the prior appropriation system, failed to protect instream values by not recognizing water left in place as a beneficial use. Decades of federally financed dam construction threatened water quality in affected rivers. Finally, the increasing environmental consciousness of the late 1960s created pressure to provide greater legislative control over the federal lands.

The WSRA initially designated ten river segments as wild or scenic. By the 1990s, the wild and scenic rivers system had grown to more than 115 segments consisting of thousands of miles. The Act is designed to preserve in free-flowing condition rivers that possess "outstandingly remarkable scenic, recreational, geologic, fish and wildlife, historic, cultural, or similar values" so that "they and their immediate environments shall be protected for the benefit and enjoyment of present and future generations." 16 U.S.C.A. § 1271.

1. DESIGNATING WILD AND SCENIC RIVERS

Congress designates most river segments for inclusion in the wild and scenic rivers system. The statute also authorizes the Secretary of the Interior, upon the request of a state's governor, to include in the federal system rivers recognized by the state as wild, scenic, or recreational. Such administratively designated rivers are managed in the same manner as congressional designations, except that only federal lands included in the segment are subject to federal control. Id. § 1273(a)(ii). If Congress delegates to the federal land management agencies the responsibility of delineating the boundaries of a wild and scenic river, the agency must set those boundaries by reference to the river's outstandingly remarkable values. Sokol v. Kennedy (8th Cir.2000).

In the usual designation process, Congress requires a land management agency to study a particular river segment for inclusion in the system and report to Congress for possible action. In the interim, federal land within a quarter-mile of each side is withdrawn from entry, sale, or other disposition and from operation of the General Mining Law. Mineral leasing is permitted under appropriate conditions. For three years, the government may not license hydroelectric dams on or directly affecting these "study" rivers. No federal agency may assist the construction of water resources projects that would adversely affect a candidate river. 16 U.S.C.A. § 1278(b). These prohibitions do not apply to rivers designated by a state but for which federal administrative designation has not yet occurred. North Carolina v. FPC (D.C. Cir.1976). The land management agencies must afford designation priority to rivers subject to the greatest threats to their aesthetic and free-flowing qualities and to those with the highest percentage of federal land within their boundaries.

See PNRL §§ 15:2–15:4.

2.   MANAGING WILD AND SCENIC RIVERS

Management of wild and scenic river areas often is complicated because much of the land in these areas is privately owned. Thus, the agencies with jurisdiction over the federal components of a designated river usually must deal with numerous private inholders. The WSRA provides limited authority to the land management agencies to acquire, by condemnation or purchase, lands within the boundaries of designated areas. 16 U.S.C.A. § 1277. With that exception, the WSRA contains few provisions that recognize the special management problems attributable to patchwork ownership patterns.

Every river included in the system must be classified and managed as wild, scenic, or recreational. Wild rivers are inaccessible except by trail, with unpolluted waters that represent "vestiges of primitive America." Scenic rivers have shorelines and watersheds that are still largely primitive and undeveloped, but they are partially accessible by road. Recreational rivers are partially developed, readily accessible by road or rail, and "may have undergone some impoundment or diversion in the past." Id. § 1272(b).

A river's classification may or may not affect its management. Subject to valid existing rights, the WSRA permanently withdraws federally owned minerals within one-quarter mile of a designated wild river from development under the GML or leasing statutes. Prospecting and mining within all designated river corridors must conform to regulations that provide safeguards against pollution and unnecessary impairment of scenery. Id. § 1280. The statutory bar on federal participation in water development projects that would have a direct and adverse effect on river values likewise applies to all three categories of designated rivers. Id. § 1278(a). This prohibition does not apply, however, to congressionally authorized dams. See Oregon Natural Resources Council v. Harrell (9th Cir.1995).

All three categories of designated rivers are subject to the Act's general management standard, which requires the land management agency with jurisdiction to "protect and enhance the values which caused it to be included in [the] system." 16 U.S.C.A. § 1281(a). The managing agency must place "primary emphasis" on protecting the aesthetic, scenic, and related features of the river. To the extent consistent with these mandates, administration must not limit other uses that do not substantially interfere with public use and enjoyment of a river's values. This flexible management prescription is similar to the compatibility standard that governs the NWRs. Even though the statute differentiates among the three categories in limited instances, to the extent that classification defines the values responsible for inclusion in the system, it should also shape management decisions. In one case, a court held that the Forest Service could not allow hunting and fishing lodges to be used as business retreats in a wild river corridor because those uses conflicted with the WSRA's clear directive that wild river segments remain "essentially primitive." Wilderness Watch v. U.S. Forest Service (D. Mont.2000). Another court refused to decide whether the WSRA bars all motorized uses on wild rivers. Instead, it deferred to the Forest Service's determination that motorized uses would not substantially interfere with fish and wildlife values due to their adverse effects on turtles and salmonids. Riverhawks v. Zepeda (D. Or.2002).

The Act requires the agency with jurisdiction over a river segment designated on or after January 1, 1986 to prepare a comprehensive management plan to protect river values. Each plan must address resource protection, development of lands and facilities, user capacities, and other management practices, but the WSRA does not define a clear relationship between the planning responsibilities of an agency such as the Forest Service under its organic statute and the WSRA. One court found that the NPS violated its obligation to address "user capacities" in the management plan. This obligation required the agency to discuss the maximum number of people that can be received at a designated river. In that case, the NPS plan included only sample standards and indicators rather than providing any concrete measure of use. Friends of Yosemite Valley v. Norton (9th Cir.2003).

Some courts have concluded that failure to complete a plan within the statutory time limit is not a valid ground for an injunction against management activities in the corridor. Newton County Wildlife Ass'n. v. United States Forest Serv. (8th Cir.1997); Sierra Club v. United States (N.D.Cal.1998). But see Sierra Club v. Babbitt (E.D.Cal.1999) (enjoining work on one segment of road reconstruction project due to "egregious" violation of WSRA planning requirements that also amounted to substantive violation). WSRA plans must be "coordinated with and may be incorporated into resource management planning for affected adjacent Federal lands." 16 U.S.C.A. § 1274(d)(1). WSRA components within national wilderness areas, parks, or wildlife refuges should be managed under the more "restrictive" of the applicable laws.

Two cases from Oregon, in 1997 and 1998, came to apparently different conclusions regarding the compatibility of livestock grazing with WSRA values. The river corridor in Oregon Natural Desert Ass'n v. Green (D.Or.1997), was classified as "wild;" the BLM prepared a management plan that allowed continued (though less) grazing in the corridor despite past damage and recommendations for livestock exclusion. The court determined that the plan violated substantive WSRA requirements by failing to consider exclusion. The court later entered a permanent injunction against all grazing in the area.

By contrast, the BLM had neglected to promulgate a management plan for the recreational river segments at issue in NWF v. Cosgriffe (D.Or.1998). The court distinguished *Green* on the facts and held that the BLM must prepare a plan, but that no injunction against grazing was warranted because plaintiffs sought blanket relief instead of attacking individual agency actions.

See PNRL §§ 15:5–15:12.

D. WILDERNESS PRESERVATION

1. THE EVOLUTION OF OFFICIAL WILDERNESS

The United States was the first nation to set aside and mandate by law preservation of pristine natural areas. The Forest Service carved out 700,000 acres of the Gila National Forest as wilderness in 1924. Periodically, Congress or the agencies required that particular areas of federal lands be maintained in roadless and primitive condition. Protection afforded by administrative action could be and was rather easily reversed, however. The Wilderness Act of 1964, 16 U.S.C.A. §§ 1131–1136, adopted after a decade of debate (and over the occasional opposition of the Forest Service), created the national wilderness preservation system (NWPS), which is one of the strongest commitments to natural preservation in the world. Intent on assuring that settlement and development do not preclude the ability to designate for preservation and protection lands in their natural condition, Congress declared a policy of securing for present and future generations of Americans "the benefits of an enduring resource of wilderness." The Act defines wilderness as:

an area where the earth and its community of life are untrammeled by man, where man himself is a visitor who does not remain. An area of wilderness is further defined to mean ... an area of undeveloped Federal land retaining its primeval character and influence, without permanent improvements or human habitation, which is protected and managed so as to preserve its natural conditions and which (1) generally appears to have been affected primarily by the forces of nature, with the imprint of man's work substantially unnoticeable; (2) has outstanding opportunities for solitude or a primitive and unconfined type of recreation; (3) has at least five thousand acres of land or is of sufficient size as to make practicable its preservation and use in an unimpaired condition; and (4) may also contain ecological, geological, or other features of scientific, educational, scenic, or historical value.

Id. § 1131(c). See generally PNRL chapter 14B; J. Hendee, G. Stankey & R. Lucas, *Wilderness Management* (1978).

Partisans have advanced many justifications for preserving wilderness areas. Early advocates of wilderness preservation argued that wilderness provides a setting for religious experiences and political reform and serves as a refuge or sanctuary from civilization. Modern supporters of wilderness preservation regard it as an important part of the American cultural heritage, a locus of biological research, a commitment to ethical obligations founded upon a biocentric view of nature, an aid to physical recuperation, and the optimal setting for a variety of recreational pursuits. The perceived benefits of preserving wilderness helped to establish the NWPS as an important federal land category. Between 1964 and 2000, the system grew ten-fold to more than 100 million acres.

2.   THE WILDERNESS ACT OF 1964: MANAGEMENT OF WILDERNESS AREAS

Congress retains the exclusive authority to determine whether an area qualifies as wilderness. See, e.g., Barnes v. Babbitt (D. Ariz.2004) (setting aside IBLA decision concluding that an area did not qualify as wilderness because Congress had already designated the area as wilderness). The Wilderness Act vests the responsibility for managing a wilderness area in the same agency that administered it before designation. With certain exceptions, the Act requires agencies with jurisdiction over wilderness areas to preserve their wilderness character and to devote them to the public purposes of recreational, scenic, scientific, educational, conservation, and historical use.

Despite the apparently absolute nature of its objectives, the Act, like all legislation, was the product of compromise. The statute permits the continuation of some existing uses and limited resource development and commercial use in wilderness areas, sometimes distinguishing among areas in the different federal land systems. Subject to existing private rights, the statute forbids commercial development, structures, roads, and motorized vehicles in wilderness areas. 16 U.S.C.A. § 1133(b)-(c).

In one case, the issue was whether the FWS violated the Act by permitting a salmon aquaculture project within a wilderness area located inside a national wildlife refuge. Wilderness Soc'y v. FWS (9th Cir.2003). The court held that the project was inconsistent with the Act's prohibition on commercial enterprises within wilderness areas, even if it had a benign purpose (assisting the local economy) and was sponsored by a non-profit trade association in cooperation with state regulators. The purpose of the aquaculture project was to advance the interests of commercial fishermen by swelling salmon runs, not to promote the goals of the Wilderness Act. The fact that the project served secondary noncommercial purposes, including enhancing recreational fishing, was irrelevant. Neither the state's maintenance of regulatory control over the project nor the fact that the commercial benefit derived from the project occurred when salmon were caught outside the bounds of the wilderness area changed the result. Because substantial and essential parts of the operation occurred within the wilderness area, it violated the Act's prohibition on commercial enterprises within wilderness areas. See also *Barnes v. Babbitt*, supra (repair and maintenance of access routes by grazing permittees prohibited because they would have amounted to road construction).

The Wilderness Act allows commercial uses "to the extent necessary for activities which are proper for realizing the recreational or other wilderness purposes of the areas." 16 U.S.C.A. § 1133(d)(5). In High Sierra Hikers Ass'n v. Blackwell (9th Cir. 2004), the court invalidated the Forest Service's decision to issue and renew a series of multi-year special use permits to commercial packstock operators. The court found that the agency failed to demonstrate that the permits were "necessary" because it did not adequately assess the impact which that particular level of commercial activity was having on wilderness character. The court also found that the Forest Service appeared to elevate recreational activity over the long-term preservation of the wilderness character of the land, in violation of its Wilderness Act obligations.

The Wilderness Act also prohibits temporary roads and the use of motor vehicles in wilderness areas "except as necessary to meet the minimum requirements for the administration of the area for the purpose of" the Act. 16 U.S.C.A. § 1133(c). When the NPS decided to provide access to historical areas under its jurisdiction by driving vans full of tourists through an adjacent wilderness area, environmental groups sued, claiming that the trips violated the Act's prohibition on the use of motor vehicles. Wilderness Watch v. Mainella (11th Cir. 2004). The NPS asserted that the Act allows designated wilderness areas to be devoted to multiple uses, including historical uses. The court, however, declared the use of the passenger vans to be a violation of the unambiguous statutory prohibition on motorized transportation through wilderness areas. It disagreed that preservation of historic structures furthers the goals of the Wilderness Act, interpreting statutory references to "historical" uses and values as referring exclusively to natural features. It concluded that the NPS failed to justify its decision to operate the passenger vans as one that was "necessary to meet the minimum requirements" for administration of the wilderness areas. Finally, the court found the NPS's action to be inconsistent with the goals of the Wilderness Act because use of a passenger van would dilute the wilderness experience for both the passengers and others using the wilderness area.

Where the use of aircraft or motorboats was established before wilderness designation, that use "may be permitted to continue" subject to agency regulations, which, in the case of the Forest Service, have been quite restrictive. See, e.g., Isle Royale Boaters Ass'n v. Norton (6th Cir.2003) (upholding NPS's decision to remove or relocate boat docks to separate motorized and non-motorized uses, even though motorized uses predated the Act). The land management agencies may use motorized vehicles for rescue missions and fire and insect control. Congress can ban motorized vehicles from state or private land within designated wilderness areas. Minnesota v. Block (8th Cir.1981).

Subject to reasonable regulation, livestock grazing that predates 1964 may continue. 16 U.S.C.A. § 1133(d)(4). This authorization is broad enough to allow the land management agencies to conduct predator control programs to protect private, domestic livestock. Forest Guardians v. Animal & Plant Health Inspection Serv. (9th Cir.2002). Aside from the Park Service, which forbids grazing in wilderness areas, the land management agencies limit grazing to levels compatible with wilderness values. The President may authorize water resource development in national forest wilderness areas, although no president has done so. The Act purports to have no effect on state hunting and fishing laws, but agency restrictions to protect wilderness values are permissible.

The 1964 Wilderness Act authorized mineral prospectors and prospective lessees to locate claims or obtain leases within twenty years after enactment, but little hardrock mining occurred and the land management agencies issued few leases. Pre–1984 locations and leases are subject to reasonable regulation. Even after 1984, mineral prospecting may be conducted in national forest wilderness areas, provided the activity is conducted in a manner compatible with preservation of the wilderness environment. In 1987, Congress banned mineral leasing in areas under consideration for wilderness designation.

The Wilderness Act does not address timber harvesting, but both courts and agencies have concluded that commercial logging is prohibited unless specifically allowed by a particular designation statute. The Act delegates to the land management agencies the discretion to take necessary measures to control fire, insects, and disease. 16 U.S.C.A. § 1131(d)(1). In Sierra Club v. Lyng (I) (D.D.C.

1987), environmental groups challenged a Forest Service program to control infestations of pine beetles by creating "buffer zones" in wilderness areas in three southern states through extensive tree-cutting and insecticide application. They argued that in order to be "necessary" under section 1131(d)(1), a control program must be effective, and that the program at issue was unsuccessful. In addition, the plaintiffs claimed that the real purpose of the program was not to protect wilderness areas but to stem the spread of the infestation to adjacent forests for the benefit of private loggers. The court reasoned that the agency lacks the authority under section 1131(d)(1) to manage wilderness for the benefit of outside commercial interests. The Act therefore required the Forest Service to provide an affirmative justification for a program that appeared to be antithetical to wilderness policy. The court nevertheless deferred final resolution of the issue pending issuance of an EIS. After preparation of the EIS, the Forest Service scaled back the scope of the tree-cutting program considerably. Contrary to the plaintiffs' interpretation, the court construed section 1131(d)(1) to allow the agency to use insect control measures that are not fully effective as long as these measures are reasonably designed to restrain the threatened spread of beetles from wilderness areas to the detriment of neighboring property. Deferring to the agency's findings, the court held that the Forest Service met its burden of affirmatively justifying the action as a means of protecting wilderness values rather than outside commercial interests. Sierra Club v. Lyng (II) (D.D.C.1987).

See PNRL §§ 14B:17–14B:23.

3.   EXPANDING THE WILDERNESS SYSTEM

The 1964 Act designated 9.1 million acres of "instant wilderness" areas. It also set in motion programs for studying whether primitive areas within the national forests, roadless areas over 5000 acres and roadless islands of any size in the National Wildlife Refuge System, and National Park Service roadless areas of more than 5000 acres should be added to the NWPS. In 1976, FLPMA required the BLM to study the wilderness potential of all roadless areas under its jurisdiction.

Each area added to the wilderness system is governed not only by the 1964 Act but also by the statute designating it as wilderness. Dozens of statutes have expanded the NWPS. The Alaska National Interest Lands Conservation Act of 1980, 16 U.S.C.A. §§ 3101–3233, alone designated more than 56 million acres in Alaska as wilderness.

a.   The National Park and Wildlife Refuge Systems

Although wilderness designation in the national parks and wildlife refuges got off to a slow start, the process has not generated significant litigation for either agency. As of January 1992, the national park system included 42 wilderness areas. About 85 percent of park system wilderness acreage is in

Alaska. The NPS has recommended to Congress that it designate another 8–9 million acres of park system land as wilderness. More than one-third of the acreage of all the wilderness areas managed by the FWS is in the Arctic National Wildlife Refuge, whose future as wilderness is threatened by periodic proposals to open the refuge to oil and gas exploration.

See PNRL § 14B:7.

b. The National Forest System

The Wilderness Act required the Secretary of Agriculture to review and report to the President by 1974 on all areas of the national forests classified before the Act's adoption as primitive areas to determine whether they were suitable for wilderness designation. When the Forest Service entered a timber contract in a national forest area that was contiguous to a primitive area and predominantly of wilderness value, the plaintiffs in Parker v. United States (10th Cir.1971), sued to enjoin the sale. The Forest Service justified the sale on the ground that it had preserved a buffer zone between the primitive and sale areas, but the Tenth Circuit affirmed the district court's injunction. Authorizing the Forest Service to continue the sale would thwart Congress's goal of providing a meaningful opportunity to add contiguous areas of wilderness value to existing primitive areas for final wilderness designation. The court relied in part on a provision of the Forest Service Manual requiring study of "contiguous lands which seem to have significant wilderness resources." The Forest Service completed the primitive area study within the statutory ten-year deadline and Congress eventually designated as wilderness most of the areas recommended by the agency for inclusion in the NWPS.

The Wilderness Act only required the Forest Service to study primitive areas for possible wilderness designation. In 1967, the agency voluntarily expanded the evaluation to include all roadless areas of more than 5000 acres or located adjacent to wilderness or primitive areas. The Roadless Area Review and Evaluation (RARE I) inventory, which included 56 million acres, was released in 1972. The courts enjoined timber contracting in these areas due to noncompliance with NEPA. Wyoming Outdoor Coord. Council v. Butz (10th Cir.1973). The final RARE I EIS retained only 12.3 million acres from the initial inventory for detailed wilderness suitability study.

In 1977, a new presidential administration on its own initiative scrapped the RARE I process and started a new, RARE II inventory, which encompassed more than 62 million acres. The RARE II EIS proposed that 15 million acres be recommended to Congress for wilderness designation, 10.8 million acres be studied further in unit management plans and protected in the interim, and 36 million acres be released to multiple use management. California sued the Forest Service, challenging its decision to release 47 RARE II areas in that state. The district court held that the EIS was inadequate to support non-wilderness designation because its consideration of the site-specific consequences of release was superficial. The EIS also failed to consider the effect of development on future opportunities for wilderness designation. The district court enjoined the agency from taking any action that might change the wilderness character of the disputed areas pending compliance with NEPA and forbade it from relying on the RARE II EIS in preparing LRMPs under the NFMA. See section 7C on the planning process.

The Ninth Circuit affirmed in California v. Block (9th Cir.1982), finding the RARE II EIS deficient on several grounds. The Forest Service claimed that RARE II was only the first step in a multi-stage planning process and that it would prepare separate EISs in connection with specific development proposals in the released areas. As a result, evaluation of site-specific consequences in the programmatic EIS was unnecessary. The court agreed with the state, however, that Forest Service regulations required that released areas be managed for purposes other than wilderness designation, at least until revision of LRMPs in the 1990s. Thus, future decisions concerning released areas would be constrained by the decision not to place them in the other two RARE II categories. The promise of site-specific EISs was meaningless because the Forest Service would not be able to consider wilderness preservation as an alternative to development at that later time. For further analysis of tiering under NEPA, see section 4E.

The injunction in *Block* purported to limit Forest Service management discretion only on released lands in California, but the inadequate EIS covered all RARE II lands nationwide. Thus, authorization of any activities that threatened wilderness areas on RARE II lands risked additional injunctions. Shortly after the *Block* decision, the Agriculture Secretary announced plans to abandon RARE II in favor of yet another evaluation, RARE III. Released areas outside California would remain open to multiple use management pending further evaluation. Congress short-circuited RARE III by adopting a series of wilderness bills that designated nearly nine million acres, most of it out of the RARE II inventory, as wilderness. Wilderness legislation encompassing RARE II lands still has not been adopted in some western states. Most remaining Forest Service wilderness studies will be conducted through NFMA planning.

The Forest Service adopted regulations in 2001 that prohibited most road construction and timber harvesting in roadless areas within the national forests. The Ninth Circuit rejected the contention that the agency violated NEPA in promulgating the regulations. Kootenai Tribe v. Veneman (9th Cir. 2002). A federal district court in Wyoming, however, permanently enjoined the regulations based on noncompliance with both NEPA and the Wilderness Act. Wyoming v. United States Dep't of Agric. (D. Wyo.2003). With respect to the Wilderness Act, the court concluded that the prohibitions amounted to a de facto wilderness designation because roadless areas are synonymous with wilderness areas and the uses permitted in the two areas were essentially the same. Most of the roadless areas were based on RARE II inventories, which were designed to recommend wilderness areas to Congress. The regulations therefore usurped Congress's exclusive power to create and set aside federally designated wilderness areas.

In another case, a different district court rejected a similar claim that President Clinton usurped Congress's exclusive prerogative to designate wilderness areas by exercising his authority to establish the Grand Staircase–Escalante National Monument under the Antiquities Act. Utah Ass'n of Counties v. Bush (D. Utah 2004). The court distinguished the decision in the roadless rule case on the ground that *Wyoming* involved an attempt by the Forest Service to use rulemaking to protect federal lands that had previously failed to achieve wilderness status after having been identified as candidates for that status. In *Utah Ass'n of Counties*, the President acted pursuant to congressional authorization.

In 2005, the Forest Service replaced the 2001 roadless rule with an entirely different rule that relies on the filing of state petitions to establish management restrictions on uses of particular roadless areas. 36 C.F.R. §§ 294.10–294.18 State governors have a limited time to file such petitions. Unless the Forest Service approves a state petition, the management of roadless areas in the national forests will be governed by the land use planning process.

An issue of continuing importance is whether a congressional decision not to include an inventoried area in the NWPS opens that area to management that might impair its wilderness characteristics. Timber and mining interests have advocated "hard release" of such lands, making them fully and permanently available for non-wilderness uses. Environmentalists urge continued agency consideration of the wilderness option in plans and EISs on development proposals so long as the area remains roadless. Beginning in 1984, Congress typically has chosen in statewide wilderness bills to adopt the latter "soft release" approach, which eliminates the Forest Service's obligation to further consider released roadless areas for wilderness treatment until it prepares the next NFMA land use plan for the area.

Forest Service proposals to develop released areas remain subject to NEPA. The Oregon Wilderness Act of 1984 released roadless areas to multiple use management until the next LRMP revision. The plaintiffs in National Audubon Soc'y v. United States Forest Serv. (9th Cir.1993), objected to timber sales in the released areas. The Forest Service argued that Congress's failure to describe the sale areas as roadless precluded the need for an EIS. The district court held that roadlessness is a question of fact, not law, and that NEPA required an evaluation of the consequences of a sale on the roadless and undeveloped nature of the tracts. The Ninth Circuit agreed that the release language did not immunize the timber sales from judicial review of NEPA compliance. See also Smith v. United

States Forest Serv. (9th Cir.1994) (reaching the same result under the Washington State Wilderness Act). In other statewide wilderness acts, Congress has directed that specific roadless areas be managed to protect wilderness characteristics until it reconsiders whether to include them in the NWPS.

See PNRL §§ 14B:8–14B:11, 14B:14.

c. Bureau of Land Management Lands

FLPMA required the Interior Secretary by 1991 to review roadless areas of 5000 acres or more and roadless islands on the public lands identified in a BLM inventory as having wilderness characteristics and make recommendations to the President as to their suitability for preservation as wilderness. 43 U.S.C.A. § 1782(a). Within two years of receiving those recommendations, the President was to forward his recommendations to Congress. Pursuant to the "interim management policy" contained in section 1782(c) of FLPMA, lands under study must be managed "so as not to impair the[ir] suitability for preservation as wilderness," subject to existing mining, mineral leasing, and grazing use, provided that the agency must take any action "required to prevent unnecessary or undue degradation" of lands and resources. See generally Leshy, *Wilderness and Its Discontents—Wilderness Review Comes to the Public Lands*, 1981 Ariz. St. L.J. 361.

i. The Inventory Process

The FLPMA wilderness area review program encompassed all lands administered by the BLM. During the inventory, the agency identified as wilderness study areas (WSAs) roadless areas with wilderness characteristics. To qualify as a WSA, a roadless area had to be at least 5000 acres of contiguous public land, substantially in natural condition, and provide an outstanding opportunity for either solitude or a primitive and unconfined type of recreation. Smaller areas with similar characteristics could qualify if they were contiguous to land with wilderness potential managed by another agency or had strong public support for identification as a WSA and were sufficiently large to make preservation and use in an unimpaired condition practicable.

The BLM inventory included more than 173 million acres, of which only about 23 million were placed in WSA status in 1980. Two years later, a new Interior Secretary ordered that lands in which the United States did not own subsurface minerals (split-estate lands) be removed from the wilderness inventory and exempted from the interim management policy. Parcels of less than 5000 acres were treated in a similar manner. These and related provisions of the Secretary's order resulted in the removal of about 1.5 million acres from WSA status. In Sierra Club v. Watt (E.D.Cal.1985), environmental groups sued to overturn the order. The court held that the exclusion of split-estate lands conflicted with the plain language of FLPMA. The Act mandates that the Secretary include in the inventory roadless areas of the public lands of 5000 acres or more with wilderness characteristics, and split-estates fit the definition of public lands. Section

1782(c)'s directive that the agency continue to manage inventoried lands so as not to impair wilderness suitability, subject to the continuation of existing mining activities, demonstrated the fallacy of the Secretary's position. Had Congress intended that split-estate lands be excluded from the inventory, it would not have provided for the continuation of existing mining activities during the review period. Even if, as the agency contended, ownership of the subsurface estate constituted a vested right (an issue the court did not resolve), such a right would not preclude assessment of split-estates for preservation as wilderness. The land might continue to be mined during study subject to controls, Congress might decide to reject any agency or Presidential recommendations that split-estate lands be designated as wilderness, and, even if it did not, it might decide to compensate subsurface estate owners. The court also held that the removal of roadless areas of less than 5000 acres from wilderness review was improper. In 1990, Congress designated many of the split-estate lands as wilderness.

Some of the BLM's decisions not to designate areas as WSAs were appealed to the Interior Board of Land Appeals (IBLA). In Utah Wilderness Coalition (IBLA 1983), the administrative board reversed many of the decisions. On remand, the BLM reclassified nearly 500,000 acres as WSAs.

ii. Interim Management: FLPMA Section 1782(c)

Several cases have interpreted the meaning of the interim management policy for WSAs contained in

section 1782(c) of FLPMA, described above. In Utah
v. Andrus (D. Utah 1979), the BLM sued to enjoin
road construction through a WSA by a uranium
mining company that had acquired mineral location
claims and begun exploration before the adoption of
FLPMA. The company argued that section 1782(c)
contains only one management standard, the prevention of undue or unnecessary environmental
degradation, and that the section's "impairment"
language was merely illustrative of that standard.
The government replied that section 1782(c) reflects
two management standards: the BLM could regulate uses that existed before FLPMA's adoption to
the degree required to prevent unnecessary and
undue degradation, while it had to regulate new
uses to the extent necessary to prevent impairment
of wilderness characteristics. The court deferred to
the agency's interpretation, concluding that the
company's construction would protect existing uses
but not address Congress' other concern, the preservation of wilderness characteristics. Under the
dual standard, new uses could be regulated more
stringently than existing uses. A carefully conducted commercial timber harvesting operation, for example, would not result in unnecessary or undue
degradation of the environment, but might impair
wilderness characteristics. Accordingly, such an operation would be permissible only if it predated
FLPMA.

The remaining issue was which standard applied
to the company's activities. The company argued
unsuccessfully that it had engaged in a protected

existing use because under the GML it had a right
of access to its unpatented claims. The court accepted the agency's view that the more lenient standard
applied only to actual on-the-ground activities being
conducted under mineral leases in force on the date
of FLPMA's adoption, not to mere statutory rights
to use. The company's claim that the BLM lacked
the authority under FLPMA to interfere with access
rights under the GML did not persuade the court
because FLPMA section 1732(b) made GML access
rights subject to the interim management policy of
section 1782(c) and the GML itself made access
rights subject to regulation. Drawing an analogy to
the *Parker* case, supra, the court deemed the company's interpretation to be inconsistent with the
Wilderness Act in that it would preclude the BLM
from preventing activity that would permanently
impair wilderness characteristics even before the
agency or Congress evaluated an area's preservation
potential. The court also held, however, that the
BLM's authority over new uses is limited to preventing permanent impairment of wilderness values, and it remanded so that the agency could
determine whether the company's reclamation plan
would cause such impairment.

Following the decision in *Utah*, the BLM modified
the interim management policy by asserting that
FLPMA precludes unreasonable interference with
the enjoyment of valid existing rights that include
the right to develop. If such rights could not be
exercised without impairing wilderness suitability,

the activities would be regulated to prevent unnecessary or undue degradation, but the activities could proceed despite impairment. In Sierra Club v. Hodel (10th Cir.1988), the court endorsed this approach, but it upheld an injunction against road construction to force the BLM to locate a right-of-way where it would have the least degrading impact on a WSA. Even though the statutory protection of valid existing rights precluded the agency from barring any construction, the BLM's obligation under section 1782(c) to choose the least degrading alternative required environmental assessment under NEPA. Distinguishing the *Alaska Wolf Kill* case, discussed in section 4E above, the court rejected the BLM's argument that its inaction in letting the road improvement proceed did not trigger NEPA.

The interim management policy also tracked the *Utah* court's holding that the BLM's authority over new uses is limited to preventing permanent impairment of wilderness values. The policy stated that temporary activities may be nonimpairing and defined temporary effects as those "capable of being reclaimed to a condition of being substantially unnoticeable in the [WSA] . . . as a whole by the time the Secretary is scheduled to send his recommendations on that area to the President." In Sierra Club v. Clark (9th Cir.1985), the court upheld the BLM's decision not to interfere with a motorcycle race from Barstow to Las Vegas because the adverse impacts it would cause in a WSA were not "sufficiently egregious" to amount to impairment. The court deferred to the BLM's interpretation that the relevant "area" for assessing the severity of the damage was the entire WSA, not just the affected race course. That holding might be distinguishable if the cumulative effects of several races were not reclaimable.

In a fourth case involving the application of section 1782(c), the Tenth Circuit reversed a district court ruling that both pre- and post–1976 mineral leases were exempt from the nonimpairment standard. Rocky Mtn. Oil & Gas Ass'n v. Watt (10th Cir.1982). The only activities not subject to that standard were pre–1976 mineral lease development physical activities, which were still subject to the undue degradation standard. Following Interior Secretary Watt's efforts to open designated wilderness and WSAs to mineral leasing, Congress withdrew all BLM WSAs from further mineral leasing. In *Southern Utah Wilderness Alliance v. Norton*, supra, the court deferred to the BLM's conclusion that a seismic oil and gas exploration project in a WSA would not violate the non-impairment mandate of § 1782(c).

Congress adopted the first major statewide BLM wilderness bill, for Arizona, in 1990. The statute released most of the WSAs in the state that were not selected as wilderness from the nonimpairment standard. That decision does not prevent the BLM from managing these areas as de facto wilderness or from reconsidering their suitability as wilderness in later planning processes. In 1994, Congress designated about 6 million acres of the California Desert Conservation Area as wilderness. Debate over how much of the remaining roadless areas to preserve as wilderness is certain to continue.

See PNRL §§ 14B:12, 14B:15.

*

INDEX

References are to Pages

---

†